The Structure of Days Out

ALSO BY TOM LOWENSTEIN:

POETRY

Filibustering in Samsara, The Many Press, 1987
Ancestors and Species, Shearsman Books, 2005
Conversation with Murasaki, Shearsman Books, 2009
From Culbone Wood – in Xanadu, Shearsman Books, 2013

ON TIKIĠAQ HISTORY

The Things That Were Said of Them, University of California Press, 1992
Ancient Land: Sacred Whale, Bloomsbury, Farrar Strauss and Giroux, 1993
Ultimate Americans, University of Alaska Press, 2008
Tikiġaq, an Early History, North Slope Borough, 2018

Tom Lowenstein

The Structure of Days Out

With storytellers, hunters and their descendants
in a Native Alaskan Community, 1973–1981

Shearsman Books

First published in the United Kingdom in 2021 by
Shearsman Books Ltd
PO Box 4239
Swindon
SN3 9FN

Shearsman Books Ltd Registered Office
30–31 St. James Place, Mangotsfield, Bristol BS16 9JB
(this address not for correspondence)

ISBN 978-1-84861-768-1

ACKNOWLEDGEMENT
This book was first published serially online, and in a different form,
with the title *After the Snowbird Comes the Whale*,
in the *Fortnightly Review*.

All quotations from "Rainey" are from Froelich G. Rainey, *The Whale Hunters
of Tigara*, American Museum of Natural History, New York, 1947. Also
from Rainey's unpublished field notes, made available to me by
John Bockstoce in 1977. A copy of these notes is now in the
archives of The University of Alaska, Fairbanks.

Contents

PEOPLE AND PLACES IN THE TEXT

Pseudonyms are in italics

Aġniin	Born ca. 1900, married to *Qiliġniq*, the first Tikiġaq cleric.
Arlott, John	English cricket commentator
Asatchaq	storyteller, born 1891.
Daisy	a teenaged girl.
Elizabeth	High Priest's wife, based in Fairbanks
Kunak	born ca. 1950
Mrs Charlotte	born ca. 1880; Elizabeth's mother
Aniqsuaq	born ca. 1940 friend to *Sarah* and Umik
Inupiaq	north Alaskan 'Eskimo' people and their language
Ipiutak	pre-Tikiġaq peninsula culture
Patsy and *Laura*	teenaged girls.
Margaret	born ca. 1950
Kayuktuq	born ca. 1930, a whale boat owner
Q	born ca. 1930.
Rainey	Froelich Rainey, archaeologist of Ipiutak; conducted ethnographic field work in 1940.
Sarah	born ca. 1930, skinboat owner
Tikiġaq	northwest Alaskan Inupiaq village
Tukummiq	born ca. 1920, translator and interpreter.
Tulugaq	a teenaged boy.
Umik	born ca. 1930 skinboat owner, married to *Sarah*
Umigluk	born ca. 1900, dancer, storyteller, historian
Uqpik	born ca. 1920

Peninsula history:

0– ca. 800 AD	Peninsula residence of pre-Inupiaq Ipiutak people
1000– AD	Peninsula residence of whale-hunting Tikiġaq people
1860	Commercial whaler/trader presence
1870	Major inter-ethnic contact leading to epidemics and game depletion
1880	Summer coast guard visits north and northwest coast
1887	Jabbertown, cosmopolitan whaler-trader station established on south beach five miles from Tikiġaq

1889	Death of shaman Ataŋauraq
1890	Missionary Driggs arrives in Tikiġaq
1891	Birth of Asatchaq
1890s	Revs Edson and Knapp substitute for Driggs on furlough
1908	Driggs deposed
1908–1919	Missionary Augustus Hoare in Tikiġaq
1908	Hoare's village census
1909	Hoare's cemetery removal

Personal chronology:

Summer 1973	Three week Tikiġaq visit, recording stories for Alaska State Museum
March–June 1975	Four month Tikiġaq visit
Autumn 1975	Inupiaq studies; meeting with Asatchaq in Fairbanks.
September 1975	Meeting with Mrs Charlotte.
Dec. 1975–July 1976	Residence in Tikiġaq.
August–Dec. 1976	Residence in San Francisco.
January–July 1977	Return to Tikiġaq.
1977–1980	Intermittent work with Asatchaq
1980	Death of Asatchaq
1998	Tikiġaq visit to research social history
2009	Final visit to Tikiġaq

TERMINOLOGY AND MYTH NAMES

aana	grandmother
Aliŋnaq	moon spirit or *tatqim inua*
aŋatkuq	shaman
arrii	exclamation of pain
ataata	grandfather
atiq	name or namesake
inua	spirit presence, literally, 'its owner'
Inupiaq	north Alaskan Eskimo. Plural Inupiat
jokes	local English from *saglu-* 'to lie', spoken casually
kiligvak	woolly mammoth, semi-Anglicised in 1891 to create Asatchaq's surname, Killigivuk
kuyak-	sexual intercourse

maktak	whale skin and blubber
niġrun	'the animal', myth-based local name for Tikiġaq
qaaq-	to use marijuana, get stoned, from the verb 'explode'
qalgi	ceremonial house. Six in pre-contact Tikiġaq
qaŋa	stoned
siqinnim inua	sun spirit
skidoo, snowgo	motorized sled
tatqim inua	moon spirit
Tikiġaq	Point Hope, Alaska
tirragiik	fresh, boiled whale skin
Tuluŋigraq	Raven Man of primordial time who harpooned the sea monster whose body became the Tikiġaq peninsula
Ukuŋniq	mythological boy shaman who travelled the south beach
ulu	semi-lunar women's knife, originally slate
umiaq	skinboat
umialik	skinboat owner, female or male
usuk	penis
utchuk	vagina
uiluaqtaq	woman who won't marry, separatist female shaman

INUPIAQ PRONUNCIATION:

The dotted g (ġ) resembles the French r
The engma (ŋ) resembles an –ng, as in 'king'
-au is spoken as in the English o
-q lies deep in the throat and draws the preceding vowel with it
-k is spoken as in English

Part 1

*Night Visitors
and Telling Stories*

He knows I know his name is Tulugaq, but still I call this mighty individual Sharva, who visits me these late spring evenings. A specialist in *kung-fu* manoeuvres reproduced from Bruce Lee movies, small hours, visionary conversation, Sharva's passage through the village keeps the girls awake and some in terror as he guns his machine to the edge of my storm-shed and opens the throttle in a final bellow. Then in the after-blast, he strides through the snow, my outer door groans and his glove smacks the lintel.

The reasons for his visits I slowly start to fathom. Drunk on night's daylight, Sharva seeks shade, and my house is full of shade. And while his path through Tikiġaq is ribald and sublime, what I offer is a margin of banality in which to convalesce from serial intensity. To mark this dull edge to his business, Sharva brings me curiosities because he knows I'll give him supper. His diet is eccentric. Abjuring *real meat* – whale, seal, caribou, walrus, fish and wild fowl – what he eats is tuna, corned beef and sardines. So in return for these, he lifts hunks of Kobuk River jade and Anchorage whiskey from his snowsuit zipper. And while I cache these, he gorges on crackers, swigs coffee, lights a Marlboro, exhales through his harmonica and crashes on my trestle.

The young god also comes to reenact his work on enemies: their legs, teeth, genitals and noses. He fought *Itqiliks* (Indians) at school in Oregon and now he's home to instruct younger brothers. Up swings an elbow caked with blood, salt, motor oil and fish fluids. A boot crashes on the lino. Hands, blackened from a leaky carburettor, sweep the light bulb. Parka nylon whistles. Typescripts, notes and carbon paper all go flying. Researched from movies, Sharva executes a high-kick and flourishing a *chako* stick, smashes my light bulb. The god transforms to housemaid, crouches on the floor, apologises, wipes glass from floor boards and then striding through the storm shed, rubs the glass-dust in the snow outside and dropping ice crusts on the lino, stamps in again for pilot crackers.

'Come! My gloves! Dry! You gonna blood 'em soon!' he cries reverting to heroic posture. He bangs his mittens and a shower of glass and ice crusts join the scabs of snow his boots drop.

Since Sharva's first visit, it helps to diagnose his mood from the sound of his approach. There's the rapid stride of a marijuana high, the heavy, agrieved drinker's gait, the depressive approach, in which his movement's drained of purpose. Finally, the quick walk of a self-possessed young man with curiosity about the world intent on intellectual conversation.

It's been this latter mood of interest marked our conversations, when Sharva sits at my table and riffles through my folders, fingering the typescripts with rightful self-possession.

'How many stories you got here? You got stories about *aŋatkuqs*?

What's this story on a brown bear?

How come you never tell me about my *atiq*?'

'Everything I know is secondhand', I tell him. 'I don't tell stories. All I know is what Asatchaq records. And these are just streaks of patterns fading on a background I can never visualise.'

'That's all anybody knows,' says Sharva. 'I see my life like that too. In lines across the snow. And what is snow? *What is it*? I don't know. I don't know where I'm going. Who were my ancestors? Hunters, *aŋatkuqs* who took journeys to the moon man. And here's me tripping round on my skiddoos. People say I'm crazy. I guess they're maybe right. But how's them different?'

I address him by mistake as Sharva.

'How come you say that name?' he asks, and I apologise.

'I know you're Tulugaq. And you have powerful *atiqs*. 'I called you that other because you remind me of someone. It's a god from India called Shiva.'

'You said *Sharva*. Not that other.'

'I know. It's complicated. Shiva has a thousand-and-eight names. Sharva means lucky. The god's names are amulets.'

'You shouldn't bother with it,' Tulugaq said. 'We're not India.'

I risked developing the conversation.

'It's not just a thousand names. He's got that many *usuks*.'

Tulugaq had a fit of coughing.

'Man, a thousand *usuks*...' For a moment he was lost in speculation. Then,

'That would be some *kuyak-*. Where does he keep 'em?'

'He was crazy for the daughter of a mountain. Parvati. She was a *uiluaqtaq*. But they married finally. And spent years in one *kuyak-*'

'What happened after?'

'One of their babies got punished. Had his head changed to an elephant's. Some kind of *kiligvak*... Fat bellied. Loved candy. One tusk broken.'

'One *tuugaq* broken. Crazy story. That many *usuks.*'

*

Tulugaq and Patsy

The teenaged Tulugaq brings a girl round. 'This is Patsy,' he says briefly. Then after some talk about their fathers' whale-boats, 'Let's go in there,' Tulugaq gestures to my alcove and they walk through the curtain.

I'm jealous of their privacy and sublimate with Heidegger, his essay on Hölderlin's *Homecoming* poem. This I'd excavated from a cache of books a teacher had abandoned in the summer: *Leaves of Grass* and *Walden,* pacifist writings of Tolstoy and Gandhi and Hesse's *Steppenwolf:* radical texts that young Americans were reading in the 1960s. These lay in a snow heap on a table in the school house built in 1900 for the traders' children, dragged five miles west to Tikiġaq and intermittently abandoned.

I'd wandered in one Sunday. A preschool programme used the east end of the building. There were toys and cushions in strawberry and banana patterns. Like a mouth jammed open to swallow a whale's head, the west end held the cockpit severed from a plane that came down in the village. Cords, dials and connectors poked out in the twilight, a telephone switchboard crammed in beside it. Some kids had set a fire here and the back wall was charred, the window frames twisted.

Back at the house, as Tulugaq and Patsy consummate their moment, I make a stab at Heidegger. The cover's pitted by an ice pick left still vertically transfixing *Steppenwolf* and I'd copied out the words the pick had skewered.

The scars to Heidegger are superficial, his essay profound and hard to fathom. More important, in Hölderlin's poem, I recognize the ice and light of Alpine Europe and an inflection of its contrasts at this Arctic moment, at once spiritually hot and deadly freezing: stanzas that illuminate the winter in an expectation of unbroken summer. The poet evokes village people in their valley 'workshops' exalted by the peaks around them which rained sacred glamour.

I shared Hölderlin's vision of community, industrious inhabitants, the encounter between communal existence and a sacred *fiat*. It expresses an Edenic anthropology of ordinary people, their lives hallowed by imperatives, blessed and expressed by divine generosity. Such people are autonomous but submissive to participation in the workings of authority, content in their share of its operations. There's eternity to this condition: where everyone *is*. Just *there* they belong with pine trees and glaciers.

This of Hölderlin, as taken up by Heidegger, musing in his peasant cabin – perhaps already having joined the Nazi Party and refusing to abandon home in Baden-Württemberg – is *Heimat*, or home's meaning, but which also demands of people that they make the effort to achieve belonging. Thus Heidegger proclaimed as excavated from the snow heap:

> Home is difficult to win.
> They're not yet ready for home's inmost essence.
> It's near, what you seek. In the end you'll find it.

How far such a venture is joyous or forbidding is difficult to measure.

*

Asatchaq

By virtue of his years and learning, Asatchaq is sage and patriarch. And yet, because he's also feared, he lives in semi-exile on the village fringes. Still, like a Buddha at the bull's eye of a *mandala*, he's also at the centre, father, village consciousness and history. *It's near, what you seek*, as Heidegger tells us, perhaps with a glance at Grimm's tale of the soldier who found gold in the kitchen he returned to.

What Asatchaq doesn't need to seek is what we can't approach without him. This, because he lives largely in the realm of fiction: in half-submerged ancestral teachings, myths, legends, narratives of ancestors, dance songs, taboo regulations, shamanistic medicine, spirit visions, sun and moon lore, supernatural histories, celebrated gestes of skinboat owners, sacred geography that maps ghost dwellings, subterranean *iglus* – birth and death rites, laws of mutuality with animals, how to butcher and ingest the soul-infused meat of whale and caribou, theories of the human spirit, its origin in previous namesakes, networks of a century's kinship, chronicles of families going back two centuries that were engaged in patterns of behaviour no-one born since 1940 follows.

He, on the other hand, living on the fringe in a cabin loaned him by a teacher and kept alive by intermittent visits by a few relations from

14

the New Town Site two miles away and an Englishman who writes him cheques for songs and stories.

Asatchaq's cabin lies due north of mine, while my interpreter/ translator Tukummiq's ex-US army quonset hut with its fence of frozen seals her son has hunted standing upright on their noses, lies roughly in the middle. The trail that Tukummiq and I negotiate each evening forms a line from my south side cabin to the north of the peninsula. Here Asatchaq has settled fifty yards from his sister Uyatauna who also lives in isolation.

'I like it better here in old Tikiġaq,' Tukummiq confesses. The half mile we walk, occasionally backwards if a north wind's blowing, is deserted. We stop to look east to New Town Site: a blur on the horizon: tract dwellings, durable and sanctioned by contemporary authority. Old post-contact Tikiġaq, improvised through nine decades of ingenuity. Autonomous, self-made, fragile, crafted out of planks and insulating paper.

North wind ('Good for polar bears' as Asatchaq remarks) is part of the landscape. It blows from Cape Lisburne, hits the Point side-on and crosses to the south shore as though connecting the two coastlines. The north wind is male, the south wind female. Like the sun and the moon, the two strive against each other and help define the Point's self-fructifying energy.

'New Town is all right,' Tukummiq continues. She is widowed, just turned fifty. 'But it's not the old village. I'd like a new home but I'll be dead before I get it.'

The identity of Tikiġaq or 'index finger', derives from its position, pointing deep into the ocean. New Town Site lies two miles inland and its geologic form has less particularity. It's part of inland. The Point, with its plunging momentum of harpoon and bird's bill, is sharper and more complex in its fabrication.

We glance round at abandoned cabins, *iglu* mounds and caches, whale bone uprights, animal bones and skins on drying racks, ruts sunk by tractors that dragged half the village east last summer, the slough and tundra hummocks where the bunting and the longspur build in April.

And we're in ghostly company. Human bones lie scattered on the tundra. Tukummiq clicks her tongue, contemplatively self-divided. It's both home and a wasteland, beautiful/ugly, things almost as they were twelve months ago but overlaid by human absence.

The New Town Site is two miles east, connected to us by the roar of snowmachines: hunters come to fetch meat from underground caches.

Sometimes I walk to New Town Site to buy goods from the store and look round Tikiġaq's reformulation. The shingle on which New Town Site is built is grey, the houses uniform. The North Slope Borough rents planes to bring in prefabs: they're tightly insulated and identical, unweathered as yet, unmarked by history.

'Hard to walk on New Town's stones till freeze up,' old people mutter. Your feet turn sideways. It's painful on the knees and hips. The feeling's precarious. Strange to remember that this stony surface pushed by dozers from the south shore is an aggregation of the old south beach: the same stones shamans trod on vision quests and where people still hunt for seal. But heaped to a pad to support new houses, New Town is the answer to impending flooding that could overwhelm the old site. The move, a rational solution, is nonetheless traumatic. The new site's also built atop pre-Eskimo remains, Ipiutak's cemetery, part excavated between 1939 and '40.

Kunak's Dream

It's the end of an era though no-one talks apocalyptically. Moves have happened since after the Ice Age. And like much history, it soon gets forgotten. Bicentennial celebrations start up in the lower States this summer. The US has withdrawn from southeast Asia and Vietnam has now invaded Cambodia. Two Tikiġaq men, conscripted to the jungle ('They pay Natives to kill Natives,' as Kunak told me) are home in the village.

The impact of both these factors has afflicted Kunak. Since seeing him last, as young, beautiful and powerful, his face is refined by thought and suffering. He shows me drawings in which he's tried to realize a vision of his people and wonders if Ipiutak which ca. 800 is blended (his word) with early Inupiaq. He also worries that the New Town Site lies atop Ipiutak ruins.

Given the unknowable extent of the Ipiutak settlement, there's truth to his anxiety and I share it. K has kept a small house in old Tikiġaq. But he lives now on the New Town Site. He's been disturbed by dreams since last summer's move. In one dream he's in an old *iglu*:

'A man came in through the tunnel. He's wearing a mask. At the centre, at the nose, there's a bird revolving.'

He told me about two other dreams, but the details are blurred. The mask dream derived from the photo of an Ipiutak mask he had been studying.

The village move involved a large adjustment. But similar places are worse affected. Kivalina, a hundred miles south and sited between sea, lagoon and river is in peril and there's nowhere local that's not threatened. Tikiġaq is fortunate. Two miles east there's higher ground. The move had to happen, but compared to the old site's history, New Town's different:

'It's a new world here. It's left you behind, man,' a boy just arrived on a skidoo tells me. Still, no separating rivalry splits the village. Everyone's involved. It's serious and painful.

'Which-way-you-always-kick-then?' I'm tempted to ask him but am glad I didn't.

I rarely indulge in ethnographic banter. This would have been unfair and arrogant. I have, after all, the luxury of books and archives. My bitten-back rejoinder concerned an ancient rivalry. Before the white man came, the village divided into parties. One group kicked towards the Point, the other team kicked from the Point, inland.

*

Inupiaq Migrations

As we cross to visit Asatchaq, I think of the migrations that brought people to Alaska. Specifically to Tikiġaq some two thousand years back, first the pre-Eskimo Ipiutak people. Then early Inupiat around 1000.

In addition to Tlingit and Athabaskan Indians and Inupiat of the interior, the Inuit have moved everywhere along the north shores of Alaska's sixteen hundred miles of coastline adapting to propitious hunting places.

Besides Tikiġaq which holds the latest wave of the late Thule people, there were, among the northern people, the flint knappers of Denbigh, Choris, Norton, Okvik, Punuk, Birnirk, Old Bering Sea, Ipiutak and Thule whale hunting people. The first migrants arrived from southeast Siberia. When the sea ice started melting about ten thousand years back, the continents separated. One story describes two distant points that once were united: here, on Tikiġaq's north coastline and somewhere near East Cape, Siberia.

*

Kiligvak, the Woolly Mammoth

In conversation about names and namesakes, we shuttle the old man's surname back and forth between us. Tukummiq laughs. The old man's birth is inscribed in a ledger as James Asecak Killigivuk. Thus missionary Driggs baptized Niġuvana's baby.

Asatchaq's father's name was Kiligvak, 'woolly mammoth'. And because he was little, people called him *kiligvauraq*, 'little *kiligvak*.' This echoed, I imagined wrongly, the presence of the Pleistocene: the beasts and early people that migrated from Siberia.[1]

Still, like ancient hunters that pursued it, the mammoth migrated from northeastern Europe and when it died out it left its presence. Ten miles north, there's beached mammoth ivory. And whole tusks tumble out of river banks. I was with Kunak's brother when he hauled into the village a set of tusks he'd recovered from the Kuukpak River. More modestly, I kicked up some gravel for a fish net and unearthed a molar.

'How old you think that tooth is?' asked one of my companions.

'Maybe ten thousand years,' I suggested, picking up, on which to place the molar for a photo, a small wooden lid from a driftwood tangle. Inscribed on the wood in magic marker was the number 10,000.

*

Time

The emptiness prompts me to imagine I feel time's passage. Like Tikiġaq's beaches, time comes and goes in oscillating repetitions. But time's always the same thing and it has no movement. We and the mammoth inhabit one medium.

Asatchaq's World View

The Ancient Mastodon, as I wrongly call him, whom we're crossing Tikiġaq to visit, lives within a gyroscope of incompatible cosmologies. Or rather, the world views coinciding in him – Inupiaq, Episcopalian, American materialist – are interchangeable, adjacent. A prayer to Jesus at the whale hunt's followed by an old charm for the harpoon float.

---

[1] People believed the *kiligvak* to have been a giant rodent. It was timid and ran underground when disturbed.

The Peninsula's Geology

People have lived here since about 0 AD and the Point has existed for millennia. Created by detritus from Cape Thompson thrown up on the south beach every summer, a new beach ridge is created every hundred years or so and thus the Point is built of mounds and troughs that stripe the peninsula, east-west, parallel: the most recent on the south side, the more ancient to the north before they're ripped off by storm waves. Cape Thompson is the endpoint of the Rocky Mountain cordillera.

Just as the peninsula enlarges from the south shore, so the north side is eroded. But while build-up from the south is gradual, the north shore collapses, summer and autumn, though there's also growth here. The same water that carries off the bluffs, deposits silt from Kuukpak River. These opposite forces both created the peninsula and render life dangerous.

The Storm of 1893

The most detailed account of a flood comes in a letter of John Driggs, Tikiġaq missionary. In October 1893, a violent storm blew across from Siberia and in Driggs's letter, we witness the storm's impact:

> On the 13th of October 1893 during a very severe blizzard, the sea came breaking on the land, driving the Natives out of the village and forcing me to desert the mission...
>
> Out of doors everything looked desolate. Along the ocean front the land had been cut away... and all the snow had been thoroughly saturated by the ocean water and spray... On the night of my return another big storm arose and the following evening I thought it best to desert the house before I was again forced to repeat my former experience of dodging waves and wading though ice water and slush, an operation I did not care to repeat...
>
> That night I slept alongside a dog sled, with a few clumps of snow thrown up as a wind break and then continued my trip back to the mountains... By the first of November... I again

returned home and opened school for the second time…A young woman who had been a pupil at the mission was overtaken by these blizzards [and] is supposed to have been blown off into the ocean… Driggs letter, June 1894

In July 1894, Driggs took Rev. Edson, who'd arrived to enable Driggs's vacation, to view the north shore and they devised a plan to relocate the Mission. In 1895, Edson wrote:

During the last four years autumn storms have driven heavy seas diagonally along this side of the point with terrific boring force, cutting off fully fifty feet of the shore in front of the house. [Driggs] believes it is only a question of a short time when, if it is not moved back, it will be washed off.

The Mission House, which Driggs had built a mile east of the village, was at the time the only Tikiġaq frame building.

Here follows a summary of a Survey Report of Tikiġaq Beach Erosion, conducted by the Alaska Corps of Engineers, January 1972. The conclusion reads:

'If problems increase, as undoubtedly they will, the desirability of remaining at the present site will dimish.'

Despite local objections outlined by the surveyor, people did agree to move two miles east. This began in summer 1975 and by 1977 most of the community had relocated.

The work I did with Asatchaq took place on the old site, which had been reduced to about a quarter of the population. The house where I spent 1976 was isolated. And when forced to move, I decamped to Asatchaq's cabin floor. I was, however, woken one morning when the cabin started shaking. Assuming this to be an earthquake, I naively welcomed this recrudescence of the geological time. But when I stumbled to the door I found affable Willie Omnik on a tractor driving a forklift platform under the cabin.

'Hey, what are you doing?' I shouted, 'we haven't finished work.'
'Oh, OK,' said Willie, and he turned away to move another cabin.

*

Secular and Sacred: The Phenomenon of Removal

'It happened here,' said Asatchaq after his first recording. It was January 1976 and he had just recited Tikiġaq's creation story. 'In the spring I'll show you the wound hole where Tuluŋigraq harpooned the animal.'

The wound, he told me, was the made by a harpoon after which the sea beast transformed to earth.

That summer I took Asatchaq to the spot he'd identified. This was the first of two excursions that we made. It was bumpy for his wheel chair and we didn't get far. 'Stop here,' he shouted at the place he intended. There was long grass and bird bone. But the wound hole had disappeared into the ocean.

Tikiġaq's *inua*

The nature of the Ur-beast was ambiguous. It was sacred, dangerous and belonged to a class of spirits that inhabited the myth world.

These beings were a species of *inua* or resident spirit, a word modified from *inuk,* 'person', meaning 'its person'. The most powerful of these was *tatqim inua:* 'the spirit owner of the moon'. Originally, this had been Aliŋnaq, a human become god and anti-hero. Having raped his sister, he ascended to the moon where he presided over a tub containing the sea mammals. His abused sister went to the sun, becoming its presiding spirit.

Inuas continued to exist. A giant flounder brooded in the waters of the inlet. The sea north of the Kuukpak river held an omnivorous mollusc. This, in summer 1899, sucked down a boat full of coal and murres' eggs that the Irishman O'Hare had gathered near Uivvaq. There were also ghostly 'families': three Itivyaaq spirits east of Tikiġaq and the Nuvuk 'people' whose support was enjoined before whaling. Dangerous spirits inhabited places where babies had died. At the cliffs were resident giants. The task of mythic humans was to visit and destroy *inuas,* thereby rendering the region safe.

Since settling on the peninsula, the people of the Point had hunted whale and Tuluŋigraq's whale *inua* was remade into the sacralising species central to subsistence.

The whale Tuluŋigraq harpooned is seldom named as such. The story takes place in the sphere of Ur-time. Things existed in transition. The earth was soft. Humans walked on their hands. Gender was uncertain.

Early creation was topsy-turvy. Caribou and seal fat existed in opposition. People wandered in darkness until the Raven man tore light from the container where it had been hoarded. Like Aliŋnaq, his mythic coeval, he ripped through taboo in order to break into creation.

Continuing with Tuluŋigraq: the animal was implicitly perceived as a whale. Asatchaq called the creature *niġrun*, 'animal'. And *niġrun* was a nickname for the peninsula. People standing on Cape Thompson looking west would say, 'There's *niġrun*:' the animal Tuluŋigraq killed.

Likewise, when the Raven struck, he sang to make the harpoon and its drag float stay in place to tether the animal. Later harpooners used the same song when they struck a bowhead: *'Uivvaluk, uivvaluk!'* ('around, around!')

This convergence of belief and actuality was concretised in *iglu* architecture: the *iglu* dome being made from whale bone, while stories evoked magical events in which whales come up through dry land to an animated *iglu*.

The notion that the Point's an animal, harmonized with the rhythm of its build and decay. Tikiġaq is made of the Ur-whale's body and people lived inside it. The whale hunt is conducted by a partnership of male and female skinboat owners. While the husband hunts, the wife sits in the *iglu*, as though in the whale's head, encountering at heightened moments, a whale rising in the *iglu*.

The Sacred and the Secular – continued

When in 1904, the priest E.J. Knapp described Tikiġaq's graveyard as 'weird', he was suggesting the place was strange, uncanny and with supernatural properties.

Tikiġaq's graveyard covered a large area of the Point and was integrated with the village, where life and death were therefore coexistent. *Weird* likewise would describe the dancing, singing and drumming which filled the ceremonial houses each October.

The anthropologist Marcel Mauss described how Eskimo spirituality was generally a winter phenomenon, summer being a more secular time when people half-forgot the spirits and taboos dominating the dark season. So in July 1909, the new missionary Hoare ordered the able bodied population to remove the relics of ancestors which lay round the village.

*

Hoare's Cemetery Removal

In July 1909, when Asatchaq was eighteen, the Rev. Hoare ordained the removal of Tikiġaq's cemetery to a space he'd consecrated a mile west of the village. Apart from the atomic threat outlined later, his action was perhaps the most drastic in contact history wherein old Tikiġaq was assimilated into Christian regulation.

To early white visitors, the village was difficult to describe in terms of original belief. The first European here was the English naval officer Frederick Beechey who noted in August 1826 that the whalebone uprights in the village looked like a 'forest of stakes', suggesting organic but uncivilised disorder.

Similarly, to Charles Brower in 1884, Tikiġaq 'looked like a forest of small trees with the tops cut off. There were thousands of these whale jaw bones'. E.J. Knapp in 1904, found this 'weird Eskimo graveyard two miles and more in length resembled trunks of blasted trees… the bodies… dissolved. Many of these graves have fallen into utter ruin and the bones and clothes that shrouded the dead lie scattered on the ground.'

Thus in 1909, the landscape of the Point changed for ever. The transformation was described by Hoare in a 1909 *Spirit of Missions*:

> One of the first duties… is the seemly… burial of the dead….
> I am sending you a picture of our new graveyard [which] was
> completed in one day. Every person of working age on the Point
> assisted. While some were building, others were patrolling up
> and down, collecting the skulls and bones of those who…have
> been laid on the surface of the ground to await decay. In one
> common grave we buried over 1,200 skulls, and about three
> cartloads of bones…. This marks the passing of a superstition…
> The people have accepted Christianity…

Hoare's was an enactment of the doctrine that Alaska's Education Commissioner Sheldon Jackson had learned from Alexander Duff whose motto proclaimed 'While we throw down, we also rebuild…'

'The white man was *pukiq*, clever. He was clean and powerful,' Umigluk told me in 1977. Some old timers held the belief that time was anyway coming to an end. This partly had to do with a self-disrespect deriving from idealized ancestral superiority. The balance between modesty and survival energy marked people with a particular character.

To minimize public expression of what you know is in part a survival stratagem. To boast is to invite nemesis.

In comparing the 1909 cemetery removal and the 1975 transfer to the New Town Site, there lies one ironic contrast. Hoare's relocation of ancestral relics to a newly plotted environment represented the removal from one sacred place to another . There is no record of what people said about the event. The cemetery removal engaged a reduced population of about 130 who were emerging from three decades of epidemics and were in the process of abandoning the shamanistic religion disparaged by the missionaries.

Hoare regarded the cemetery removal as an act of purging. Missionary language contained frequent reference, to cleaning and rebuilding. Driggs's temporary replacement, Elijah Edson, was preoccupied by a relationship between physical and religious purity: 'For God's sake,' he wrote in 1895, 'send us towels.' Hoare's new cemetery was an orderly, contained space. Birth, death and resurrection could now proceed along a coherent trajectory.

The 1975 site-move was predicated on a similar imperative. This time it was federal government not the priesthood that initiated the transition. And Tikiġaq by now had moved further into the modern world. And while the 1975 move was agreed in coordination with the village council and the North Slope Borough, cemetery relocation had been the act of a church autocrat.

The two events nonetheless shared one key element. Both constituted removal from a sacralised environment. And the 1975 move took the living population to a secular environment with modernizing potential.

*

The Shaman Ataŋauraq and Disease

For almost ten years until his murder in February 1889, the shaman and self-proclaimed chief Ataŋauraq created a goods exchange monopoly

The commercial whale hunters who penetrated the Bering Sea in 1848 not only carried these diseases, but through the use of repeating rifles and exploding bomb harpoons, reduced the whale and caribou populations, leading Native communities to an increasing commercial dependence.

The inflow of manufactured goods continued and Frohlich Rainey's notes of 1940 enumerate many non-local articles that circulated.

Many imported goods acquired Inupiaq terminology and these neo-logisms entered the linguistic repertoire. Much of this was inventive. It wasn't, however, for entertainment that mustard became *iligam anaɲa,* 'baby shit' or the word for sausage was built from *usuk,* 'penis'. Such words, along with terms for different kinds of imported oil, household equipment, nails, string, hammers, firearms and their components, became assimilated into the language. People might comprehend the English terms but many of these didn't fit Inupiaq phonology. There is, for example, no Inupiaq phonological matrix which fits words like 'rifle' or 'stove oil'. Some English phonemes could be harmonized into polysynthetic compounds: 'seal,' 'sea', 'tea', 'coffee,' 'cup','get', 'go' and a number of others could be slipped into Inupiaq.

*

The Village Council and Social Order

In 1920, partly with Church intervention, Tikiġaq elected a village council. As Vanstone wrote in 1960, 'The council is surprisingly effective as an enforcement agency. The pressures of public opinion, together with the prestige of council members, are important factors in encouraging compliance with village rules and regulations. The United States Marshall at Nome has jurisdiction over the [Tikiġaq] area and he may come to the village to arrest individuals who have committed crimes against the American legal system. Cases of this kind, which are relatively few, are handled with the cooperation of the village council.' (Vanstone 1962: 103).

Social control during the traditional period had been exerted by older people and behaviour was regulated by example. With suffering that followed epidemics and the dissolution, by ca. 1900, of the last ceremonial house, the formation of a village council was a major initiative.

The first council consisted of seven survivors of the epidemic period. These were men from ceremonial houses who had close connection with the old dispensation but who also lived effectively in the modern period. Samaruna and Peter Kunuyaq, two of the remembered council members exemplified this self-assured identity. These were hardy individuals whose dictat was reinforced by example.

Asatchaq grew up during this transitional period and successfully negotiated bicultural loyalties. Educated in Tikiġaq lore, he comprehended and assimilated pre-contact tradition, while also taking advantage of manufactured goods that helped support life. By the mid-1970s his insistence on the centrality of Inupiaq order and his disdain for what he perceived as mid-century disorder, was therefore in reaction both to a semi-idealized culture which preceded his birth and also to the 'golden' period of Inupiaq/American cultural coexistence as realized by his own elders.[2]

*

Wasteland — School Ruins

Asatchaq inhabited a wasteland on the edge of school house residue abandoned on the north side when the classroom portacabins were transported to the New Town site. These light prefabs were made for inexpensive transportation and were deposited into urbanizing New Town culture until they were replaced by an up-to-date school building in the 1980s.

To reach Asatchaq's cabin you must first pick your way across wrecked bits of piping which had fed stove oil and drinking water into the school buildings. There was also wreckage from a pumping shed, a ruined workshop and rectangular patches from where buildings had been lifted.

The white man, like this architecture of impermanence, was himself a migrant. While Native people had long settled in their territories, white men were, as the U.S. 1976 Bicentennial attested, modern visitors. Tikiġaq's school teachers in the 1970s came mostly from the mid- and southwestern states, and lured by generous salaries, most stayed only so long as they could stand the cold and isolation.[3]

The detritus round Asatchaq's cabin differed from other signs of village removal. Walking back to Tikiġaq from New Town Site, I saw how the airstrip cut the slough that fills with water every summer.

---

[2] Ivrulik Rock, a Tikiġaq elder in a Fairbanks shelter became so Christianised that he wanted nothing to do with pre-contact history. In 1933, he worked, with Asatchaq, as an extra in W.S. Van Dyke's MGM movie *Eskimo,* some of which was shot on Tikiġaq's south shore. See https://en.wikipedia.org/wiki/Eskimo_%28film%29. Both Ivrulik and Asatchaq had a vivid time when they were briefly transported to Hollywood. Ivrulik commented on Jean Harlow: 'Jeanie… she sure made good hotcakes.'

[3] I understand this because I'm one of them. But as a teenager once put it, 'Taam's not a *naluaġmiu*. He's an *Inglagmiu* (English). He's a Native from his own country.' Another boy added, 'You lived in England? They taken away your culture too?'

'There were thousands of skeletons', one man told me. 'What do you do with them? And next to each grave would be hunting gear, sewing kit or cooking equipment. Their old things. Whose is it when they're dead?'

I walked round in the gloom. A mist had come in, the cloud was low. The remains of overlapping cultures strewed the village: earth and gravel churned up by removal machinery is rutted, gouged, humped, ditched, scarred by Kat tracks, and the contours of the Point with its troughs, ridges and old *iglus*, grasses, wild flowers, are dislocated and shapeless, scattered with abandoned house bits, hunting gear and imported manufacture.

*

Daisy's Narrative

I watched, in diagram, the overture to Daisy's tragedy. This started on the north side, next to Asatchaq's cabin, at Nanny Uyatauna's.

Uyatauna is Asatchaq's younger sister. Pale-skinned and emaciated, she stretches painfully to sit up in bed but can only just cry out and wave her arms and speak in abbreviated Inupiaq that three years ago I'd heard her talking briskly. Nanny lives with her daughter Rose-Marie. They were Tikiġaq's last *iglu* dwellers and vacated their earth house in August '73.

Nanny inhabits a nineteenth century trader's cabin which was hauled into Tikiġaq from Jabbertown around 1920. It's a tight little building insulated with black tarp and has an attic, originally a storage space for bear skins, ivory and baleen. Accessible by ladder, the attic also functioned as a social annexe.

The transition for Nanny from her *iglu* to a cabin, repeated the experience her elders witnessed. Her parents, Kiligvak and Niġuvana, were in the vanguard of these changes. Selling whalebone with trader John Backland, Kiligvak took delivery in autumn 1912 of lumber from Seattle and the following summer built the first native frame house. It survives to the far west by Samaruna's *iglu* ruins, the furthest northwest building on the continent.

Asatchaq and Uyatauna moved into this house in their twenties and while Asatchaq continued to live there until about 1974, Nanny joined her husband in an *iglu*.

Rose-Marie, who's fifty, small and hunchbacked, runs Nanny's household. In Dickens's phrase in *Our Mutual Friend* for Jenny Wren, she's 'the person of the house'.[4] And Rose would agree, though she'd never complain, as Jenny Wren did: 'My back's bad and my legs are queer.'

But while Jenny's sharp and critical ('I can't bear children. I know their tricks and their manners'), Rose-Marie is cheerful, friendly, non-judgemental, her movements neat and animated. Once when I had eaten what she'd shared, she ran to the stove, swept up trash with a gull's wing and ran outside to throw this in the snow, returning to feed Nanny. Like Jenny Wren, she makes her living as a seamstress and wears a snowshirt she's embroidered, flitting between tasks around the house as though she's sewing things together.

I asked, in my hunger for Inupiaq, 'What you call these?' and pointed to the moons and stars and flowers she'd stitched into calico. I knew words for lunar phases, the guttural and liquid word for star, and excitedly anticipated a term for the branching flowers she'd stitched into her shirt hem.

'We call that kind forget-me-nots,' said Rose-Marie shyly. For the next few minutes she composed a sentence and I wrote this from dictation: 'I-sewed-moon-stars-and-flowers-on-my-*atigiluk*.'

'Good Eskimo language,' said Rose-Marie, 'but I never spell it.' The long, single compound with its inner transformations was a string of complex balances and harmonies as though created for a concert aria, while to the speaker it remained a simple sentence, one of millions spoken daily.

I thought of the engravings that Tikiġaq people once did on snow knives and bow drill handles: beautiful and ordinary, scratched on bone and ivory and highlighted with lamp soot.

Later I told Asatchaq I knew of a girl called Jenny who reminded me of Rose-Marie.

'Ya, Jenny. *Yiniiraq*, Little Jenny. I call her *Qupaluuraq*, "little long-spur". Lays eggs in old *iglus*.' And he fluttered his lips with a song-like trilling.

*

---

[4] There's a coincidence between Dickens's locution and an Inupiaq idiom. *Inua* 'its person, spirit', is used for two phenomena. Animals revealed their *inua*, 'it's person', represented by a human face emerging from a non-human countenance (*tuttum inua*, 'the caribou, its person'). Someone could also be the *inua* of the place over which they presided. Dickens's locution thus homologises the personalities of Rose-Marie and Jenny Wren.

Daisy at Uyatauna's

Inupiaq engraving, nineteenth century

On a mid-March evening, Daisy, aged fifteen and three teenage boys burst into Uyatauna's cabin. I'd met Daisy on her visits earlier this month to Asatchaq. Once she'd come down from the New Town store with groceries, but as soon she came in the old man started shouting. 'He always *suak* (scolds) me,' she said sadly. Asatchaq was unrelenting; Daisy passive, made no effort to defend herself.

She was with the old man on a morning when his stove had flooded. It was thirty below and Asatchaq was sitting on the carpet trying to refit the carburetor. There was stove oil everywhere and he had burned his forearms. Before I left to find help, Daisy was cleaning the old man's forearms. She addressed him as *ataata,* grandpa, and was gently saying: '*Arrii ataata,* it's *alappaa* in here for you! How cold, alas, it is here, grandpa.'

A day or so later Daisy crashed in to Uyatauna's with a trio of young men. I knew one of them. A big lad. He'd come to visit me once in my cabin and asked unanswerable philosophic questions.

And Daisy: delicate and dressed as though for skiing in blue snow suit. The four ran in to Nanny's as if from one century to another.

The boys had no family connection with Uyatauna. They might have been at school or been working for their families. They hadn't arrived with fresh pond ice, snow for laundry, meat from a meat cache or a barrel of stove oil, but thundered after Daisy because Nanny was Daisy's great aunt and she implicitly belonged here. The household was safe.

Asatchaq described a similar visit.

'Some boys. They came in. They looked at me and stood there doing nothing. I said "What do you want?" But they said nothing. And they went away again.'

But Daisy and the boys, I heard later, had broken a window into the clinic and rifled the cupboards. Now without stopping to acknowledge Uyatauna, they swarmed up the ladder and into the attic.

Conversations with Daisy

Daisy and I had two conversations.

'Hey, I'd really like to have a conversation with you. Not for you know…'

'It's all right. It's not what I do here.'

'You tried out Eskimo girls already?'

'No. I've got a girl friend. White girl. She's in Juneau.

'Wow. Modern person. Why you come round here then? We're kinda old fashioned.'

'I'm recording Asatchaq's stories.'

'Yes, he knows the stories. But I never hear them. I'll come listen maybe.'

'We listen in the evening.'

'OK, I'm coming. Since I never hear those stories.'

I was nervous when she turned up two days later. This was following a *contretemps* involving Tulugaq. I hadn't seen him since he'd come round with Patsy and I thought perhaps there'd been some trouble.

But he arrived, as we'd arranged, to visit Asatchaq and charmingly he brought seal meat. Not that they acknowledged one another. And clumsily, I failed to introduce them to each other.

That didn't seem to matter. Tulugaq maintained his distance and crouched by the door as I placed a cassette into the recorder.

'Ready,' I said, hanging the mike on a string from the ceiling.

The old man cleared his throat and said 'Ready' in English.

Then fixing on the visitor, 'What's he doing here?'

'He's come to listen.'

'He doesn't have to listen. He's got his own grandfather.'

'Can't he listen?'

'Let him ask his own *ataata*.'

Since his name was Tulugaq (Raven), I tried an ethnographic gesture: 'He's come to hear about the *uiluaqtaqs* in your stories.'[5]

The joke didn't work and Asatchaq refused to start till Tulugaq left.

*

---

[5] Tulugaq, raven, is the short form of Tuluŋigraq, the trickster shaman who, having seduced the *uliuaqtaq*, 'woman who won't marry,' harpooned Tikiġaq.

Daisy at Asatchaq's

After the embarrassment of Tulugaq's dismissal I was anxious that Asatchaq might dismiss Daisy. But I didn't understand the tie that made her presence natural. Family connection made the difference.

From the moment she came in she seemed at home and though she still hardly knew her grandpa, she gave the impression of belonging. It was strange, this transformation of the cabin from a lonely outpost to a household. It hadn't occurred to me how out of character the old man's life was. Inupiat live close to one another in extended families.

Daisy made tea and sat down to listen. I'd overlooked this comfortable, domestic aspect of what stories meant to people.

'I sure want to learn this Inupiaq language,' Daisy muttered.

'I thought you understood it.'

'I know some words, all right.' She mimicked singular and plural object suffixes: *aŋuti*mik ('man' in the accusative), *aŋuti*nik (plural) and repeated '*mik, -nik,*' in smiling sing-song.

'You know those words?' she asked me.

'I'm trying to learn slowly.'

'People in the New Town've been talking on you. You're an interesting guy. Kinda weird, maybe. He's funny when he's *qaŋa*, they told me.'

'I shouldn't use *qaaq* (marijuana). Your *ataata* would scold me.'

'You gotta do what you like. You can go kinda crazy. Like some dreams I'm getting.'

'Everyone has funny dreams,' I said.

'Not like my dreams.' She changed the subject. 'Did you know I'm half-breed?'

'Yes, I knew that. Most of us are half-breed. Me too. Everyone.'

'Gee, I bet you'd like to *–kuyak* with a girl like me.'

'I can't talk about those things.' I was embarrassed.

'Gee, I bet you'd like to *–kuyak.*'

'I wouldn't and I couldn't.'

'You're all right, then. That's what you're supposed to. I'm like you though.'

I've forgotten most of what she said except this last bit:

'I'd sure like to *qaaq-* with you and hear you joking.'

'I'm not going to do that with you.'

'How come?'

'I'm too old and you're too young.'

'Maybe when I'm older. You'll be younger.' Then, as though she thought she had offended me, 'I jokes.'

'It's all right. I don't mind being older.'

All this happened in Asatchaq's cabin. He dozed on and off. And anyway he took no interest in our conversation. He knew that Daisy didn't understand his recitations and that I also comprehended little. The event was one thing, the translation another and when Tukummiq was absent, I carried the performance to her cabin and played it on my little Sony. It seemed natural to transport the old man's voice across the Point in a Japanese cassette machine and convert his polysyllables to modern English on my Olivetti.

Daisy's friendship made me happy. She was alive and clever, instant in communication. Her last words I remember were:

'You gotta tell me about Shakespeare.'

I might have answered:

'One day you can teach me about Whitman and Thoreau.' But that wouldn't happen.

*

Daisy died just one night later. Someone saw her walking by herself round Tikiġaq. She was tearing off her clothes and weeping. The next day, Uqpik and his Search and Rescue team found her body on the sea ice.

*

The Aftermath

Much of February was pleasant. The mornings were clear and the wind intermittent. March brought storms and blizzards. The sun inched every morning off the ice horizon. The story Asatchaq told in December described the Moon Man's violation of his sister. She'd escaped to the sun, re-emerging, vengeful, towards the end of each winter. I'd watch the sun at ten each morning climbing from the sea ice. At first just a glimmer, then in crimson, orange, yellow and in a molten interfusion before dropping away in furious exhaustion.

'That's *siqinnim inua* (the sun spirit) showing us her mutilations', Piquk explained to me.

Asatchaq had told the two origin stories one late December session. First the harpooning myth. And then its companion, the sun and moon story.

The rituals of the sun and moon were complex. There was, in Ur-time, a taboo infraction. Historically, on winter mornings, women used to climb their *iglus* and shout greetings to their Sister/Mother. They held up their babies, with a baby boy's *usuk* sometimes pointing southeast and shout: '*Siqinnim inua!* Make him a good hunter! Make him a fast runner!'

I thought of Daisy. Uyatauna. Rose-Marie.

In a multiple twilight, at the centre with its sheets of blizzard, lay the wounded goddess unappeasable and shaming.

*

Contemporary Religion

Daisy's death has so shocked the village that both churches are holding extra meetings. I've attended two. First with the Episcopalians and then at the *Assemblies of God,* listening to prayers, hymns and confessions from grief-racked women. They unpack sins they think have led to alcohol and drug use. They throw down knives and *ulus* that they use for cooking as though to purge themselves of things they think they've done.

There are guilt-stricken testimonials like confessions to taboo infraction that the shamans once extracted in subsistence crises. All are untrue. But still they reflect the horror that Daisy's death could happen in the village.

There are starker ecstasies. The influx in the past two years of Native Land Claims dollars, Borough revenues from Prudhoe oil, the trauma of the village move: all these have escalated the drug and alcohol presence. The quiet village of 1960 has now entered a world of larger connections: federal, Alaskan, North Slope Borough. Autonomous Tikiġaq is now subject to powers outside.

There are floods of new money. But no-one's taking care of the community. Tikiġaq's both part of a new world and lost within it. When things go wrong, the great powers are absent. It's natural at such times to translate a crisis to apocalypse. And thus visionary weepings ascended from the churches:

I saw Jesus on the *Assemblies* roof!
I too saw lights there. Jesus is arriving!
It's finally coming. It's the Final Judgement!
Save us, Jesus!

I visit the preacher Qiliġniq and his wife Aġniin. They live in the beach
house the church brought here in the 1920s. It's now the Mission
building, the main room filled with fifty years' of tracts and bibles. We sit
in silence. Aġniin is reading the Inupiaq bible:

> *Tiŋmiaqpak tiŋmuruaq qutchiktun: silami nipattuaq nipaturluni,*
> *'Iluilliugutipak! Iluilliugutipak!*
> *Qaŋutua iluilliuqtiginiaqtut innruat nunami.*

'Then I looked and I heard an eagle that was flying high in the air
say in a loud voice: "O horror! Horror!"'

Aġniin murmurs, '*Revelation.*'

*

Patsy and Laura. Teenaged Mystics

Next midnight, Tulugaq returns with Patsy and her cousin.
    'This is Laura,' says Tulugaq pleasantly and leads them behind the
curtain. When Tulugaq dozes, the girls come out and talk.
    They are of Daisy's generation. It's two weeks since her disappearance.
She was victim of insecure liaisons. 'Half breed girl' as she'd described
herself. Brought up part in 'southeast'. Daisy came to be our patron angel.
    There was… I hear Daisy, as though lecturing from death where
Uqpik found her –

> 'There was a childhood back then: games, songs, *ayahgaaq*, the
> *qalgi*, learning to sew with mother, sisters, mittens, boots and
> parkas, bead work, walking out in summer to dig cotton bulbs
> from lemming burrows…

> No hope, no time, no husband and no children.'
> *History echoes her lamentation.*

'We had our thousand years', she sings.
'Our years of freedom and of meaning.'

Fly away Peter, fly away Paul.
Through dead empty space we half-consciously whirl.

In whispers on her fate, the girls, haunted by their love and terror, muse, as though alone, on Daisy's life, her death, irreparable. What they say is visionary, exalted. I don't understand and sit frozen.

'I'm not just myself,' Laura murmurs.
'I'm in my bones, my hair and my skin.
'But I'm not in myself,' impatient she whispers.
'Why don't we go lost then?' answers Patsy.
'Nowhere to get lost!' moans Laura, empty.
'Shine with your glasses!' Patsy whispers.
'And see clearly?'
'See *anything*,' (Patsy).
'But there's nothing,' answers Laura.
'Should we take that step, hers, Daisy's then?' says Patsy, humble.
'The last!' breathes Laura.
'To *siku*! To the ice and sea!'
'I'm not myself. But I'm not *her*,' says Laura, sinking.
'You'll find that,' whispers Patsy.
'But it's nothing,' Laura.
'Up and down. Or half way. Maybe in the middle.'
'Maybe *he* can help us,' whispers Laura.'
'*Him*… Maybe. But bring luck too,' Patsy brightens.
'To be *aŋatkuq*…?'
'The *aŋatkuq* is powerful. But he suffers.'
'Yes, the *aŋatkuq* suffers.'
'You unhappy?'
'What's that? Is it funny?'
'No. You're happy. I mean when you *sleep*.'
'The sleep that *goes on*!'
'That sleep *out there*.'
They measure the prospect.
'What about the others? When you leave them?'
'They forget soon enough. We all forget – people.'

'You remember Daisy.
'*Arrii*! I forget her.' The girls weep together.
'But then,' says Patsy…'I could go school.
To the U. At Fairbanks. Get things done. Get them right.'
'Yes,' says Laura, 'You could do it.'
'And come back. Different.'
'Older. *Arrii,* horrible. How do you fit back again?
Once you've gone there?'
'There is no place for us.'
'Like for Daisy.'
'Daisy.'
'Daisy.'

*

At one and the same time, wrote Heidegger,
It is the clarity in whose brightness everything remains.
And the tranquillity by whose strength everything high stands firm.
And the joyfulness in whose play every liberated thing hovers.

As I eavesdrop on the girls' despairing wisdom, I hear in their voices sages of old Tikiġaq: those virtuosos of survival who enacted forms the girls potentially inherited. These, their brilliant children, muse amid the uninterpretable ruins.

*

The Story of Ukuŋniq

It's 1976, a mid-June evening and I'm wearing old grey thrift-store boots. They're 1960s National Guard footwear and the toes are split open.
'Ukuŋniq!' Asatchaq remarks, pointing at the toe holes. 'Ukunniq's toes came out like yours. They ate people!'
While Asatchaq drinks tea I set up the recorder.
'Where's Tukummiq?' he asks me.
'Tukummiq's sick. She has a cold.'
'Sick. Ah.' Asatchaq sniffs and starts reciting.

When later, Tukummiq translates, I learn this shaman narrative from Ur-time. Ukuŋniq's world is geographically familiar. A boy leaves the village and walks south. He stops at the creek at the north end of the cliffs to compete with spirits. The spirits challenge him to split a driftwood tree trunk for which they give him whale bone wedges. Around the trunk lie human skeletons. These are the bones of previous shamans.

Ukuŋniq's hammer strikes a wedge. It flies up and misses his head. Ukuŋniq's overcome the spirits. He shows them his toes. They run off in terror.

'Run!' shouts Ukuŋniq. 'My toes! They'll eat you!'

Ukuŋniq walks on. He joins a group of inland travellers and sleeps with a woman. But when he wakes the blanket's vanished. Ukuŋniq had slept with a ptarmigan woman.

Ukuŋniq walks further and collects more amulets. Another spirit owns a pair of copper snowshoes. Ukuŋniq fights and takes the copper. The snowshoes sing: '*Ipuputima! Ipuputima!*'

It's nonsense but magic. Ukuŋniq travels to the river where there is a woman who won't marry. She's a shaman. When she combs her hair, the men she sleeps with vanish. Ukuŋniq finds her *iglu*:

> The woman asked Ukuŋniq what he wanted.
> 'I heard, he says, 'about a woman and I came to see her.
>
> '*Ii...Ii*! Yes! Let's fight,' said the woman.
> And they got on the floor.
> Now while they were fighting, the woman lost him.
> She was fighting the floor.
> When Ukuŋniq returned to consciousness,
> The first thing he heard was *Ipuputima, ipuputima.*
> It was the snowshoes.
> They took him to the *iglu*. There was his sled that was made of
>   copper.
> He entered the *iglu*.
> 'Well. You came back,' said the woman.
> 'Others before you didn't make it.'
> 'Yes, I've come back,' Ukuŋniq said.
> 'You can have me,' said the woman.

The story takes place in the travelling season. The sun never sets and everyone has left the village.

So with Joseph and Piquk I walk south and we pitch our tents where Jabbertown stood in the 1890s and Jabbertown graves have sunk in buttercups and poppies. The wind smells of honey. A few bees stumble between clumps of saxifrage.

For twenty miles along the bluffs are canvas-wall tents. The bearded seal migration's started and men walk out and shoot them on ice floes. When Piquk's killed one, we haul it in and carry driftwood up the beach-head. I build a fire while Aakuq pushes meat into the embers.

Neighbours bring a sack of caribou the women have preserved in seal oil. The meat's dark and chewy and the thick bits have a sweet, soft centre. We eat at midnight. The sun burns low. The kids flubber their lips in imitation of a longspur couple, chase ptarmigan and run round barefoot.

I lie down on saxifrage. But the permafrost reaches. I try the longspur call that Asatchaq applied to Rose-Marie and which the children have been calling:

Quppaluk
Quppalaaluk [6]

Everything's alive and in migration. The lagoons beyond the bluff fill with snow goose, scoters, harlequins and bufflehead. On the marshes that surround these, phalarope and godwits, knots and whimbrels. Summer migrations draw people inland. After the whale hunt, they live with smaller species.

I'm touched by the season. An old vertebra crops up between beach stones where I'm lying. This is where Utuaġaaluk murdered his brother-in-law. Maybe that's a bone.

From south to north along the beach, men are shooting guillemots. Piquk chops firewood. Children holler. Kool Daddy, in his trilby's in the tent at cards. Dogs bark. Rifles. I take my boots off. Longspurs perch on a driftwood upright. The sun pours light along the promontory.

I think of Rose-Marie, who's back in Tikiġaq. Born to his sister in 1920, for Asatchaq she'd been a little longspur, so little she fit into her mother's palms, then darting and stitching one thing to another. Now, like Jenny Wren, she is the *person* of her mother's house. Its animation. As though the house walls are the cupped palms of a string game player, she weaves between them: a small, spirit ensconced within the village energies.

It's late afternoon and four cranes fly towards us – perhaps from Nebraska. Aniqsuaq and Piquk run to meet them. They crawl up the

---

[6] Lapland longspur. The *-aaluk* suffix expresses an affectionate 'funny, big old'.

bluff and stand against sky with rifles.

They fire and two cranes rise, flying north until they've vanished. One of the birds stands between the hunters. The crane lunges at Piquk who turns towards it shouting. Its legs spiral and its body cartwheels. Kool Daddy has arrived, still wearing his trilby. He runs against it, man and bird entangled suddenly. The bird's kicking and stabbing. Someone shoots it.

*

'Snowbird' and Whale and *First Poem Legend* [7]

Crane, German *Kranich,* Latin *grus*: the latter the genus given by Linnaeus. Presumably he knew the word derived from Sanskrit *kraunca,* the demoiselle crane, a vision of whose love/death gave rise to the *Ramayana* epic:

> At the beginning of time, as evoked by the *Ramayana* poet, two *kraunca* birds are sporting in the forest and as their amorous debate proceeds, a hunter stands up and shoots the husband.
>
> The sage Valmiki is witness to this spectacle and with his compassion aroused by the widowed love bird's lamentation, anathemises the hunter. 'You,' he cries, 'who killed the husband of this couple, may you not yourself live long!' And from his reaction emerged a *shloka*, rhythmic measure.
>
> Thus the first song arose – and by some freak of etymology, Valmiki's verse, because it arose from *shoka* 'grief,' was called *shloka,* a verse. Poetry's origin was thus lamentation. Returning to his hermitage, Valmiki was visited by the god Brahma who bade him employ his new *shloka* for the opening measures of the *Ramayana.*
>
> The first poem arose from this sequence, which, starting with erotic bird song, was followed by the wife bird's threnody and ended with Valmiki's poem which synthesised the previous utterances. Love, death, bereavement and compassion thus inform the first song's origin, and perhaps all subsequent poetry. One other constituent is the curse the sage directs towards the hunter: a wild tribal fellow who plies a sanguinary existence outside Hindu society and its vegetarian ethic. Valmiki's com-

---

[7] This passage on the birth of song is adapted from my *From Culbone Wood – in Xanadu,* 2013. The term 'snowbird' is Tikiġaq dialect for snow bunting.

passion thus represents only one aspect of his utterance. For the sage who approves the *kraunca* birds' bliss and who responds to the wife's bereavement is one and the same who issues a malediction – while this latter parallels the hunter's action.

And this curse represents no casual reprobation. Its words are shot, parallel with the hunter's arrow, at the hunter's own being, outside the Hindu *polis*. And now he is condemned, by means of the *arrow shaft* of the poem itself, to more extreme exclusion.

Here it's poetry, not Hindu *mores* that detain us. And whether those primordial notes came from the *kraunca* couple in their love or from the widow in her mourning, or whether they arose from human sympathy and an anger which was deflected from compassion into anathema, each declaration contains elements which have a preternatural character. The fact that these declamations come at the threshold of time, lends them mythologic weight: for they are spoken on an empty stage, and thus suggest, in that environment, creational doings.

Love, grief, anger and compassion. What more, might there be to express? I hear each of these arguments in border ballads and Shakespeare Sonnets. They persuade me that I might one day comprehend *Lear, Antony* and *Hamlet* in all their tortuous grandiloquence.

To conclude. In Valmiki's story, we read of a drama which stands at the threshold between two genres. In the love-and-death narrative, we recognise the folk. With the intervention of Valmiki into what so far has taken place in the language of birds, we witness a translation from the forest into the sacred environment of an *ashrama* and Sanskrit.

Thus while the *kraunca* story comes through the high-flown medium of the *Ramayana,* my suspicion that this little tale must have derived from folk lore is confirmed by the discovery of its parallel among a 'primitive' people. This I learned from C.L. Giesecke, Professor at Trinity in Dublin, who recorded a narrative of a bird wife's bereavement while he was travelling among the 'Esquimaux'.

Giesecke records that a Snow Bunting is shot by a hunter and his widow laments – just as did the *kraunca* bird. This story of the bunting or some other bird, as determined by environment, raw and untarnished, must be the *Ursprung* or the origin of *kraunca*.

Tersely wringing its long, brown neck, Aniqsuaq walks back, the bird slung round his shoulders. *Grus, Kranich, kraunca:* the demoiselle crane, *tattilgak* in Inupiaq, whose love/death in Sanskrit gave birth to the first poetic writing. Present cranes had arrived to breed in Arctic marshes. Now coiled on Joseph's rifle they wait for a woman to eviscerate and cook them.

*

Avatiliuuraq, Snow Bunting

'Taam, you know what is a *avatiliguuvaq*?'
'A bit. Though here's the only place I've seen it.'
'You know that snow bird comes round here and make nests in *iglus*? I'd anticipated Tulugaq's message.
'We hunt other birds. Every kind we hunt. Snipers, *qupuluuraq*, ptarmigan. I hunt all those when I was younger. My uncle even give me an old style sling. *Qilamittaun*. Me and my brother sure killed ptarmigan and snipers.'

He drew out a silence that continued what had happened when he'd been at Asatchaq's.
'Maybe I never heard Asatchaq tell story. Gee, that was scary... But I visit my uncle and he told a story.'
'You mean Isigraqtuaq?'
'Yah. Good harpooner.' He says, "I'll tell you stories. But then you forget 'em. Today we don't need those. Sometimes stories, the old timers told us, those stories will get you. They will come get you. The stories are like *aŋatkuqs.*"
'So he told me to watch out. "The stories. They will come and get you."'
Tulugaq continued. 'They got *aŋatkuq* power. You know those stories and you're gonna be some kind of *aŋatkuq*. Those stories they are like *aanguaqs* (amulets) you carry on your body. But those stories get inside you and they gonna eat you.' Then he told this story:

A snow bunting sat on a hummock and wept for her husband who'd been killed by a hunter. A snowy owl approached and sang:

'What a fool to lament that wretched little husband with his spears of grass! I'll be your husband!

The Bunting replied:

Marry an owl? With those coarse feathers,
fat beak, thick legs and forehead, no neck!

The owl stabbed at the bunting and when she cried, he taunted her:

That's women for you! Sharp-tongued all right,
but one little poke will start them whimpering!
And off they flew in their separate directions.

'You hear that story?' Tulugaq asks sharply.

'Yes, I first heard in Tikiġaq. But I'd read it before. Canadian Inuit tell it.'

Journal April 1976

The buntings arrived three days ago, skimming across the point and coming to settle in the ruins of old *iglus*. They are brown-and-white passerines and fly in sweeping patterns expressing confidence that they're secure here. The males arrive first and gather feathers and dead grasses to line nests for their bird wives who'll arrive in a day or so.

Snowbird: *avataliguugaq*. The dictionary gives five dialect versions. Tikiġaq's six syllables are affectionate with music suggesting light, quick movement:

two short a's in *ava*
short a and i in *tali*,
the long u of *uuvaq*.
followed by short final *a*
and the end stop guttural.
Before the q, the final *a* lies deep in the throat, expressing finality.

The bunting is a spring and summer visitor. It's the single creature that can't be hunted. Boys practise shooting .22s at snipe, longspur, ptarmigan and squirrels. Squirrels and ptarmigan can be eaten but the smaller birds are useless.

Buntings in flight appear white from below. 'They come from above,' said old people in the missionary period: local spirits Christianised to angelic beings.

Because it is the whale's attendant, the bunting is associated with the whale's divinity. Because it nests in family houses it also has historical character: its own forebears colonizing *iglus* owned by previous families.

Early this century, people called the bunting *Jiisauraq*, 'little Jesus'.

'My mother,' Aġniin told me, 'she was sitting by her *iglu* when that bird landed, right here.' Aġniin touched the crown of her head. 'My mother didn't move. She sat and did nothing.' As though grace had descended.

Aġniin and Qiliġniq. Qiliġniq was Tikiġaq's first Native preacher.

Later that evening, 'After the snowbird…' Aġniin murmurs in the gas flame, 'After the snowbird comes the whale.'

The south wind sets the chimney knocking.

'That wind needs oiling,' Aġniin mutters.

'What kind oil?' asks her five-year-old grandson.

'Whale oil,' says Qiliġniq.

I'm sitting at the window. Snow blows against old *iglus* and skims across dark spaces that the wind's exposed.

'How about one song?' asks Qiliġniq. 'The old man teach you.'

Qiliġniq wants north wind to keep a channel open for the whales to travel. Deep in the preacher live old connections which priesthood's rendered difficult of access.

Before they were Christians, *qalgi* dancers wore masks depicting spirits they had seen in visions. Two years ago I watched Qiliġniq dancing and watched his ancient face-disc slide out from a surface Christian presentation as he stamped and gestured. While this ancient, pre-Christian feature slipped back to a past identity, the archaic figure and the Christian feature danced together.[8]

---

[8] There's vivid precedent to the coexistence of Tikiġaq religion and Christianity. When the Driggs arrived in 1890, he was befriended by one Anaqulutuq. Anaqulutuq continued to practise as a shaman and Driggs colluded with what the missionary called his friend's *hoodoo*. In his 1894 journal of a trip they took to Cape Lisburne, Driggs wrote: 'Very stormy. I staid in iglu all day. Anaqulutuq did the *hoodoo* act to change the wind.' This is followed by an entry that describes another shaman: 'Wind south. Changed to N.W. [The shaman] Ayauniq changes the wind.' Driggs's leaning towards shamanism coexisted with his Christianity. And Driggs was one of the few 19th century missionaries who didn't suppress Native dancing.

Jabbertown

The south beach evokes journeys. It's a barren shoreline. There's nothing ahead but beach, lagoons and inland country. Hidden to your right, just sea or sea ice, the cliffs forming a horizon thirty miles south.

To travel this strip is to retrace Ukuŋniq's path that led him to the woman he would marry. The journey also led the young initiate through meetings with birds, animals and amuletic objects.

The south was a source: the region from which sea mammals, fish and summer birds migrated. It was also both the symbol and the region of the female. Souls went back there for their reincarnation. The south shore also served as Tikiġaq's main hunting region. To both honour the profusion and harvest it were one thing, not separate.

For more than twenty years, the south beach changed when in summer 1887 Peter Bayne, a hunter from New Brunswick set up a hunting/trading station five miles from the village. A cosmopolitan community of hunters, traders, boat hands, beach combers and southern Inupiat – some for a season, others, for two decades; and at its most prosperous the settlement consisted of ten or fifteen cabins, sheds and Native *iglus*.

Tikiġaq people called the place Jabbertown, most likely for the English, German, Scandinavian, Inupiaq dialects and Pacific island Pidgin spoken here.

Jabbertown hunters killed whales for oil and baleen: the former to sell as lubricant and lighting, baleen or 'whalebone' for corset stays, umbrella frames, whips, buttons and other accessories. Unhindered by taboo or animistic sanction, the Jabbertown hunters went straight for the bowhead in small boats from the sea ice with harpoon shafts from a Pennsylvania foundry.

Both big-time hunters in pelagic ships and smaller land-based crews like those at Jabbertown had, by 1900, disastrously reduced the bowhead herd, while simultaneously, the kerosene trade in the lower states was replacing whale oil as a lighting fluid. With the creation of tensile steel, whalebone was squeezed out of the corset market. As the bottom dropped from both markets, Jabbertown, by 1910, no longer existed.

The southward shamanistic journey was a construct of imagination and only survives in shamanistic stories. Jabbertown has vanished likewise into stories.

Today's Tikiġaq hunters continue to set up hunting camps where the trader Koenig's cabins stood till 1900. And while nothing is left of the old community, I picked up a rusted door hinge on the beach bluffs there one evening. Perhaps it had opened one of Koenig's storerooms.

Jabbertown and Native Cabins

In the first two decades of the twentieth century, six Jabbertown cabins were dragged by dog team to the village. It's easy to distinguish these. Their black tarp cladding and geometric regularity express resolution to withstand the weather. But for all their sturdiness, these cabins proclaimed transience.

Native houses were built roughly on the traders' model. But Tikiġaq people, unlike Caucasian incomers, had no access to American suppliers. Once Natives began to abandon their *iglus,* local architecture became haphazard. And in the absence of lumber, houses were irregular, insulation scanty.[9]

The peninsula lies above the tree line. And whereas the Kobuk and Noatak valleys are forested with spruce and birch, the tallest plants in Tikiġaq are marrain grasses. It was partly this flatness that rendered conspicuous the 'forest of stakes' that Beechey described in 1826. Since the missionary Hoare cleared the village of whale jaw bone markers in 1909, Tikiġaq's houses became the only elevations on a horizontal landscape – apart from Ataŋauraq's monument and the whale jaw bones that mark the positions of the two last ceremonial houses.

Trickster's Landscape

Everything in Tikiġaq arises and then visibly falls away. Some things lie around to weather. Memory retains a few and memories transform to stories. This general truth is represented by the Point itself, the limits of whose two containing beaches intensify the process and whose own enlargement and decay are visible.

Just as people have inhabited this spot for two millennia, so there are archaic stories. These are brief fables in which animals confront each another in what seems aimless conflict.

---

[9] Once driftwood supplies on the south shore were depleted by whaling steamers in the early 1900s, Tikiġaq people in American-style cabins with wood-burning stoves became dependent on stove oil. This continues to be catastrophically expensive.

45

Beast Fables

'Animals pop up unexpectedly,' said Kunak one day *en route* to Cape Lisburne. His expression was not simple. He understood we'd see caribou and brown bear. An animal's appearance is exciting. And while its appearance may not be anticipated, its scale in the landscape has large implications. These join some event beyond village life where some of it you eat, other parts you wear. An anonymous creature from out in the cold enters the body and warms the skin.

Inupiaq animal stories express a cruel wisdom. Whatever its species, all living beings are alone and suffer. Life presents obstacles; there are rival species. Animals are headstrong, quick to quarrel. Life is short and folly's punished.

Inupiaq fables are archaic but not all of them northern. Versions are told by people elsewhere and tribal narratives are converted into texts like Aesop's *Fables,* La Fontaine, the Sanskrit *Hitopadesha,* the Grimms' *Maerchen.*

While the 'household' tales of literature sometimes supply a moral, such endings are foreign to Native idiom and fables outline things that simply happen. True, there are didactic stories about fools and lazy children. But there's no ethic to animal fables: they're raw comedies of existence.

In Tikiġaq, it is tempting to imagine that fables, like animals that 'pop up', were themselves in residence and they inhabited the earth whether or not in human company. They have quickness, life force. While animal behaviour may seem pointless, fables are representations of being, animation.

Thus the meaning of a bunting story corresponds to the existence of the bird. Story and animal are equivalent, and this simply *is* until the bird ceases to be and the story is over. When there is nothing, there will be another.

String Figures

Elders today sometimes describe the beast fables as 'children's stories'. This is appropriate. The stories have the immediacy both of children and things that children like. And the beast fables are the children of the early world. They hop round as component players of first principals.

The fables are often crude descriptions of an interaction and many have been absorbed into fast moving string games: the *ayahaġaaq* (cat's cradle) about which Daisy is imagined to dream.

In *ayaháġaaq*, a circle of seal line held between the palms is manipulated into semi-abstract transformations. The string moves in coordination with the narrative and when the string collapses, the space between the hands is empty.

Just as there is nothing once the pattern goes slack, so when a live animal disappears, the environment it had animated returns to quiet. The stories have restless, sometimes convulsive movement. Their often simple climax is soon achieved.

*

Absence of purpose in stories is matched by the emptiness in which fables are enacted. Each drama happens in a void which animals animate. This contributes to a sense that the stories take place at time's experimental beginning.

The environment in which these events happen might be called Trickster's Landscape: a void in which the painful or deceiving action of an animal or a spirit, generates life. Death, eating, copulation and survival are all without much affect.

Inupiat admire animals for their completeness. An individual may achieve perfect form. But there is little to do except exist. This is in the nature of things. The Trickster deities of origin myths, in their vague, heroic outline, are magnifications of the mischievous animals of the fables. And these animals of origination achieve creational success through the same egotistic means as the minor species that quarrel merely for the apparent reason of an other's existence. In this landscape, life simply happens, and when it happens, it clashes with coincident phenomena on the world's uncertain surface.

Five Tikiġaq Fables

1.

Here's a seagull with a song. It tied a stone round its neck and flew across a river. When the seagull got across, it said, 'They sometimes have games. But I'm no good at anything. When they start to play, I won't have a game to challenge them with.'

So the gull thought: 'Next time I cross the river I'll take a larger stone to carry.' When it reached the other side it found a larger stone and hung it round its neck. Then it started to cross.

Where is the song?

Archaic song unintelligible.

The gull went across again and looked for an even larger stone.
Just when it was half way across, the gull fell in. It shouted:
'There are kayaks coming! And two skinboats. They're coming
to help me!'

But it thought its own feet were kayaks. And its wings he
thought were skinboats. That's how it died. *Told by Asatchaq*

2.

A lemming,
running round and round
the skylight
round in a circle
fell through the skylight
and started crying:
Sung-ang-ang-aa!
Sung-ang-ang-aa!
My ribs! My ribs!
I think I've broken them! *Told by Umigluk*

3.

There was a lemming which spent sunny mornings outside a
brown bear's den. One morning, the bear emerged and found
the lemming. 'Watch out,' said the bear, 'I'm coming to get you.'
'Come on', cried the lemming. And then shouted, 'Come out all
you lemmings!' And they came.

New ice was forming on the nearby river. And the lemmings
chased the bear towards the river. The bear tried to run across. But
the ice was too thin and it fell in the water. 'Come and help me,'
shouted the bear. But the lemmings just laughed and the brown
bear stopped struggling. When it was dead, the lemmings were
happy. 'Now we have a year's food supply!' *Told by Qimiuraq.*

4. Raven and Loon Story

Taimmani, back then when animals were people
Raven and Loon were partners
and agreed to tattoo each other.
'Me first,' said Raven.
He was white at the beginning.
So Raven took lamp soot
and drew fire sparks
on his partner's feathers.
That was how Loon
got the pattern on his feathers.
But Raven tired of painting
and grabbed some soot and ashes
and tossed them over Loon's back.
That's why it's grey now
Loon was angry.
He scooped soot from the pot
And threw it over Raven.

Raven had been white.
But now he's black.
And stayed that way. *Widespread in the Arctic.*

A Modern Folk Verse – 1973 Journal Entries

Another beach. August 1973. A fish net's pegged into shingle and extends through the water where a float holds it vertical. Every few hours we haul the net in, sometimes with jellyfish, otherwise loaded with Arctic Char.

'They want to know why you come round here,' says Samaruna suddenly.
'What brings you round here, white man?' echoes one of the players. Everyone laughs.
'Looking for a party?'
'Maybe you've brought *qaaq*?'
'What's *qaaq*?' I ask.
'Yah. That's what we call *badweed*. We call that *qaaq* because it makes your mind explode'

'No *qaaq*, sorry…'

Another voice, more challenging:

'You CIA or FBI?' A painful silence.

'I don't think they'd employ me, I'm English, not a Yankee.'

The oldest of the men addresses me in Inupiaq. Everyone chokes. I'm confused and frightened. Nervously infected by their laughter I produce a strangulated giggle. Someone comes to my rescue.

'His name's Q. He wants to know if you brought your girlfriend with you, because if you have, he wants an introduction. Right now!'

'Sorry, I didn't bring her this time. I'm still looking unfortunately.'

'Aym-still-looking-unfortunately!' declaims a man in educated Cambridge.

The men lie down laughing. 'My ribs!' someone chokes, 'My ribs-they-gonna-bust-all-right! The wind picks up and the dingy lurches. All jump into action and drag the boat higher.

'OK, stop that!' shouts a man called Aviq.

Then, 'Can you stop it white man?' A man named Suluk, with a face as though cast from bronze, explains:

'We want you to stop that wind from blowing.'

The older man, Q: 'Tell it blow round the other way. Or maybe stop it blowing for ever! If you don't have *qaaq*, we want to see your white man's power!'

August 21 1973

Uqpik came in this morning with a pot of sea slugs. He sits eating them raw and says, 'You're a poet aren't you?'

'I try now and then.'

'How many you got?'

'What?'

'How many poems you got?' (chewing).

'You mean how many have I written?'

'Yah.'

'I haven't counted them.'

'We don't do that at Cambridge,' he says satirically between mouth-fuls.

'Well, here's another that I made about you:

'Tom Lowenstein come to Tikiĝaq.
Goes down on the beach.
Looks up at the sky.

Sees a sea gull.
Sea gull shits in his eye.'

Later in the store, an old man approaches and stands with his face in mine.

'You the white man?' he asks softly.

The question pushes coldly at me. 'Because if you are,' his voice descends to whisper, 'maybe I can help clean that bird shit out of your eye.'

Suddenly the man's face opens and light pours from it. Invisibly, beyond the store shelves, anonymous voices quote Tulugaq's poem. It has become folklore.

Snowbird and Crane

The snowbird fable and *krauncha* story are parallel, and similar in presentation of a love-death drama. Erotic pairing in both narratives is violated by a hunter and the happiness of partnership is followed by the survivor's dirge. At the core of each story lies love-death sorrow.

Sanskrit culture has adopted the Valmiki/*krauncha* episode to claim the origin of poetry. The bunting story makes no such assertion. Instead, Tikiġaq custom reaches back to the snowbird fable.

'Children! Go hunt longspur, snipe and squirrel. But don't shoot the snowbird,' goes the elders' warning, renouncing the bunting fable's outcome.

Here follows an imagined sequel to the elders' precept. It brings together the arrival of the buntings which herald the whale's arrival:

> Don't shoot at mating couples. The buntings have arrived at their reproductive moment. They've migrated for that purpose and make their home in human *iglu* ruins.
>
> Refrain from widowing a breeding couple at the moment when the bowhead's coming. The snowbirds raise their children in old *iglus*. These are the days when Tikiġaq will hunt the bowhead. The men take their skinboats to the sea ice. The women sit at home in silence. They contemplate the hunt and draw whales to them. This happens as snowbird couples nest around them.'

*

Journal. South Beach, July 1976

Someone jabs my shoulder.

'Taam! Wake up. You gotta tell a story!'

I'm stretched on a mattress someone's sledded from the village.

'I don't know stories.'

'You know stories!' It's Margaret who'd claimed I'd come to steal the language (see below).

What Margaret had said was childish. But her scolding contained truth. You can't steal language. But you can create conditions in which one language dies and another replaces it. Margaret herself was a victim of this history.

'Since you learned 'em, you gotta tell us,' Margaret continues.

'But listen. It's not for me to tell your stories.'

'You belong here now,' says Margaret casually.

'Anyway, we want to hear 'em,' growls a stranger. 'We want to hear those stories.'

'You better tell us. In Inupiaq. We won't understand if you tell them in English.' Paralysing tension binds me. It's five in the morning, the sun is high and it's cold. Someone dumps branches on the fire. A shocking heat cascades across the body.

Words form in the throat and are trapped on the larynx as though birds' wings stuck there. I grasp a verb stem and grope for an infix. Parts of a sentence start to separate, then hold together. I detach another verb-stem that was threatening to drop back and inflect its ending which grafts itself onto the next one till the sentence emerges.

'You talk our language like a baby,' gasps Margaret when I've finished. She's weeping with laughter.

'And when will you find yourself a woman, down there on the river?'

'She might cut off his *usuk*!' groans a voice from the mattress. The fire has collapsed as the laughter continues.

Part 2

Fairbanks
Finding Asatchaq

Fairbanks, September 5 1975

I swing through the doors of the Care Home with the casual self-assurance of a thirty-five-year-old with no anxiety about his legs and who doesn't expect to lose his balance. An octogenarian whose legs and hips have been worn out on the sea- or river-ice and by transporting heavy animals, observes the mobile arrogance of a younger man with blazing and reflective recollection and sees deep, through cataracts and semi-blindness, as if by x-ray, into working joints and ligaments.

'I'm gonna borrow your cheeks,' an old man scarred with frostbite barked at me one Tikiġaq winter. Another growled, 'I'll have his legs. He can try mine. He won't like 'em.'

Dead air and the smell of thrift store seconds hit me. Still, the bungalow is light, clean, up to date and situated at the edge of town in undeveloped woods, footpaths, meadows and log cabins.

I walk down a passage and stop briefly in the common room where half a dozen Natives and a black man sit in wheelchairs. The TV's inexhaustible. *Charlie's Angels*, rerun for Alaska, is playing. A Yupi'k woman, dark blue tattoos round her face and hand-backs dozes in a wheel chair.

A Yukon River man in check shirt sits by her. His eyes are white with cataracts; his lips mumble. He may never have seen a coastal Eskimo till he came to Fairbanks. His ancestors reached Alaska eight thousand years ago; hers perhaps two thousand later. If they share any language and happen to talk, it must be in English. She would be Orthodox, perhaps Moravian, he Episcopal or Catholic.

The men are in shirtsleeves. One Inupiaq man wears seal skin boots. The Athabascan man wears moose skin slippers. The black man is Henry, an ex-rail-coach steward, retired in the nineteen fifties from the Burlington Northern, to chance his hand 'Where Northern *means* north, man... Ready to go, to go out now,' he whispers, as though humming a blues line.

I stand in the doorway. There's a man in the corner slumped across a copy of the *Daily Telegraph*. I peer through his fingers at the date of his paper. It's five months old now. The old man wakes, adjusts the paper and starts talking. Name of Alfred. Cockney. Merchant seaman.

'Wot's yor nime, ven? You fr'm London? Long way, ain't it? Come to live wiv Esky-moes? You'll find plenty of old Esky-mo codgers rahnd 'ere, nice lot mainly... This ain't such a bad place. Wot's ve difference where you die, eh? Bye now, Tommy.'

The *o* of Tommy's drowned by wheezing. Alfred lives his days with philosophic courtesy. He's brought his character in perfect order to this terminal contraction and has started to unload it.

I go to the desk and ask if Jimmie Killigivuk's available. 'Jimmie? *Sure!*' says the woman with a friendly downward intonation. 'He's down this corridor, then to the left in Room Nineteen.' For seven months I'd searched for him in Tikiġaq and Fairbanks. Locating him now is disarmingly straight forward.

*

I find Asatchaq asleep on his bed. His room is small, square, quiet and uncannily remote from routine care home business. It's lit by a window which stands open onto spruce, birch, willow bush and fireweed. He might be camping in the forest.

I stand watching a jay bird in a dusty willow. Aspen and cottonwood crowd against a rough lawn underneath the window. Chickadees play in late summer foliage. Bees stumble through a clump of ragweed. A man with a toolbox emerges from the generator shed whistling a Dolly Parton number. A White Admiral shimmers past him and a dragonfly shuttles to and fro through grass moths. Late summer is precarious. Winter could arrive tomorrow.

Asatchaq's curled in a rough arc on his bed top. He's a small man, stocky, thin, bowlegged. He has short grey hair; his hands and feet are arthritic. He wears a white shirt and black worsted trousers. There's a walrus tattoo on his left inner forearm. Below the walrus hangs a loose, gold-plated wrist watch. The room's sunny and retired. Apart from glasses on the bedside table, I see no belongings. He's dressed soberly, as though anticipating company.

Now I've found him, I am disappointed. Is this all? Just this old man, by himself, asleep here? No agents, ethnographers or heads of department competing at the bedside?

As for the person I intend to be informant, maybe he'll be more than I can handle. Why not slip out now before he sees me? If he wakes before I exit, I'll pretend it's a mistake. 'Sorry, I was looking for Alfred.' The old man would turn over. I'll never have existed.

These thoughts zigzag between larger questions. (Why here, my life, and not in some European garden, at some library table?) More immediately, there's etiquette. Approach him with speech? A cough, a shuffle? There's village gossip. He's miserly and autocratic. White men, in the past, have flown to Tikiġaq. They seek ethnographic conversations. A mean, withdrawn look overcomes his face and suddenly the stranger's on the air strip waiting for the mail plane. In what guise do I approach this person?

There are kind, well-meaning Christians, the university professional, the ethno-hipster come to groove on palaeo-linguistic vibes. There's the principal investigator, anxious not to waste a grant from Washington, investing his sabbatical on insider views which speak from the margins.

I've encountered some of these personae in myself already. Westerners who've lived in Third World villages uncomfortably struggle with their privilege. Of equal non-importance is the nature of the Westerner's identity. Set down on the Kalahari or the tundra where your psychology's invisible, you realize, that to people round you, that you could be anyone. Or simply you're a type. This echoes ways that you see 'them': less individuals than representatives. You're a white man. They are 'Bushmen', 'Eskimos'. Types that resist exfoliation.

I hover on the threshold and contemplate the patriarch. Potentially he's dangerous. We'll start work together; then he'll slam the brakes on. Then I too will shuffle towards the mail plane. Last year I had an office at the university. Students called me Dr or Professor. In London, I found filing clerk work, then taught on 'supply' where five years back I'd headed a department. Late summer, as I calculate vicissitude, blazes through the window. It is beautiful and transient.

Both this redoubt of Caucasian America and, outside, the sub-Arctic struggle to prolong the season, accentuate the old man's isolation, far above the tree line. Trees to the old man are irrelevant. A story he recorded later tells how trees once grew in Tikiġaq.[1]

---

[1] In February 1895, the missionary Driggs travelled south from Tikiġaq to the Noatak valley and wrote: 'Yesterday was the first time I have seen trees in nearly 5 years…It seems good to be in the woods and out of the wind.'

Asatchaq's secluded from this phase of boreal ecology. But he'll recognise the winter. The two of us, in mutual separation, hang within a four-part structure:

There's the care home, stone-built following the flood of 1967. Framed in geometric section by the window there's this afternoon of summer. In the foreground, Asatchaq's asleep, enclosing in his body, as though carrying a microfilm, an ancient culture. Anxious and ambivalent, I cross the threshold.

I know his surname *Killigivuk* was thus converted to a surname after Asatchaq's father, *kiligvak*. Father *kiligvak* was small, the Pleistocene beast from which the missionary derived a surname was enormous. Tusks and molars ancient hunters chased across the Land Bridge emerge from the earth through river banks and beaches. This last human mammoth lies in semi-exile.

Daylight's faded. I cough and call his name politely. Asatchaq half-rises and casts round for his slippers. Then sitting straight in quizzical anticipation, he recruits awareness and extends a hand that grips mine softly. I'm gratified and disconcerted.

I think later of the work this hand's accomplished. The meat, blood and fat it has harpooned and hauled up, skinned, dragged, butchered, given with self-deprecating generosity and eaten. The nets and rifles, spears, slings, snares and harpoons, dogs, harnesses and packs, the sled lashings and skin boats it's managed. The drummings, dances, rituals, sexual escapades it has engaged in. Soft, yielding and domesticated, this hand now stretches out to greet the possibility of friendship.

'What's your name?' His words in English accompany a handshake.

'Tom. Aniqsuayaaq,' I offer him in shorthand.

'Who gave you that name? Aniqsuayaaq was *Taam* too. My father's harpooner.'

'Kayuktuq named me.' It happened last winter. We were vacuuming the school room. He said I looked like Tom Goose, Aniqsuayaaq, who wore the same blue woolen hat as I did. Our hats were *atiqs*,' I joked unwisely. Asatchaq ignored my sally. *Atiq*, namesake, also means a soul component.

By the time he's aligned my presence with old Aniqsuayaaq who'd died in the 1940s, I gather Asatchaq's agreed to know me. Or he's retrieved some parallel identity on which to mount my presence. I am, via *atiq* theory, a version of old Tom Goose.

'My father's skinboat. Aniqsuayaaq always worked with him.' I tell him that I've come to work in Tikiġaq.

Asatchaq replies with memories of Aniqsuayaaq. 'I last saw him on the south side. 1930. June time. After whaling. His camp was this side.' He gestures with his forearm, as though measuring an angle drawn along the south beach.

'He was walking slowly. Carrying a *tattilgaq* (sandhill crane). Legs round his shoulders. Its wings hid him.

'I thought that bird had come to get me. It was like a *puguq* (ritual figure*)*. Just the head and feathers. I saw his hat then. And his gun stuck out. Bird, hat, gun. Beak hung across his *usuk*.'

What the *puguq* was, I didn't know yet. I learned later how Asatchaq and other ten-year-olds lay on the *qalgi* roof and watched autumn rituals through the skylight.

'Pogok,' wrote Rainey, 'is the name applied to... carved figures which were made at the time of [a *qalgi* meditation]...' (Rainey 1947: 247)

The *puguqs* invoked souls of animals and brought luck to hunters. Tom Goose at that moment was a compound: man, crane *pugaq*.[2]

Artists and statesmen live in revolt against obliteration. Not so Aniqsuayaaq who just worked to live and was leveled in death with billions like him.

His name's retrieved briefly in a single image of a hunter walking west past skin tents, meat racks. Once back in the village, he vanishes entirely.

The people in the care home know Asatchaq as Jimmie. His family called him Asatchaq in memory of two late forebears: one was an aunt, the other was the shaman Asatchaq, a distant uncle. The name Jimmie and his surname were donated by the missionary. According to the parish register, early converts took names from the Bible: Sarah, Eva, Judith, Isaac, Simon... Powerful namesakes.

As, through the weeks, I sit with Asatchaq, I close my eyes and imagine Kuukpak River, north of Tikiġaq. From the banks on the river, tusks fall into the water. Two years later, as I'm pegging out a fish net I scoop a fossil molar from the gravel. The surface ridged for grinding *Artemisa* grasses. *Kiligvak*, back then, was hunted and propitiated. First the mastodon perished, then mammoth.

---

[2] I thought of Mozart's Papageno with his wild bird costume who had entered stage and musical existence on C.L. Gieseke's return to Dublin with his specimens from Greenland.

We drift into silence. I stammer news from Tikiġaq and he listens with indifference. I'm desperate for home and am doubtful of the future. Then the old man says abruptly: 'Sure. I'll tell stories. We'll go back together.' I gather my things and walk back to supper. He seems scarcely to notice.

*

The care home's at the town's edge off the airport highway. Sometimes en route, I stop at Macdonalds to fetch him a hamburger. This goes with beer we drink together. At first, we wrap our cans in paper bags but when I realise that it's legal, we don't bother to disguise it.

The road to the home starts with roaring traffic dust and peters out in scrub land where the railway meets the river. This is the stretch I like walking or biking. Town life dissolves. There are ponds, gravel pits and little cabins.

One landmark near the home's a herbalist. I once knocked on the door and pressed my face against the window. Spearmint, yarrow, willow bark, dried mushrooms stand in preparation.

Another cabin sports *bodhisattvas* at the window. What Buddhists live here, or are the icons ornamental? A group of pot-heads live across the meadow. In blue-and-white gingham, Darlene, on the front porch, sorts through berries and a-fixes of her winter pickles. Brad's come from Five Mile Line Camp where he spent his free time welding a small suit of armour. Halberd extended, the iron man stands rigid on a whiskey crate from which flourishes a bush of marijuana fed by outhouse oozings. A window *mandala* proclaims *Om* in a lotus.

Opposite the nursing home, the Dept. of Parks and Recreation has reclaimed some wasteland and ringed a softball pitch, complete with baseball diamond and a stand of benches.

Before biking home, I watch the women playing in the dim September evening. Tonight's the final between Swann's Drilling Team and Frith's Fossils. They're union women from the 'Over Thirty-five Geritol League'. Husbands, boy friends, children, colleagues crowd the benches and lean on their pickups with cans of beer and Coca Cola, shouting their teams on.

'O.K. girls! Come on! Let's play ball! That's the way, Trudi! Swing, girl, swing! Go! Go! Go! Let's catch that ball! Force the third! One way now! Swing! Stay ready out there, girls!'

Trudi, forearm bandaged, skies the ball into the wasteland. Two home runs. The league's over for the season. The women cluster round a stand of trophies on a pickup. A speech, with wisecracks about tits and fannies, follows, raising cheers and whistles as Trudi steps up to accept the trophy.

*

It's two p.m. and thunderously muggy. I'm thirsty from my walk through town and then the outskirts. In the care home carport there's an ice-cream van. It's flaringly painted with transcendental iconography. Planets, UFOs and Third Eyes float above a paradise of temple gardens. Yogis and *yakshas* sprawl in foliage round the driver's window, where a scholarly young man in army fatigues sits reading comics, smoking.

An Athabascan girl, lured out by Schumann's *Träumerei* on the ice-cream bell, limps through the swing doors, buys a strawberry, lights a Camel and reenters, smoking. The ice-cream music modulates to Brahms's *Guten Abend* and the van drifts off towards the river.

*

The track by the river twists into scrub past cabins where Native men spend summer and autumn. They come to Fairbanks for work as drivers, linemen, carpenters, electricians. Their families travel south to visit and then cousins and brothers fly down to replace them.

It's a tranquil spot. The men walk home evenings and check the snares they've fixed for rabbits, ptarmigan and squirrel between birch and willow. Moose and coyote blunder through them. People fish through the ice, October onwards. No-one stops them.

I walk down here on sunny afternoons and stroll round the ponds. I recognise some dragonflies that correspond to European species. The huge *Anax* that feeds late in autumn and the blue winged *Agrion* of European rivers. Owls take over from the loons and pintails in the evening. Yesterday I stumbled on a pellet of coyote scat in which I found a vole's skull, whose own defecated body packed its cranium.

*

Imagine an old folk's home for multinational Nobel laureates. Powerful as they were in their time, they spend their last days paralysed, incontinent, dressed in cast-offs, penniless, dementing.

Since science was abolished fifty years ago, the world, in my imagin-ation's, in an improved way, on a new, reformed system of which these old women and men have no conception. Here they sit, respectful and compliant, while with patronising self-confidence, the kindly peons of the master-race bustle round to make them comfortable. The arrogance of this new breed, limited as it must be by an absence of historical awareness, is not cruel. How could they understand what their present masters have obliterated?

The old scholars, nonetheless, remember vaguely the principles by which they once lived. Smiling and nodding obediently to their keepers, they're wheeled into the common-room each morning, and as the TV raves, they sit contemplating the tremendous theorems which brought them joy and suffering.

Their attendants bounce in and out, shouting in their ears and tittering. Since each one of these old folks comes from a different part of the world and are specialists in separate fields, they scarcely communicate with each other. Sometimes, a couple who spoke cognate languages find their wheelchairs touching. But the TV's roaring and they're too exhausted to raise their voices.

*

'The simplicity,' I scribble in a notebook as I once leave Asatchaq. 'Above all the simplicity. And behind the simplicity, realms I can't imagine.'

Another old Inupiaq sits staring at the window. His life is finished. He dwells in the coda of existence in which work and 'doing nothing' counterpointed one another.

That double rhythm is expressed in stories. The word *suŋitchuq*: 'does nothing'. First there's work, love, dancing, danger, violence. Then suspension. Each segment of experience an act of being. The violence and stress of travel, hunting, butchering. A journey to the village. Hills, rocks, cliffs, snow, blizzards, marshes. The wind blows against them. The hunter fills space and then leaves it empty. Space, too, has its being. At home there's more work. Distribution. Storage caches. The women scour the hides and tan them, stretch them out and peg them tight above the beaches. Then cutting and shaping, measuring and sewing. They eat, sleep deeply. First work, and then nothing.

A glimpse at the vastness of Tikiġaq culture. I've been reading Rainey's 1940 field notes. One of his informants was Niġuvana. Died 1942. Here is a list of things she kept by her:

— fish skin sewing box with bleached seal skin bottom
— needle case
— steel *ulu* (woman's knife) with whalebone handle
— sinew from rump, back and front caribou legs
— jade needle-maker
— bow drill with ivory mouthpiece and sinew bow
— seal skin bag for keeping clothes
— brown caribou skin boots with seal-skin soles
— striped caribou waist-high boots
— boots with white at front and back, brown on sides; white stripe up
        thigh, with wolverine skin fringe
— women's mittens
— belt from caribou throat skin
— bearded seal skin belt for pants with knotted thong
— long underwear pants from summer caribou skin
— seal skin pant-boots, up to waist, bearded seal-skin bottoms
— hip length seal skin boots
— waterproof seal skin boots
— winter boots up to knee or waist
— short pants to below knee
— men's knee-length socks
— fawn skin boots
— ceremonial caribou and wolverine boots with stripes and checks
— short boots with beluga skin soles
— bird skin socks
— caribou-ear underpants
— seal pants for winter with strip of reindeer above belt
— insoles of shaved, wadded-together baleen
— two parkas
— short baby boots
— seal skin diapers, with moss
— seal skin baby's sleeping mat
— polar bear mittens
— thin caribou skin gloves
— caribou mittens, hooked to belt
— caribou-leg mittens, fur on back outside
— wolf and wolverine parka ruff
— seal-gut rain parka
— scraped seal skin rain parka

— walrus-gut rain parka
— waterproof boots, high and low
— spotted seal skin bag for clothing
— sleeping bags for winter camping
— caribou and reindeer mattresses
— iron pots
— big wood pot for lamp-oil
— stick for hanging blubber to drip over lamp
— wooden mallet for smashing lamp blubber
— wooden spills for carrying light
— seal skin bag for fire-making equipment, includes two kinds of flint, charcoal, cottongrass
— big wooden spoon
— sheep-horn ladle for drinking water
— wooden platter for large hunks of meat
— men's eating dish
— big wooden pan
— children's plate
— soup bucket with handles
— wooden spoons
— seaweed for hand-towels
— moss for wicks
— pot for lamp-soot and discarded bones
— wooden slop bucket
— boy's slop pot with handle
— husband and wife's night-pot
— girl's pot
— gull's wing brushes
— woven whalebone strip mat for entrance
— wooden frame for entrance hole
— wooden windbreak for entrance hole
— entrance passage frame for hanging parkas
— log-splitting wedges of four sizes
— adzes
— hammers
— skin-scrapers of wood and mammoth ivory
— scraping-board
— caribou horn and ivory combs
— knife-sharpener
— ivory and bead ear-ornaments

— copper bracelets
— bead necklaces
— animal amulets
— reindeer skin tobacco bag
— entrance passage drying racks
— iglu interior drying racks
— stone lamp by entrance
— stone lamp under drying rack

Rainey also cites a list of men's equipment, excluding sleds, skinboats, kayaks, masks and figurines. There are forty-six items. The lexicon describing each and the elements that make up the equipment matches the material culture. Each artefact had its terminology. I note one example:

Five different shaped stones on leather thongs, composed a bird sling. To find each shape, boys crawled along the south beach to find the pebbles. Each shape had its name:

- *qutchuŋuaq*	like water drops
- *manniŋuaq*	egg shaped
- *qivluinnuuqtuaq*	square
- *satuquyaq*	flat one
- *uqatuġa*	leaf-shaped

Stones and thong today are simplified and reduced to *qilamitaun*, and this sling is what young Tulugaq used to hunt snipe and squirrels.

*

I'm here at the care home with beer and burgers and I wander through the corridors. They've moved Asatchaq to share with an old Yukon man who sits up and shouts his own dance song: *Ayaya! Ayaya!* On the second occasion, Asatchaq scolds him in Inupiaq, then in English: 'We're trying to work here!'

Asatchaq is always hungry. Here in Fairbanks, six hundred miles from his coastal village, he's starved of 'real meat'. 'That's what I call it.' He thrusts out his jaw and grabs the Macdonalds with strong back teeth.

'These teeth,' he gestures to his canines, 'they're called *kiugitiik*. They're like a polar bear's. I always had these long front teeth. And when

I was born, I never ate whale meat. Only caribou, bear or seal meat. Until I was twenty.'

'Which shaman put you in taboo?' I ask him. The old man cocks his head and squints. He drags the left side of his mouth down when he's thinking. It's as though, as he does this, broadening a screen within him, scenes and people enter. They've been gone sixty years. When they enter fresh and lively, he projects them.

'It was Tiguatchialuk. He was the shaman. He showed my mother the three Itivyaaq spirits. My father paid him ivory and seal skins. When my father caught a whale in 1920, they found Tiguatchialuk's tooth marks. He'd bitten that flipper when he visited the spirits.'

It's mid-September and just weeks ago, I'd come from Tikiġaq. It's hot in the interior. No one knew where Asatchaq was. 'He's having a rest,' was the neutral opinion. He's eighty-five, his breath is short and his knees are paralysed with arthritis.

Asatchaq is vague about the future. 'I'm going back. When you go back, we'll go back together. Then I'll tell stories.'

He's started to prepare some recitations. And since, at our first meeting, it was as though he had reentered an abandoned history which reached into the nineteenth century, then further back to myths and legends. Born at the start of the Christianising dispensation, Asatchaq associated with the values of both the traditional and the American regimes. And feared as he was by many as the last local 'heathen', he was honoured as a scholar.

Meanwhile, this Fairbanks bungalow is his refuge. And to white folks, Asatchaq is just another pleasant-mannered ancient. Not that any resident's neglected. Their native past is nonetheless unreachable.

Inupiaq, Yup'ik, Gwitchin, Koyukuk, Tlingit, Ingalik, Aleutic. Most native groups are represented here, living out their final days in virtual silence. Stranded in their rooms and in front of the TV, the old folk sit, in thrift-store shirts and trousers, a patchwork map of tribes from a country the size of Germany and Scandinavia, and whose people, in their riverine and coastal villages, seldom meet except when they come to be cured of white men's diseases or to die in isolation.

As for me and this archaic stranger, I'm as innocent as the high-school kids who clean the room and change his linen. I'd spent six months in the village and now I've found him in this ordinary environment, the quest seems both too complex and too easy.

Our meetings continue through the autumn. As other Tikiġaq narrators used to say: 'I don't know much. But if you want stories, you'd better find Asatchaq.' This was a conventional disclaimer. Tradition demands modesty. The spirits wreak vengeance on a braggart. Dancers and singers must likewise be prudent. 'There are those who are better. I can do little.'

And just as animal spirits report back to their spirit families, so stories, songs and dances are performed according to precedent. If gestures or words are casually performed without respect to detail, then ancestor souls will show their displeasure.

Just as animal souls must be returned contented to their 'countries' where they'll be reborn, so stories are living entities. 'Watch out,' one man warned me, 'Don't make mistakes. Don't leave things out. Those stories otherwise will get you.' By which he meant that narrative itself has shamanistic energy.

The death of a seal brings life to humans. Stories, likewise, restore life from 'back then'. The order of things depends on right conduct.

Remote as this might be to Big Macs in Fairbanks, my relations with Asatchaq depend on such proprieties. He anticipates my deference, expects submission to his age and status. I must acquire appropriate behaviour.

Sketches of pre-contact life emerge in semi-formal ethnographic conversations. These sketches don't approximate a recitation. Meanwhile, Asatchaq experiments with conversation in mixed English and Inupiaq. And to locate his ancestry he starts with his great uncle Asatchaq, a late pre-contact shaman.

His English isn't good. My Inupiaq is rudimentary. The history is complex. I get tangled. He's talking about Asatchaq, one of the last shamans to make spirit journeys and who 'flew' to fight a rival in Siberia. Mid-autumn's taken over. As we sit on his bed, the window dark behind him, the opaque tale unfolds in fragments:

> *There is travel to the further shore, probably East Cape in Chukchi Siberia. There are fights, gestes, murder. Someone's flying. The traveller adopts a weird flight posture, one leg bent backwards. Asatchaq's familiar, a biting rodent, executes the killing.*
>
> *Counter-shamanistic visits happen. Tikiġaq and East Cape swing unsteadily across the sea ice between Alaska and Siberia. Shamanistic competition. Power issues.*

'I'll carve you a *kikituk*,' says Asatchaq one evening. The *kikituk's* the rodent-like familiar that a shaman harboured in his armpit and which he dispatched to eat into a rival's heart, before it scuttled back into its owner's parka.

'I'll make Elizabeth one, too,' the old man added. Elizabeth, the high priest's wife, was one of Asatchaq's visitors. He didn't get round to giving her a *kikituk*, though he carved one for me. There's no point in asking Asatchaq the meaning of the gift intended for a pious Christian. In a good, eventful life Elizabeth's acquired no enemies.

*

These twilight evenings are unnerving. The Inupiaq I've learned comes quickly unravelled. Asatchaq's talk is arcane, involuted. I shift restlessly, ask baffled questions. Asatchaq is disappointed. He sees how little that I understand. He's irritated, withdraws, resorts to silence. He turns his back. I stumble out to walk through Fairbanks. 'You should listen,' he would growl, 'then you'll learn the story.'

Internal Exile: Alfred from London and Henry from Chicago are both a long way from their homes of origin. Almost all of White Alaska shares this distance. By contrast, Native people became displaced in their own country. There were, however, in Alaska, no wars of conquest and extermination. Unlike Lower States Indians whose lands were stolen or appropriated, very few Alaskan Natives lost territory. But contact changed their settlements unrecognizably. Riverine nomads were 'settled' into villages where trade and Christianity could happen. Autonomous people became dependants.

The late nineteenth century was the heavy contact period. Most summers, they stood as children, these wheel-chaired men and women, on Arctic beaches or river banks and watched bearded men row towards them. These men carried firearms, exchanged beads and tobacco for furs, ivory and 'curios'. In small groups, they seemed harmless. They were often useful and some forged friendships. Some white men settled in the villages, others moved south, their boats riding low with lucrative products. They were few in number. What remained in Native cultures were European habits, manufactured things, new technologies.

Some villages were obliterated by diseases. Others, like Tikiġaq, endured and patched a compromise together. Those who lived through epidemics travelled and continued hunting. But they also attended schools the whites established.

Tabulated below are some of these exchanges from a page of Heinrich 'Cooper' Koenig's journal. It's from Jabbertown, July 1889. Hard to ignore, given the subsistence crisis, how small were quantities of goods that Tikiġaq let go.

Received from natives	Given by Koenig
Whalebone 25 lb	425lb flour
Dogskin boots	1 yard drill
1 large, 1 small sealskin	250 primers
1 coil seal line	5 yard drill
6 deer skins	50lb flour
whalebone 16 lb 5 foot long	75 lb flour, 4 ?drill?
seal line	1 package matches
whalebone 18lb, 5ft long	25 lb flour, 100 .44 cartridges
1 seal skin	1 small tin cup
frame for small canoe	100 lb flour, 5 yards drill
large sealskin	25lb flour
1 larger seal skin	25lb flour, half lb tobacco
1 white fish skin [beluga]	25 lb flour
2 small seal skin	150 primers
1 spotted seal skin tanned	3 lb flour
1 seal poke [bag]	1 lb flour

September – October 1889

Received from natives	Given by Koenig
9lb small whalebone 5 foot long	3lb powder, 250 primers, bar lead
3lb whalebone do	200 primers, 2 bars lead
1 pair deerskin boots	half lb tobacco
1 deer skin	5 bars lead
underclothing	3 bars lead
6lb whalebone [skullbone & jaw]	20lb flour, 11 b?
1 white fox skin, 1 mink	5 yards print
110 white weasel skins	6 yd print, 5 bars lead, 1 tin cup
1 dog	25lb flour, 1 qt molasses
2 deer skin artiga [parka] &	
2 pair pants	75lb flour +?
1 pair deer skin boots	half lb tobacco
? seal line	4lb tobacco
2 fishnets	25 lb flour 1lb tobacco
1 red fox and 1 white	2 knifes [sic]
1 white fox	half lb tobacco

1 squirrel skin shirt	?
3 white fox skins	half lb tobacco
1 coil seal skin line	3 lb lead
1 dog	some sugar and little other things.[3]

The journal for the next two years is relatively uniform. Then in 1893, the food inventory's more varied. Koenig notes lard, baking powder, fresh and dried potatoes, syrup, dried tomatoes, apples, peaches, bacon, butter, oat meal, corn meal, ginger, cinnamon. Such was the beginning of the composite diet. Most people still lived in *iglus*. Some built quasi-European houses. Christianity and shamanism coexisted. Hunters took seals with both harpoons and rifles, wore calico snow shirts over skin parkas. Rifle shells jangled against tooth and bird claw amulet necklaces.

Material life was soon visibly changed; the people themselves changed more slowly. Village people spoke Inupiaq, preserved some old ways that tied them to the landscape, ancestors and animals. And in spite of Christianity, stayed in touch with local mysteries. Thus while they entered American time, they also continued to live beyond recorded time, where they moved within patterns out of reach of white men.

I look round these shrunken figures in their secondhand clothes. Within each body, intelligence still plays, rehearsing, in silence, incommunicable systems. Like Asatchaq, these are heirs of two traditions.

Native communities take care of their old people. But behind each person in the nursing home lies a complex of events which displaced them.

A woman from the Kobuk had three children. Two daughters left for Anchorage. The son stayed home and hunted. Then on the river, he broke a leg and died of exposure. The old woman went crazy. One night in her grief she set fire to her cabin. A social worker brought her to Fairbanks. Now she sits waiting for transfer to a home in Anchorage.

A man aged sixty from a Yukon village. Three years ago he crushed his rib-cage. He was taken to hospital, convalesced in the nursing home and then suddenly gave up, refusing to go home. His son travelled to town to fetch him, but the old man said he'd die pretty soon and might as well do that here as anywhere.

An old woman of eighty-five: spry as a fifty-year-old, she lived with her disabled daughter and then had a stroke. Paralysed and dumb, she came south, lay six months in room 15, while her daughter in the village

---

[3] Koenig trade journal: 1880–1914, University of Alaska Library Archive, Fairbanks.

died of pneumonia. So she lies staring at the ceiling.

And the storyteller Asatchaq? What brings him to Fairbanks? The kindly competence of social services accounts in part for this privilege of upkeep. Here are care home notes that summarise his recent history:

*

Medical Notes for James A. Killigivuk

Born: Tikiġaq ?March 189. Religion: Episcopalian
Admitted with bronchitis, September 1974

11–74	Discharge planning
	depression
	inability of care for self & manage funds
12–74	Intraoperative cardiac arrest
1–75	Irregular pulse
7.75	Bells palsy, left cheek
	cataracts
	old TB
	arthritis; pain both knees
7.75	Anemia
9.75	bronchitis

Comments: Apparently no-one at home can take responsibility to have James die at home. Any future travel there would certainly be temporary, but definitely therapeutic for him.

Historical Interlude

Frohlich Rainey was one of the 1939 archaeologists who with Larsen and Giddings uncovered the pre-Eskimo Ipiutak houses and burials of the people which had lain within the peninsula since about 900 AD. Rainey returned to the village in 1940 and recorded elders born in the 1870s, one of whom was Asatchaq's mother Niġuvana.

I have edited Niġuvana's account of Asatchaq's birth and added some paragraphs about the social and religious systems to which Asatchaq became affiliated. It is hard to imagine a contrast greater than between life as Niġuvana describes it and late twentieth century existence.

At the height of his power, 'chief' Ataŋauraq planned to build a Euro-American house with lumber and a stove that he had ordered for summer 1889. It was not to be, and Ataŋauraq was shot dead on St Valentine's Day 1889. Ataŋauraq's household had included several adopted children. One of these was the teenaged Siuluk, and Ataŋauraq contrived a marriage for him with Niġuvana, then about fourteen. One function of this marriage was to bring a clever young woman into a modernizing household.

This marriage was without issue and just outlasted Ataŋauraq's death, when Niġuvana was taken by Siġvana for her son, Kiligvak. There were three surviving children: Asatchaq, Nanny Uyatauna and Piquk.

'My mother was capable and clever', Asatchaq told me. 'My grandmother was also strong and could outrun a caribou fawn.'

Siġvana's was a gesture of hope. Both spouses' families had opposed Ataŋauraq, and the village needed a new generation.

The village population was disastrously diminished and had, by 1890, reduced the population from ca. six hundred to a hundred and sixty. Worse was to come during the 'Great Sickness' at the turn of the century, reducing Tikiġaq's population by 1906 to 121. But the new family thrived. Kiligvak survived until 1925, and Niġuvana until 1942. Here is a genealogy:

Siuluk = Niġuvana = Kiligvak
(ca.1875–1942) (ca.1870–1925)

Both Kiligvak and Niġuvana came from skinboat owning families who had weathered contact with the white man since the 1880s. And while Ataŋauraq had terrorized both families, their dealings with the white man had enabled them to prosper a little. To deliver a son at this historical moment was a major event.

*

The Birth of Asatchaq

Late spring 1891. Niġuvana and Kiligvak left the village with about fifteen relatives and travelled north towards the Utuqqaq River. Stopping to gather eggs at Cape Lisburne, the party reached Cape Beaufort in early July. Here Niġuvana went into labour, and while her husband and brothers were building a hut where she and child would be secluded for the summer, Niġuvana gave birth.

Four women, Utualuk, Aglaq, Qiina and Sininaluk were present as Niġuvana delivered. They sat and watched as she knelt behind a mound of earth and the child came out on a skin. Niġuvana, who would later become a midwife, started to get up, but the afterbirth had not fallen.

'Wait for the placenta!' shouted the older women. Niġuvana obeyed, then picked up the boy child. The women ran over. Qiina cut the cord and tied it with sinew. Niġuvana wiped the child with sealskin. Then they dressed him in a fawn-skin parka and slid him inside a sleeping bag. Niġuvana crawled into the hut and the child was handed in. There she sat in taboo – 'to keep the child alive' – until September when most of the party returned to Tikiġaq.

On the night of Asatchaq's birth, Niġuvana's father Piquk came to hold the baby and he put it inside his parka while she rested. Later, when the baby wanted milk, Piquk woke his daughter and she fed him.

On their way up coast that summer, Niġuvana's father had made a clay pot for her. On the fourth day after the birth, the older women built a fire outside her hut and started to boil water. Niġuvana had been fasting. Three small bits of caribou meat and a piece of whale skin with blubber, no bigger than a finger-joint, were cooking in the pot her father had made her.

Niġuvana was thirsty but didn't feel like eating. The women offered her two spoonfuls of broth. She drank these and then kissed the baby's nose and genitals to keep him from making too much water. Then she blew on his right hand and his left foot and stretched him long. 'T-t-t-t-t!' she whispered.

Next, Niġuvana ate whale skin, followed by the bits of caribou. Then she drank some more broth and threw the rest away. If she had eaten before the cord was dry, the child would not have grown up to be a good hunter.

The Spirit Guardian (*Qumnaaluk*)

Soon, Asatchaq's guardian visited the birth hut. The guardian was non-family and would be the child's main spiritual mentor. Baby Asatchaq had two guardians, the shaman Nuiġaaq and his daughter, who were to give the baby his social and spiritual identity. The guardian would present the baby with name, amulets, taboo rules, ritual affiliations and membership of one of the village football teams.

The guardian's visit would also constitute the child's first social event. Until now, the baby existed outside the framework of village identity. The act of naming was also important. With name, the child became allied to several Tikiġaq namesakes. One of these was an aunt called Asatchaq, another was the recently deceased male shaman. A third was a maternal great-grandmother, long deceased. In naming him thus, the newborn was bound into a continuum that had both historical significance and present urgency. Namesake connections had to do with soul theory. Humans were animated by three main souls. Two of these were personal, but the name soul was shared by both living and dead individuals. The naming process sometimes involved whispering names into a baby's ear until it smiled at the one it wanted, thus enacting a process of transmigration. At this point the infant *became* the deceased namesake.

Given that the child was also associated by name with two female relatives, the baby's identity incorporated both male and female, shaman and non-shaman, living and dead souls. Thus within the texture of the society, each individual enjoyed a multiply textured self, and was defined by three older people who anchored him in local genealogy.

Amulets and Taboos

The guardian's next gift was a squirrel skin, representing the baby's first amulet animal. The parka squirrel, which was one of the first animals that boys hunted, is a small, harmless creature, with moderate soul power. Later, Asatchaq became associated with polar bear.

A second amulet was determined by the child itself. This was the moment he laughed for the first time – perhaps the baby's earliest communication. At this moment, one of Asatchaq's uncles tied a sinew bracelet with a flint attached to the baby's wrist. This could have represented a traditional stone amulet bestowing physical strength. Or it might have come from one of the muskets currently in use. Or it could have been an old arrow head. But the fact of its having been donated at this moment, placed the action within traditional practice.

This was true of another amulet: a scrap of umbilical cord, which identified to Asatchaq's amulet *class*. Most people belonged to one of two classes relating to birth and death – plus a third group connected to menstruation.

Perhaps to reinforce the optimism with which his birth was received, Asatchaq was assigned to the birth class. This meant that to activate the potential of personal amulets, he must rub them on the body of a pregnant woman, a woman who had recently given birth or some object connected with birth.

People in the death or menstruation groups empowered their amulets by bringing them to grave goods, human relics or menstrual pads. This system with its existentially profound implications was perhaps the most extreme of Tikiġaq's taboo regimes and it fell into disuse soon after Asatchaq's birth.

The guardian finally determined the child's avoidances. For Asatchaq, this involved a taboo, lasting nineteen years, against eating whale meat. That Asatchaq should have grown up within a whale hunting family as a non-whale eater suggests an abstinence that harmonized grimly with the subsistence crisis into which he was born.

It is also significant that Asatchaq stressed that he ate polar bear meat when he could have mentioned seal, walrus and caribou which he also ate. Not only were polar bears plentiful, but the bear was a source of hunting power whose meat, skin, teeth and claw amulets bestowed success.

Building polar bear meat into the young man would thus enable him to become an adept in both the polar bear and the whale hunt. Asatchaq was also believed to have kinship with polar bears and grew unusually long canines.

Lastly, Asatchaq was assigned to a football team. Everyone belonged to one of two groups, and Asatchaq joined his paternal grandmother in the team carrying land amulets and kicked away from the Point. Games of winter football usually happened when someone spontaneously started to play. At this signal, both young and old climbed from their *iglus* and joined a struggle between land animal people and those who had sea mammal amulets – the latter kicking, often over several miles, towards the peninsula point.

The one social affiliation for which the guardian had no responsibility was ceremonial house membership. A boy joined his father's *qalgi*; young women entered their husbands'. To avoid the guardian being accused of recruiting future hunters for his own group, custom dictated that the *qumnaaluk* the came from a different house to that of the child's parents.

These affiliations complete, the child was ready to enter society. This followed the mother's period of seclusion which generally lasted about three months. Asatchaq would probably thus have arrived in Tikiġaq in September.

Fairbanks Again

He lies on his bed. Slippers by the bedside table. I sit quietly. Still, in desultory fashion, we've started work together. I'm pleased to have a name that ties me to the namesake system.

A Tikiġaq name ties its owner to both past and present. My local name is also a fictional extension, a local self, a mask connecting me to village history. I'm both sceptical and acquiescent. I am and am not Aniqsuayaaq. It doesn't matter. My other self has no existence.

Asatchaq discourses on my namesakes and their families. 'Aniqsuayaaq. His mother was a shaman.' His narrative extends to genealogies. He orders me to write the names down. I trip on spellings and lose track.

Now that he's fixed me in my namesake's history, he sits up as a courtesy and pulls on slippers. His English is hard to follow. When he puts in his teeth, the words take form. But English doesn't fit his mouth. Words, like letters on a crumbling wall, are deformed and faded. My Inupiaq is still less efficient and my ramshackle proficiency renders what the old man says more frustratingly ambiguous. His gestures likewise. The movement of hand to eye or a gesture of his forearm, evoke relationships within a story whose connections he expects me to interpret. Almost everything is dark to me.

Darkness is our medium and it's what we share. I've spent four months in Tikiġaq, walking the surface and chattering in English. Suddenly the village history yawns and the present floods backwards, sucking the central heating in his bed room into prehistoric winter.

Somewhere in this void, subverting my comfort, a Tikiġaq shaman, the old mastodon's namesake, wanders the coast of northeast Asia engaging rivals in a game of violence. Or he's on a soul-path to the moon, freezing in the radiance of the lunar spirit.

But the journey to the 'other side', (Siberia), and moon-trip, collapse across my hemispheres. Stone lamps, harpoons, masks and shaman effigies circulate in darkness and are swallowed by the same abyss that generated history. The past spirals like a cinder.

I take him beer and we sit watching chickadees outside his window while a vacuum cleaner moves towards us in the corridor. To Asatchaq, both bird and vacuum cleaner are foreign. He has knowledge of all Arctic species and a grasp of genealogy that stretches through the nineteenth century. The chickadee and vacuum cleaner are anonymous phenomena, as is the white man from London. This nescience is mutual.

Part 3

Fairbanks
Starting Work with Asatchaq

Fairbanks Autumn 1975

I spend mornings in the campus library where instead of studying ethnographies, I evade the challenge, browse Virgil's *Aeneid,* and ponder a line I'd written out from *Monsieur Teste* by Valéry that a teacher had dictated. 'Que peut un homme?' the teacher read. A haunting question.

It was autumn. In three or four months, I'd be back in Tikiġaq, and optimistically assuming that hard necessity would shape my work.

Still, I was disconcerted by the convergence, on the one hand, of my ethnographic unpreparedness and by the demands of Arctic living. Should I not either be better academically prepared or headed for somewhere, like a Japanese coastal village where I might construct an ethnography of seaweed gathering and its relationship to poetry.

There were logistical preoccupations – food, money, housing, cold weather clothing. I was also preoccupied by recollections of a 1960 meeting in Tel Aviv, when Helena, a clairvoyant, had spontaneously read my character.

'So long as he does things,' said Helena. '*Taten*: actions. Right now, he's nothing. Do things,' she said vaguely.'

She'd glanced into my skeleton and muttered, 'Not much there yet.' '*Taten!*' she repeated. '*Du musst ein Mann der Taten werden!*' [1]

Later I dreamed that Asatchaq and I were stranded on an ice floe. He was paralysed and I was helpless. The voice of Helena echoed round the Arctic Ocean.

*

The Pict no shelter now shall find
Within his party-colour'd mind.
          —Andrew Marvell, *An Horation Ode*

---

[1] 'You must become a man of action.'

These lines were quoted to me by Mrs Charlotte, the missionary widow I met in September. The poem was part of a long harangue that Mrs Charlotte delivered at me in the High Priest's garden. Her words, like Helena's, continued to echo.

I'd never understood the *Horatian Ode*. And while I didn't know whom 'his' referred to, Mrs Charlotte was categorical.

Was it, I asked, the rebellious Pict, against whom Cromwell had opposed his forces, or was it the Lord Protector who was party-coloured? And what, anyway, was party-coloured? What Marvell impressed on Mrs C was that our minds are composed of contradictory elements and to pretend intellectual unity is self-deception. We're all diverse personae. And Mrs Charlotte comprehended the split loyalties of Native people like Asatchaq and Sioux she'd known in South Dakota.

I knew Asatchaq better than she did, but when Mrs Charlotte described him as 'an old pagan', she was also alluding to the old man's party- (or parti-) mindedness. As Mrs Charlotte understood, a German Jewish Londoner working in an Inupiaq community represents self-contradiction. Everything to such a person is of interest and no one thing remains entirely true. Agnostic paradox offered the foundation of nothing.

*

I think of my father and his exiled elders much of whose conversation lay between quotations from Heine and Goethe, as though poetry, even in the Anglophone UK, could express any phenomenon. I thought, too, of his army mate whom my father described as spending the war reading Proust in defiance of Hitler.

All this returned when my father appeared in my Tikiġaq cabin one night. It was shortly after Daisy's disappearance and my father had died fifteen years earlier. I'd shown him some of my university poems and we listened to music together.

Then I lost touch with him and it was only once, that he returned in spirit, and requested an account of what I was 'up to'. And pointing to a volume of poetry that lay on my table, remarked sardonically,

'Well at least you're reading something worthwhile in your spare moments.' And he quoted Hölderlin's *Die Kurtze* — of which this is a rough translation:

My song's like my luck. Surely you're not happy to go swimming
at twilight? Everything has gone. The earth is cold. And in your
face the night bird, in disquiet, is whirring.

'So what's this Eskimo business about?' he mused as though thinking aloud.

'It's OK, is it,' I replied in modest supplication, 'to spend time on things that may not be entirely relevant?'

'Frankly,' he said, casting his eyes round the cabin, 'this is ridiculous. You could catch an extremely severe cold. Think of your poor mother. Besides, this is a dangerous, hare-brained exercise. Get home to where you belong where there are libraries and music. Find yourself a woman who will bear you children. You're good at teaching. And you can spend your spare time reading poetry. Then there's cousin Riekchen. She'll talk Hölderlin with you. You're a quietist,' he concluded. 'A European. Leave this sort of expedition to Americans: their anthropologists these days who measure things scientifically. And wilderness mystics. You're unsuited to it.'

His spirit visit lasted a few minutes. Then he vanished.

'I don't understand that poem either,' came his voice beyond the window.

'That way's south,' I shouted. 'Left at the National Guard building.'

*

Sortes Vergilianae Alaskanae

Cumae was where the Trojans made landfall, northwest of Naples. It was wild country, from where the Sybil led Aeneas on his underworld journey.

My reading during this pre-fieldwork period consisted largely of displacement activity. More relevant was Cumae's equivalence to Tikiġaq as a site of multiple pre-habitation. Both Tikiġaq and Cumae were wilderness regions, both marked with signs of early occupancy. Ruined temples, sanctuaries and the statues marked Cumae, just as the remains of ceremonial houses and archaic burials marked what early visitors observed in Tikiġaq.

Meanwhile in Fairbanks I was bored with walking through the evening traffic to Asatchaq and noticed local registration plates had numbers starting AEN or AED, followed by three digits, as though referring to lines from the *Aeneid*. I started at that moment using Virgil as an oracle.

I'd been 'conning my Virgil' as school masters described that activity and was enchanted by the texture of Virgil's verses, and that the pliability of his hexameters was also monumental, as though carved from stone: the noun relationships, as if magnetized to one another, held together by case endings that attached themselves to one another in mutually fructifying oozings.

The Aeneid Book VI opens with an evocation of the cliffs, flints, forests, chapparal and caverns rising over south Italian beaches, while Aeneas's men leap between rocks and the hero looms among shrines scattered round the Sybil's sanctuary.

I was also preoccupied with the verb *sulluk-,* which the linguist Larry Kaplan translated as 'the sea travellers come ashore briefly': Arctic landscapes and Virgilian travellers thus converging in my imagination. So Virgil's poem came alive as I contemplated the seas and landscapes through which Native peoples travelled.

The *Sortes Vergilianae* (Virgilian divination) was an old divination practice based on opening the *Aeneid* and applying random lines to questions. Just as the Romans read animal entrails and bird flight, so medieval clerks used lines from the *Aeneid*. Sir Philip Sidney in *Defense of Poesy* wrote in 1595:

> ...so far were the late Romans carried into the admiration of poetry, that they thought in the chanceable hitting upon any such verses great fore-tokens of their fortunes were placed. Whereupon grew the word of *Sortes Virgilianæ*, when by sudden opening Virgil's book they lighted upon some verse of his making.

Thus prompted by the Fairbanks traffic and limiting play to passing numbers, I built a collage of Virgilian omens, as follows:

> Given that the *Aeneid* is divided into twelve books of 700–900 lines each, and that a three-digit registration suffix is too short to suggest both book and line number above ninety-nine, I improvised two methods : the number AEN 612 referred both to *Aeneid* Book VI:12 and line 612 from the next book opened randomly. Thus if the page falls open at Book II, the second reading will be Book II, line 612. The two readings are thus:

Book VI, line 12
Delius inspirat vates aperitque futura:
The Delian seer breathes ... and opens the future.
Book II, l. 612 *eruit. hic Iuno Scaeas saevissima portas:...* 'uproots.
Here most savage Juno ... the Scaean gates...'

Because some single lines make no sense, we must sometimes refer backwards and forwards to derive the original meaning. The temptation to gather too much sense should however be resisted. The system depends on a haphazard method, and the point of the game is less to arrive at a truth than to decorate a passing moment.

Thus a line of Virgil, interlarded with a number from the Fairbanks traffic, becomes a new kind of registration: the vehicle in its path across my own trajectory enters the continuum of Latin *poesis*.

One other reading:
Registration AEN 966 outside Super Rexall Drugstore leads to
Book IX. 66
ignescunt irae; duris dolor ossibus ardet.
'indignation burns in his hard bones'

AEN 396 leaving a university car park:
Aeneid III. 96
accipiet reduces. antiquam exquirite matrem.
will welcome you back. Seek your ancient mother.

This was whimsical and threadbare entertainment. Still, I practised the game for the happiness of keeping Virgil active. The game also coloured hours that I walked through Fairbanks once snow had settled and like footnotes engineered to literary prognostication, AEN and AED distracted me from vehicle exhaust that froze round the nostrils.

These loaded prophecies meant nothing. There were multiple things that any one of their images might have connoted. And while lines from Virgil could return to their places in the epic, traffic came and went uninterpretably.

*

Asatchaq had lived actively until he was eighty, but his wife Kate and his later partner Sally were dead and his three children had moved to Anchorage and to southeast Alaska. Tauttuk, Daisy's mother, had died in Juneau.

Asatchaq was the oldest Tikiġaq elder and while he was related to almost the whole village, there seemed no domestic arrangement for him. The context of this lay in several areas of estrangement. He was estranged from modern Tikiġaq which had moved away from the traditions that he associated with social order. He despised modern life and had no connection with the New Town Site while sitting in an old Tikiġaq he could scarcely step out in.

*

Another aspect of Asatchaq's isolation lay in the fact of his age. It is difficult for younger people to grasp the reality of aging. One tendency of youth is to view age as a Gestalt. It's alien from mainstream experience. Just as casually we walk past old buildings, we take age so much for granted that we assume that someone has always been old and that this – while paradoxically we request archaic memories – is who they have always been.

Likewise, we take casually the fact of near-death status and efficiently make use of the short time we have to record an elder's knowledge. At other times, we regard old age as a condition which people should have been careful to avoid. Still, we venerate them for the accomplishment of a status that actively they have done nothing to achieve.

In this respect, the phenomenon of aging is passive. Just as a plant withers, so in age we start falling to pieces. There's no mileage in repining. And while I divined Asatchaq's regrets and he talked of friends he'd never see again, he never complained of his limitations.

Still, one thing is marked among Tikiġaq people with peculiar intensity. While children's lives are protected, the ordeals of adulthood are relentless.

Boys accompany older relatives onto sea ice. They go about their business in a storm of challenges. Every moment requires life and death decisions and in order to emerge as the person who entered an ordeal, the hunter cultivates a core of self-possession. A supporting and illuminating shaft of light sustains mind and body and connects each individual to the village.

But youth exhausts itself early. The transition to old age is absolute. But in Asatchaq's case, internal exile exacerbated aging.

Many of these generalities are truisms of which Tikiġaq's experience represents just one example. But in Tikiġaq life, the change from one state to another, represents a dramatic separation. The hunter who exercises social generosity, will become its recipient.

Yet this is only one aspect of the old man's alienation. Elements of Asatchaq's care home isolation are common features of aging experience.

Health workers in even relatively homogenous cultures will have little time for residents whose language and culture they can't share.

*

Another aspect of Asatchaq's alienation lay in his relationship to me. I arrived as a stranger and so I remained, albeit a friend, until his death in 1980. My Inupiaq name helped enable our relationship because this placed me theoretically within local genealogy. I was at his side to take an interest in his narratives. I was a surrogate ceremonial house audience and as my knowledge grew, so our intimacy deepened.

Asatchaq also sometimes called me *partner,* while Tikiġaq people referred to the old man as my grandfather. And when finally I did address him as grandfather, I was moved by the way he replied in a voice of recognition,

'You called me *ataata.'* But I was proud of our partnership, as Asatchaq called it, though Asatchaq may have used that word crudely. 'Partner' was a word used by traders to sweeten the commercial nexus. It had a western tang which I liked for its cinematic character.

But 'partner' in English is also crude. In Inupiaq, there are many different kinds of partnership each with its function. Some were intra-societal trade and spouse exchange associations, with children therefore having near sibling status.

One of the jokes that made me popular, was to say about someone that he or she was my *qataŋun,* 'out-of-wedlock-partner-generated half-sibling'. It gratified me to be able to make learned jokes. But it was perhaps patronizingly easy, because I was committed to fitting in. And perhaps I also thought that anyway we're all the children of sexual partnerships and this makes everyone part of the same family.

Still, I was a stranger, despite what one of my friends said to me as once I was leaving, 'Don't be a stranger!' This was a version of what Qiliġniq said, and who once thrust his face into mine and whispered: 'You Eskimo!'

This latter occurred several times. And while aching to be in a string quartet or kissing a girl in San Francisco, I longed for village integration. I was taken into Tikiġaq society as though I was an intriguing variety of meat. And while I allowed myself to be digested, I, in turn, ate Tikiġaq, digesting the experience in harmony with cuts of me they relished. All this happened as a part of my relationship with Asatchaq.

Much of Tikiġaq lore had been lost by the twentieth century: repudiated by Christians and *iktaq'd* (thrown out) as unnecessary and in part simply allowed to fall to pieces. The past was linguistically inaccessible to the younger generation. Transmitting it to a white man both authenticated it while rendering the material safe.

In this respect, I was a harmless, neutralizing container and my possession of the lore rendered it biologically dead. Traditional knowledge contained organic life and this previously was kept alive by an interconnected audience. People passed it on alive and thus sustained the lives of hearers.

That life for me would exist in tapes and footnotes. I was part of the machinery of transformation. And I was instrumental to the culture as a whole, at once securing the lore artefactually and, in separation, sterilizing it in separation.

To Asatchaq, I was largely instrumental. Perhaps this was how he related to everyone and in that I too was *using* him, I reciprocated. But I was, in his company, less myself than with most other people. Partly because our limited language skills made it difficult to touch, I remained as remote to him in my deference as he remained distant as his self-possession demanded.

Asatchaq was unvaryingly courteous except when he was scolding someone of the younger generation. But I could not imagine him reaching beyond who he consistently remained in his self-affirmation, and for example, doing anyone a kindness. Kindness flows from an empathic consideration of another's similarity and/or their difference and thus connects people who otherwise might remain isolated. Asatchaq accepted kindness graciously. But partly because he was in no position to extend a kindness, this did not come naturally.

In this way I remained, like his nursing aides, an outsider. When Asatchaq, Tukummiq and I completed our first period of work, Asatchaq dictated an Inupiaq statement declaring that 'Three sticks can't be broken.' By which he meant that our partnership had the coherence of a composite tool.

This touches on the question of loneliness. We all belong to the global population and however solitary we may feel within the fragmented passage of experience, we remain part of a collective. In Asatchaq's case, however, I became aware of an isolation that lay within particular elements of social and historical alienation. To observe him sleeping on a neatly made care home bed with the knowledge of the old man's separation both from Tikiġaq society and from Fairbanks, was to become aware of a separation from virtually every social group to which he might have been connected.

*

I was also aware of the privilege that enabled Asatchaq to have landed in this quiet room, a comfortable bed, good food and medical attention. This, he too, appreciated and was grateful to his sponsor, 'Lady Elizabeth', the priest's wife, for getting him into a good residence. Perhaps he felt like the English merchant seaman Alfred that 'it didn't matter where you died.'

But Asatchaq had no intention of dying. He clung to life and his anticipated betrothal to Lady Elizabeth's near hundred-year-old mother represented to him a new beginning. The care home and his separation from Tikiġaq provided him, paradoxically, with a platform for a fresh start. My ethnographic involvement also gave him a motive to continue. He seemed not to recognise the close horizon. And when he was dying in winter 1980, he showed no sign of accepting the finality of his moment.

Human connection, friendship, mutuality are perhaps our highest goods. And in this regard, Asatchaq accepted the limitations of who and where he was, lived stoically in solitude but grasped every possible relational connection. He regarded his alienation both as a phase and as a reflex of his guardianship of truths which he thought would recondition society.

And my appearance as his amanuensis appealed to him as part of a historical continuum. He understood the importance of what he knew and it seemed natural that an earnest young white man should come along and validate that knowledge.

'Take it to the Governor,' he enjoined me. He wanted to establish Tikiġaq lore as a component of good order, perhaps throughout Alaska: as though traditional knowledge would provide a foundation for the reconstruction of life as it had once been.

In this connection, I sometimes experienced what he told me as solids. Perhaps it was because I carried notebooks and tapes that I entertained the fantasy that I too was building something. I had a vision of the physical presence of a book. And I experienced even story fragments as objects.

This, on account of my own solitude, was no doubt a projection and I found myself repeating 'These fragments I have shored against my ruins,' and it was my happiness both to inhabit ruins and to imagine building something from them. Thus our solitudes met.

I also experienced Asatchaq's presence in Fairbanks as a representation of Tikiġaq. It was less that he brought information with him, but that he *was* Tikiġaq, or perhaps that he was, and carried within him, a piece broken from the peninsula.

*

I loved the old man. But many didn't. His younger contemporaries were very different. There was sweet natured George Omnik who sat alone through his eighties weaving baleen baskets. Uyaġaaluk, overwhelming and satirical. The visionary intensity of the preacher Qiliġniq who expressed through dance and drumming a pre-Christian identity which he balanced with his priesthood. Wise and knowledgeable Umigluk, skin-boat owner and oral historian with his repertoire of songs and dances and ironic humour. The self-deprecating Roy Vincent, whose biological father had been a white whaler. Piquk, Asatchaq's younger brother, a sage of modestly undisclosed knowledge. Each expressed the often boisterous self-confidence of Tikiġaq character as though ready to embrace a whale or at least struggle with it.

The older women I admired were as wise and knowledgeable as their husbands. The most imposing was Ayagiiyaq, a large old woman who lived in Kotzebue with her husband Saġana, who shared with Asatchaq the status of master historian. Saġana had been Ernest Burch's main informant in the 1960s and was as courteous as his wife was sarcastic.

For several decades Saġana and Ayagiiyaq had travelled widely before spending their final years in Kotzebue. Ayagiiyaq came occasionally to Tikiġaq. She was blind, and while she walked clumsily, she was a wonderful dancer and had inherited a men's dance.

It was frightening and unnerving to watch Ayagiiyaq dance. Female dance movement is conventionally understated. It serenely accommodates the accompanying two-in-a-bar drum percussion. Women dance in legato gestures without moving their feet far. Their movements participate in the flux of time and express acknowledgement of life rhythms. Spacially, it is more restricted than the boldly enacted male dithyramb.

Men's dancing is heroic and confrontational. It enacts the dramatic character of hunting and shamanistic vision. One foot stamps in time with the drum while the dancer flings himself through angular, often defiant postures. The male dance keeps time with life-death relationships with animals, arduous travel, killing for food, exhausting travel. And the often terrifying ecstasy of visionary experience within which the souls of animals and ancestors interact with humans. Whatever the wilderness experience, which often prompted the character and narrative of dance, the dance and often its accompanying song represents a self-confident social and aesthetic resolution.

The men's dance that Ayagiiyaq inherited she enacted with what Lorca described as *duende:*

> '[which is] a power… It is a struggle…. I have heard an old maestro say, "The *duende* is not in the throat; the *duende* climbs up inside you, from the soles of the feet." It is not a question of ability, but of true, living style, of blood…'

Following a dance, Ayagiiyaq completed her performance with gestures of self-dismissal, as though to suggest that it lay beyond comprehension.

*

Just once I visited Ayagiiyaq and Saġana in Kotzebue and needed a guide to find their house. I was greeted by a young man I had never met. He was large-eyed and intense and on one forearm, was a twisted leather phylactery. 'Taam!' he shouted, 'We've been expecting you,' before vanishing. While Saġana told stories, Ayagiiyaq sat beside him, making song-like gestures. It was as though she were still dancing.[2]

In varying degrees of intimacy, I got to know about a dozen older men and women and most refrained from offering opinions about Asatchaq. Many old people lived in semi-isolation, their households maintained by younger families, the boys hunting, fetching stove oil and water, the women sewing, cooking and looking after children. Asatchaq's isolation was, in this regard, semi-conventional. He commanded no household, but like his contemporaries, he lived indoors.

When I last visited Tikiġaq in 2009, the community had constructed an old people's home. During the 1970s, one could plot village composition on a map representing about thirty households, each converg-

---

[2] Later, in a back room of the Fairbanks museum, I saw trays of objects found in 1960 during the Cape Thompson excavations. Amid these were cartridge shells, a broken knife, damaged scissors and bits of a fox trap. Ayagiiyaq and Saġana had lived at this remote location in the 1940s and some of these leavings came from their *iglu.*

ing round elders. Even in easier environments, old people tend to confine their mobility to their immediate surroundings. Older men in pre-contact times could spend winter in their *qalgis,* while old women continued to live in *iglus.*

Asatchaq seemed not to mind his isolation and I learned to ask him, 'You are all alone?' to which he replied casually as though I were asking the location of an object.[3]

Part of Asatchaq's distance from his contemporaries had to do with rival story versions whose differences derived sometimes from lineage issues, family disputes, meat distribution or arguments over protocol.

To be in the right, as Asatchaq's uncle Samaruna determined, was the important thing. Procedural correctness was a component of the self-assurance which contributed to Asatchaq's sense of self and even social integration.

There is a photo of Samaruna taken in about 1935 and it is not a portrait of a joker. Contrastingly, a photo that hung in Qiliġniq's kitchen shows old Quwana, ca. 1940, sitting on the grass, an open letter lying across his boots. The old man smiles radiantly into the camera, as though greeting the person before him and responding to the attention of the lens.

Samaruna, on the other hand, does not give the impression that he would want to be photographed informally. And while the two men had a historical connection – both had confronted Ataŋauraq – they represented contrasting extremes of Tikiġaq character: the nimble-witted Quwana as opposed to the implacable Samaruna who had posted himself with a rifle outside his *iglu* and dared Ataŋauraq to demand tribute.

While Quwana radiates a smile consuming his entire person, Samaruna stands in front of his *iglu* in a pose suggesting the integration of physical and psychological power of a man who even in this micro-second is still at work.[4]

*

---

[3] There is a verb *alianniuq-* 'to be lonely'; and *aliasuk-* 'to feel lonely' and *alianaq-* 'to be boring, not enjoyable...' (MacLean 1980:25). The last of these was sometimes applied to white people because of their difficulty with casual socializing.

[4] I saw Quwana's smile reproduced in 1976 by his son Uqpik who, entering a room, approached a newborn baby, thrust his face close to the baby's and radiated a smile of solar brilliance.

The Phenomenon of Belonging

My visits to Asatchaq in Fairbanks were predicated on a shared assumption that we'd only discuss village history and his gestures suggested that he had oriented himself and was sitting not in Fairbanks but somewhere on the peninsula.

I was able to follow these gestures better when we were in Tikiġaq. But even here as when, for example, he raised an elbow and angled it to indicate the site of *qaġmaqtuuq qalgi,* he expected me to position the reference. Following word and gesture, as together they were intended to conduct me to where he assumed I knew he was, I was mesmerized by the precision of his experience and hypnotised into collusion.

*

'nos patriam fugimus, we are fleeing our home land', Virgil, *Eclogue* I.4

If my project was farfetched and jutted absurdly from the trajectory of a previous life which had existed in the classroom, Virgil's presence was perhaps the most extreme absurdity.

My first visit to Tikiġaq had been in summer 1973. I arrived on the day that Nanny Uyatauna and Rose-Marie abandoned their *iglu* and moved into the trader's cabin where I met them later. And once, I crawled into their old earth house and sat, in an attempt to imagine the two women's lives here, among the reeking whale bones , green with moss. The bones leaned inward and jostled one another like a mouth of decaying teeth.

*

A person in relation to their place: this is one great issue. But Asatchaq expresses a mater-of-fact kind of belonging. This is articulated not in the manner of the western consciousness with scope to openly proclaim dissociation, but rather as a quietly accepted given, as though an Inupiaq is a portion of the missed place, and while stranded in unknowable country, continues to represent its reality without having to remark on it.

But I'm better acquainted with the kind of heartbreak evoked by Eichendorff and which Schumann rendered in *Liederkreis:*

From my homeland clouds drift in.
But father and mother are long dead now.
And no one there knows me.

Here the speaker both glances at previous harmony and expresses exiled individuality, while previous identity is acknowledged from a place of dislocation.

*

Interlude with Narrative Poem

It was mid-October in Fairbanks, 1975. I was running out of money and needed a job. But while everyone I knew was either salaried or earning pipeline dollars, I must slip into the service economy. I found two positions. First in a pizza hell. And then as a bellhop in a big log-cabin motel.

Offering a flavour of both Fairbanks life and Tikiġaq, I'm inserting here a comic poem focusing on the weeks I worked as a night shift bellhop. Thus far, I'd funded my Alaskan trip with savings and London rental income. I wasn't conscious of how bell boys figured in Kafka's *Amerika* and Proust's Baalbec. Although here, motel life more resembled the Florida of *Some Like it Hot.*

The Bellman's Story – largely as narrated to a group of Tikiġaq girls

I was snowbound in my Tikiġaq cabin in March 1976 when six girls rolled in and requested a story I'd told some other people. The following tale, more or less as I spoke it, is written in village English in affectionate imitation of local language and Asatchaq's stories. Most of the action takes place in Fairbanks where I had previously lived in 1975. *Booster*, written the previous winter, is a game of divination containing 150 apothegms and mottos. Not all this comes into the telling.

> *Uqaluktuagniaqtuŋa!* I'm going to tell a story.
> I told this to Piquk, Cool Daddy and Konrad.
> The story is a true one. It happened in Fairbanks.
> The story's about me. I lived down town. Near the log cabins.
> On Third Avenue. A small house. Old.

Built in the forties. Five of us lived there.
We shared the rent and sometimes ate together.
I was getting ready for my trip to Tikiġaq.
I went to college in the mornings. I went to learn Inupiaq at college.
A white man taught us. Larry. A good teacher.
He really knows Inupiaq.
After I ate lunch I studied in the library. I worked on Inupiaq.
That's how I lived. I'd saved some money.

It wasn't enough.
My cheque would come in New Year, only.
I needed the money to pay Asatchaq for stories.
I needed more money for rent and travel.
So I looked for a job. There were several in Fairbanks.
Most of my friends had jobs on the pipeline.
The jobs I could get were in hotels and restaurants.
So I went to *Jake's Cabin*.
It's down by the river.
I went and talked to Jakey. He's a white man.
'OK,' said Jake, 'you start this evening.
Get here at six. You can work in the kitchen.'
So I got there at six. And they taught me to make pizza.

Lots of people came to eat. That kitchen was busy.
We rolled out the dough and cut it in circles.
There was lots of cheese. It was in flakes and it came in boxes.
We threw on cheese and mushrooms, meat and pepper.

The orders came on paper through a window in the kitchen.
It was hot in the kitchen. There were four other cooks.
All five of us were white boys:
but all of *them* were Jehovah's Witnesses.
All they talked about was Jesus witnessing.

I didn't join in. When they asked me my religion I said nothing.
'You must be a pagan.' That's what they told me.

So in my breaks I walked to the river.
    The banks were muddy, the weeds were dying.
The weeds and the reeds had frozen: bending, broken.

I'd been here with my girl friend earlier that autumn.
We sat by the water and watched migrations.
    Ducks and geese were coming from the Arctic.
That place on the river was no good for fishing.
    To do any fishing you had to go up river.
There are moose there too. In a couple of weeks,
    hunters who had licences would go up river.
There are plenty of moose there feeding by the water.

You asked me about Ernie. Ernie didn't have a hunting license.
Ernie shot one.
Went to prison three weeks for it.
That moose had come into his garden.
Ernie and Kora had a garden.
They lived high on a ridge, twelve miles from Fairbanks.
They'd bought some land and built a house.
Kora did the garden in the summer.

Lots of white folks like to eat vegetables. They can't help it.
They fenced in the garden to protect it from rabbits.
But that moose just stepped through it.
It ate most of their vegetables in just five minutes.

Ernie went in and fetched his rifle.
He walked right up to that moose in his garden
and point blank shot it.
The moose died right there. Just one shot killed it.
It fell down in the carrots and they skinned it:
cut up the body and put it in their freezer.
They kept their freezer in the garage.

Then a man called Owl Claws called the Troopers.
Owl Claws was a white man. Big one.
He wore owl's feet on a string.
He hung them round his neck,
like old timers here in Tikiġaq.
'There's a dead moose up the Ridge,' he told those troopers.
'Somebody has shot it. He didn't have a licence.'

The troopers drove in a four-wheel-drive pickup.
They came and opened Kora's freezer.

She and Ernie had butchered the whole animal.
They'd wrapped the pieces in freezer paper.

When the Troopers saw the meat, they said:
'Is this moose meat?' Kora was crying.
'Is this meat moose meat?' the troopers asked Kora.
'It was eating our garden. We'll have nothing to live on.'
So they took away the meat.
Kora and Ernie were left with nothing.

Then Ernie and Owl Claws started to quarrel.
First they quarrelled on the moose meat.
Then they quarrelled about fences.
Ernie chartered a plane and flew to Valdez.

He went to Valdez: at the end of the pipeline.
The pipeline people were selling equipment they had finished with.
People flew down to buy it at auctions.
Ernie flew down with his cheque-book.
He bought three hundred fence posts,
a tank for getting the salt out of water,
and a dome that came in five thousand pieces.
The dome came in pieces. Polystyrene.
I saw those pieces. Ernie never built it.
As part of the deal Ernie had to take some other things:

sugar dispensers, restaurant trays and salt and pepper shakers.
Thirty dozen. More than three thousand.
I saw them myself a year or so later.
The packing had burst:
the ground by their garage was covered with salt and pepper shakers.
Both kinds.
But they couldn't use them.

Ernie rented a plane and brought the whole lot back to Fairbanks.
He unloaded on his land,
and the very next day his house burned down.

They lost the house, their books and records, clothes and pictures.
They moved into their garage where they kept their freezer.

So they started to keep rabbits.
They grew vegetables all summer.
All summer and fall they bottled and canned them.
They ate nothing but rabbits: with peas, beans, beets, and lettuce,
carrots and tomatoes.
They got money on insurance,
and Ernie grew *qaaq* which he sold in Fairbanks.

Ernie had been to school in Boston.
He'd studied the aurora.

He'd lived in the Antarctic.
It was cold like here there, maybe colder.
He spent two years studying aurora.
He lived down there with other scientists.
All they knew, those men, was scientific knowledge.
They lived in isolation.
They all went crazy.
They became little boys.
They pretended to be trains.
They ran through their housing and made engine noises.
They made railroad schedules.
They talked engine language.

They pretended to be aeroplanes and whales and penguins.
Maybe Ernie, too, went crazy with them.
He wrote to a friend to send him *qaaq* seeds.
The seeds took six months to come from Berkeley.
Ernie planted them in pots. He grew bushes in a window.
It's light there all summer.
Their summer is our winter: their winter is our summer.

When Ernie tried his *qaaq* out, it was strong and tasty.
He got really *qaŋa*.

He packed some up and sent it to America.

His friends in Berkeley got *qaaq* from the Antarctic.
Then another plane flew down. Ernie went to New Zealand.

He gave up studying.

He could have been a big professor.
He came to Alaska. He built a house with Kora.
Three years it took them.
When it burned down, they slept in the garage and lived on rabbits.
Then they got tired of it.
'Let's go to New Zealand!'
That's how they planned it.

When he came out of prison,
Ernie found that Owl Claws had taken some land away.
Owl Claws had moved the fence posts Ernie had planted.
When Ernie saw what Owl Claws had started,
he loaded his shot gun and got on his dozer.
Kora ran after him.
'Don't shoot him, Ernie! Don't shoot, Ernie!'
Kora ran ahead. She threw herself down.
She lay in the mud between Ernie and Owl Claws.
Ernie stopped the machine.

And Kora made Owl Claws move the fence back.
It was Kora who made him. Just by talking.
That's how they lived. They quarrelled with their neighbour.
They planned to leave Fairbanks: go to New Zealand.
Still they lived on in their garage, eating rabbits.

I was working on a late shift, making Jakey's pizzas.
But I couldn't get on with those Jehovah's Witnesses.
Those Witnesses boys had a kind of leader.
His name was Orville.
One night Orville got me by the pizza oven.
He tried to make me come to their meetings.
I told him I wouldn't.
This made him angry. He said:
'You'll roast! You'll roast in hell just like that pizza!'

He beat his knuckles on the oven.
So I went to the boss. I told Jake I was leaving.
'Okay,' said Jakey. 'Can't say I blame you.'

Now I looked for work again.
I walked through Fairbanks.
The snow had started.

It was almost evening.
I came to a hotel they called *The Trapper*.
It's a big log building near the edge of Fairbanks.
I went in. To the desk.
'I'm looking for a job.
A job for the evenings.'

The woman at the desk said:
'We've got an opening for junior bellman.
'What's a bellman?' I asked.
'Bellman's a bellboy. He sits in the lobby.
When guests come in, the bellman carries their bags to their
    bedroom.
It's three bucks an hour. Tips are extra.
I'll introduce you to the senior bellman.'

The senior bellman was high school student.
A boy called Rick. Some people called him Ricky.
Rick took me to a cupboard.
It was full of bow-ties, vests and towels.
The corridor was empty.
The corridor smelled of vaccuum cleaning.
Rick gave me a bow tie and a waistcoat.
We each took a towel.
'You can wear your own pants. Black pants. White shirt.
And this vest and bow-tie.'

Next day I went to the Salvation Army.
I bought a shirt and blue cord trousers.
They fitted me well.
I've got them here. I still wear those trousers.

And this is the shirt I bought that morning.
It was made in Montana.

The work wasn't hard.
I started at six and worked until midnight.
I sat in the lobby and waited for guests.
To pick up their cases.
There weren't very many.
The next evening I brought my Inupiaq homework.
I sat and did my homework in the lobby:
I sat opposite the desk.
The lady did crosswords.
I did my homework:

Tautukpigu: 'Am I seeing it?' Tautukkiga: 'I am seeing it.'
Qilakpisigu: 'Are we knitting it?' Qilakkikput: 'We are knitting it.'
Akkuaqpiun: 'Did you just catch it?' Akkuagiga: 'I just caught it.'

That's the homework Larry gave us.
I learned lots of words and some of the bits that go inside words:
How *piqsiq* + *niaq* + *tuq* makes *piqsiġniaqtuq*
(There will be blowing snow.)
How *aqpat* + *nit* + *lutik* makes *aqpaŋnillutik*
(Because the two of them did not run.)

How *itqutchiq* + *niaq* + *tugut* makes *itqutchiŋiaqtugut*
(We will breakfast.)

I wrote out my homework for class next morning.
'You getting some smarts?' the woman asked me.
She was someone to talk to.
'I'm not too sure. I'm trying to learn this language.'
'What language is it?' the woman asked me.
I told her I was learning some Inupiaq.
'Never heard of it,' she said.
'It's the Eskimo's language.'
'I've lived in Alaska these fifteen years,' the woman said,
'and young man, I assure you, they don't have a language.'
'Look, this is their language.' I showed her some typed pages.

'These words are Eskimo.' And I spoke them to her.
'That's just nonesense,' said the woman.
'No-one talks like that. I don't get a word of it.'
'What are these words then?'
'Some smart-assed professor's made those words up.

You've been taken for a ride, son. Go and earn a proper living.'
'But this is my work,' I tried explaining.
'There's this old man. He knows a lot of stories.
I'm going to his village. When I've learned his language,
it'll help me translate them.'
'A drinker, I reckon, spinning you a snow job.
That's all they're good for. Go down Second Avenue.
All those Eskies know's the inside of a bottle.
And where's their dollar coming from?
A fat monthly cheque from Social security. Out of my taxes.'

Most nights I worked alone.
But sometimes on a weekend shift the head bellman came too.
His job was to train me.
He showed me how to raise Old Glory and then bring it down again.
He told me the Stars and Stripes must never touch the ground.
If the flag touched the ground it would lose its power.
Its power would drain out. The earth would harm it.

So one afternoon we went outside.
The flagpole stood opposite the hotel coffee shop.
People sat behind the windows, eating and smoking.
Outside it was cold. It had started snowing.

A store sign opposite read: 'Parking for Gulls'.
Gulls was a store for vacuum cleaners.
I thought that sign was funny. *Nauyaq. Nauyaaluk.*[5]

I tried translating the sign into Inupiaq.
But Rick wouldn't listen. He stood to attention.
He saluted Old Glory and undid the lanyard.
The flag started running. It rattled down the flag post.

---

[5] Inupiaq, 'common gull' + *–aaluk,* 'big, old'.

'Catch it bellman!' But the it fell on the gravel.
'Shithead! Asshole!' the head bellman shouted.
'You did that on purpose!' 'I'm sorry,' I told him.

Then I had to learn to fill the notice-board with letters.
Some dentists were having a conference at *Trappers*.
Their meetings had to be shown on the hotel notice board.
The board stood on an easel.
It was lined with black velvet.
Rick gave me a box full of white plastic letters.
You picked out letters and stuck them in the velvet.
Rick had all the day's announcements in his pocket.
That's when I started to quarrel with Ricky.
We quarrelled over spelling.
There were conferences and meetings that I had to spell.
Meetings of dentists and business people.
Rick told me I'd spelled 'Annual Conference' wrong.

I'd used up the *n*'s. I should keep them for later.
I told him I was an English teacher. I needed those *n*-s.
Both words needed two of them.
'Oh yeah? Catch these spellings!'
And he shook my sentences onto the carpet and made me start over.

The next day it froze.
The snow turned to ice in the motel courtyard.
I'd gone to the bar to fill some orders.
I was crossing the yard with a tray of cocktails.
There was ice in the courtyard. I was trying to be careful.
Then a big Dodge roared in through the archway.
It was going at 30.
It was Ricky, the head bellman.
He saw me in his headlights, but he didn't stop driving.
I was straight in his path.
I was carrying those cocktails.
There was nowhere else to go. I jumped into the doorway.
I got rid of the drinks tray.

There were two Bloody Marys.
They froze on his windshield. The ice hit my waistcoat.

'Nice shot teacher!' Ricky shouted.
I guess he'd been drinking.
I went back to the bar to get more Bloody Marys.
I thought I'd be fired.
I ordered a Jack Daniels.
I ordered another.
But no-one said nothing.

I filled a new tray and added some peanuts.
A man and woman had come down from a pipeline camp
for rest and recreation and had ordered cocktails.
I got in the lift and took their drinks up.
When I got to their door, I could hear that they were high
                    on something,
cocaine maybe. They *kuyaked*, sexed up, giggling.
I didn't want to interrupt them.
I rattled the ice in their highball glasses
and set down the tray in the empty passage.

It was seven at night and I'd just sat down to my Eskimo homework
when a string quartet arrived from the airport.
It was the Guarneris. I knew they were coming.
They'd flown in from Osaka. On their way to New York City.
They were playing at the U tomorrow. Haydn, Mozart and Dvorak.
I'd bought a ticket. I had leave for next evening.
I was upset still from my quarrel with the bellman.
I stood up. I was shaking. I was going to meet them.

They checked in. I'd seen them ten years back in London.
'Come to give the folks some good ole tunes?' said the woman
                    at reception.
'Which'v youse guys does lip-synch?'
They were quiet men, friendly. They chatted to the lady.
I picked up their bags. They carried their own instruments.

I mooned past their bedrooms late that evening.
    Michael Tree on the viola intoned 'Seid ihr nicht der Schwanen-
        dreher?'
Steinhardt the leader dreamed through a Szymanowski *Legend*,
    Dalley and Soyer bowed darkly through the Kodály duo.

After the concert I went to say hello with Larry.
'Our hotel porter!' exclaimed Arnold Steinhardt, 'what a range
        of interests!'
We talked for a while. Arnie asked us at once about Inupiaq.

I wanted to say: 'I'll never learn properly. That's for virtuosi.
      You on the fiddle and Larry here, in language pyrotechnics.
We poets stagger through creation's bits and pieces: farceurs, flâneurs,
      butterflies: we browse figments and fragments – ultimate or rudi-
      mentary –

and try to fuse these, in some coalition of a relative and intermediate
      samjna,[6] with a circumstantial and haphazard colour and our
      own chaotic rhythms.

You work technically, with consciousness broader than we'll ever stretch
      to in our self-enclosure,
We speak from solo ipse and non-knowledge: one eye half open to relative
      truth and the semi-unconscious:
the other beating the corpuscular muddle thrown up on our eyelids by
      indecipherable photons:
images from half-truth crystallised in sacred fear at having the
      chutzpah to approach sublime kingdoms.'

I walked out late, and stood beneath Orion.
      The crusted spruce looked dwarfish and sullen.
'How many kingdoms know us not?' the words came.
      'We must match their indifference with burning solicitude.
This must be the motif of my work here.
      Have courage and be tranquil,' I scolded myself, shrinking.
'Acknowledge you may learn, but most likely achieve nothing.'

Logistics took over.
      Worries about packing, clothes, equipment, plane flights, money:
what to do about polar bears and rabid foxes, trichanosis.
      'What good's a book?
A single tile, like one of Ernie's geodesic dome slabs
      in the heap that welters round the world tree.

---

[6] Pali: 'limited human perception' as opposed to insight.

What matters is now: not some test,
*   nor yet the crucible of ice and darkness:*
but whether I can rub along,
*   live graciously sans greed or competition:*
hunting in peace like a Tikiġaq hunter:
*   this project: exercise and tactic:*
walking any layout given, then tactfully leaving
*   to contemplate the structure of the stories' cosmos,*
the design of this ancient people's thinking:
*   their shape in the context of a world imagination.'*

The *taaqsipaks*[7] arrived three nights later.
Two sets of two-tones lowered from a taxi:
tan-and-white spats,
and pair of squarer black and white deals.
I recognised the spat man. Name of Arnie:
Arnie the pusher, not Arnie *Guaneri.*
I'd seen Arnie the pusher at the U.S. Dewline base at Barrow.
I'd gone there with Hanky, an education salesman.

Barrow was dry, so we'd gone for a drink.
The barman was English.

A technician from Yorkshire who did radar systems.
The men at the base all belonged to a club.
The bar was part of it, with a cage in the corner
for a Go-Go dancer. They paid subscriptions,
and took it in turns to serve behind the counter.
Drinks were quite cheap: beer 15 cents, $1 for spirits.
Then Arnie arrived.
He wanted a bottle, but the man from Yorkshire wouldn't serve him.
Arnie hadn't paid his bar bill. He refused to pay it.
The man from Yorkshire didn't mince words.

Arnie, he said, was a son-of-a-bitch twister:
all he knew was skyving and scrounging.
He told him not look for favours
because he (the boffin) gave nary-a-toss for the junk

---

[7] black people; literally, 'grown dark'.

that Arnie fixed the boys with.
'So gimme a drink,' said Arnie smiling.
'Go fuck yourself backwards' the barman whispered,
'or I'll sling your black guts round the radar mushroom.'
Words continued. But after each of the Yorkshireman's *fuck-offs*,
Arnie leaned forward on the bar and whispered:
'*Eat mah shee*-yet. Smiling but emphatic.

So here was Arnie, five months later, checking into the Fairbanks
    Trapper,
green jacket, pink flares, cuff links in diced abalone.
Cyril, Arnie's partner, dressed in black and orange.

'*Hey, bellboh*, take these boxes, don't leave them in the wet,'
    said Arnie.
It was snowing in the courtyard.
They had nine cases, thereabout, including some open cardboard
    boxes.
It looked as though they'd been through Pay'n'Save
snapping up knick-knacks as they passed them.
Arnie was still cool.
But Cyril, the partner, was restless and nervy.
He rocked on his heel, kept one hand in his jacket.

I started to lead them through the corridor.
My trolley was groaning.
'Don't drop those, son,' said Cyril (in orange),
'we don't want bad herb on the carpet.'
'You want bad herb, man?' said Arnie.
'I just roll in and visit this cat in his crib and he laid 20 on me.'

I'd packed the trolley high and clumsy
so the luggage tottered and the wheels sank in the carpet.
To make matters worse I got lost, and the doors of the lift stuck.
We stepped out for a moment to see where we'd got to,
and the lift ran off with their trolley-full of cases.

When it came back, the doors got stuck open.
Bored and frightened, I tried making small talk.
The conversation zigzagged up to Barrow.

'How's your friend at the bar who wanted your tripes
for the radar mushroom?' I dangerously asked him.

We were miles from reception, in a maze of bedrooms.
Arnie froze the jive-ass component.
'This bellboy is something!' I was flattered.
He pulled out two wallets in burgundy and crocodile.
Each cheque book had a different name and P.O. number.
'I'm *boss*,' he said darkly. 'Both of me is.'
'You crazy?' Cyril stabbed in, 'This guy could – '
whipping out a small revolver.
The gun was tiny. I thought he'd picked it up from Woolworths,
like the stuff in his boxes from Super Rexall.

Then Cyril spun the chamber and I saw the hammer.
'That gat: don't sap me with it,' I managed to stammer from
Raymond Chandler.
'Who is this guy?' snapped Cyril in a whisper.
'Some punk. I don't know,' muttered Arnie, half-frowning.
Cyril marched round by the open lift cage flourishing his pistol.
He wasn't pleased, unlike the fellow in Mae West's, to see me.
'This cat. I don't believe it! Stuck here, and he knows your…
This guy's getting fired, I'm telling you…'
'But not that gun I hope,' I tittered.
Both of them were stoned, drunk, out of it, I realised,
and the Barrow encounter jarred their memories,
collapsed and drifting, in the usual marijuana tangle.
I slipped round the edge and came out as bellhop with their luggage
        trolley.

The rest of that evening I spent running errands.
Arnie and Cyril had jugs of vodka.
I shuttled them ice, I changed their glasses.
The glasses were wrong. They needed more ashtrays.
They wanted cigarettes from Turkey.
I ran out to get them.
When I got back, they had two girls with them:
Tiffany and Sunshine, sporty-looking in their underwear.
Arnie gave me a dollar, a joint and a vodka.
This was stingy but fun. I enjoyed my evening.

Next night, quite late, Arnie called reception.
They wanted me up there.
'This room's no use. We need a new one.'
I ran upstairs and found them sweating.

They'd packed already.
I called down to confirm the booking.
'It's someone on their tail!' the lady whispered.
She was excited.
To Arnie it was just a game still:
'You want to earn a *real* tip this time, bellman?'
He leaned back in his chair and fished up his wallet.
He took out five bills and laid them on the carpet.
'You move us in five minutes, bellboy: and you get *these*.'
They were new, crisp centuries.
I took up the challenge. I wanted those dollars.
I might have done it if I'd known my way, and not dropped too
     many boxes.
I hurried the corners. The two *taaqsipaks* followed.
The trolley wouldn't run straight.
Cyril slung a rolled-up copy of the evening paper with his pistol in it.
Arnie sang the minutes. He knew I couldn't.

We had one more meeting. I'd told them about *Booster*.
That's my book of questions.
Cousin Lazarus and Piquk played it.
It's a book of funny answers.
The men wanted to see it.
So I took them the dice, and mottos in typescript.
'Will the Man get us?' That was Cyril's question.
Cyril shook the dice and threw Bell-Orange-Cherry.
Dice rattled on his pistol.
'That's the empty combination,' I told him.
'There's no motto for it.
Lay down your gun if you want an answer.'

Cyril liked the hierophantic posture.
He did as I told him, and shriven, he threw clearer.

It was Orange-Orange-Cherry. I read out his answer:
Someone with clear eyes is tired of watching out for you. Cultivate self-
love.
'What's that mean?' asked Cyril, excited by flashes of his mother in
        Chicago.
'That's for *you* to figure out,' said Arnie.
'If we play properly,' I said, 'you get four answers.'
'No, no. No time,' said Arnie, impatient. 'Give me my turn.'
'What's your question?'
'This is my question: 'How come I'm here now?''
He scattered the dice and threw up Plum-Lemon-Orange:
'*The texture of all flesh from Mae West to the Eskimos is one,*' said *Booster.*
'Oh,' said Arnie.
'Let me give you the companion motto. Number 84.
It's one of my favourites:
'*Extreme alternatives. Untidy circus of emotion:*
the glamorous equipment is exhausted by display.

or:

The whips and harnesses rot in the night dew with neglect.'
'I'll meditate on that,' said Arnie.
He wrote down his answer in his crocodile skin cheque book.
'Huh,' said Cyril.
That's where I left them.

At the end of the telling, the six girls left the cabin.
'Goodbye,' I said.
But Inupiat don't say goodbye.
They just walk into silence.

The Harpoon that Ejaculates

It is a source of wonder that an ancient society, whose survival had been
the outcome of a harpoon thrust, should likewise also itself derive life
from the harpoon-like action of the male genital.

To the elderly who have lost interest in sex, eroticism can appear
extravagant and even bizarre behaviour. But the scrawny but ithyphallic
male form is one of the marks that humans recorded in cave sanctuaries.

This, beside the rotund female figures whose archetypes are scattered through ancient history.

These latter arrive sculpturally, while the man with an erection, is often realized in two-dimensional scratches. This is appropriate to the tendency of the male to thrust and run away as opposed to the more stationary, philosophical character of women's post-coital experience which takes into the body a studious posture of more portentous consequence. Men are fertile. But the *usuk* is fickle. It is powerful but slight. As Duncan says in *Macbeth*: once planted, it requires the supervision of growing.

With Dido interred, I continued to engage with Virgil. This offered reentry to an ancient world I had observed since childhood without understanding it. My Latin was bad. Still, the texture of the poetry, built as though from stonework whose foundations reached the inferno, was intoxicating. A modern reader could inhabit the upper levels only of a complex *Gestalt* whose interior, like the inner parts of polyphonic music, was hard to access.

Once I'd spent more time in Tikiġaq, I started to see this as a part of my training. It was the deep modelling of Virgil's poetry, its part organic and part artefactual glamour, that translated a notion of the *Aeneid's* internality to a version of what Tikiġaq earth comprehended. Embedded in this, lay multiple worlds dispersed through the centuries and which converged in a bric-a-brac of bones, *iglu* ruins, masks, tools, carvings, flints, knife blades, spear heads, beads and bird-bone needles.

Nivarana – Hindrances

A helpful Buddhist term is *nivarana*. Breaking the word into a primitive etymology, the *ni-* suggests 'without', while *varana* derives from *vr-* 'to move or flow', the two parts suggesting blockage. Buddhist theory teaches that hindrances to development derive from human weakness. Whether or not that's true, *nivarana* is a description of the relationship to time as the individual moves through unknowable future spaces.

The path ahead is never clearly open. We all produce our idiosyncratic interferences, whether or not these are projections like the delusional obstacles in the trajectory of a picaro. And in a real sense, we are all picaros shambling through ordinary landscapes loaded internally with libraries of outdated 'how to do it' equipment.

Essentially, we inhabit a featureless and flat landscape with no contour, a space without limit, a colourless expanse which has neither margin nor definition, a featureless emptiness onto which phenomena imprint themselves: things, people, structures and natural objects whose forms and colours are characterized by phantasmagoric projection.

The most normal day presents itself in the morning as a transparent, simplified aether as evoked in the first line of a folk song – 'As I walked out one morning…' Anything then could happen. The landscape is open.

Which is to say that we wake into an environment of nothing and that into this space move our plans for the next accessible period plus accretions of previous activity. All this suggests that much as we love our plans and that these keep us interconnected, they get in the way of the only perfection we know, which is the phenomenon of nothing: an unbroken, featureless simulacrum of death which compromises things we normally engage with.

It is a monkish preoccupation to exist doing nothing, with accretions of nothing in the past and with the prospect of nothing happening in the future except release into a greater nothing. The latter occurring ideally 'with no residue' of previous accumulation or psychic deposits.

My own mundane interest in all this has to do with the bother of things filling what otherwise might be the unlimited space of a day. For as suggested, time does not really move, it's rather that we move along and notch up eventualities which are defined by identifiable concretions.

This reminds me of a poem by the eleventh-century Hebrew poet Shmuel Hanagid:

A woman said: 'Be happy that God has helped you reach
The age of fifty.' What the woman didn't know was
That there is, to me, no difference between my own past
And that of Noah or any of the ancients.
There is only the hour in which I am present.
This stays briefly. Then like a cloud it moves on.

The actuality of this is hard to acknowledge, perhaps because we experience the consequence of things, establishing everything in an indelible historicity. Both in Tikiġaq and Fairbanks, I'm painfully aware of the impositions with which I've loaded myself. But I collude with the experience as described by the poet. Still, this represents an abstract rather than a life supporting logistic. I need, after all, to assemble some warm clothing. And to avoid getting lost, I should number notebook pages. These little things constitute the *nivarana*, obstacles that take place in a time that has its transient existence in the featureless and eternal nothing.

*

From Letter to Joanne, November 22 1975

Meanwhile, I'm learning Inupiaq and beginning to get some idea of how almost impenetrable a language can be. I look forward nonetheless to being able to communicate better when I get back to the village before Xmas.

What I can say is still limited, since it's not the case, as in some European languages, where you throw nouns and verbs together and learn French in days.

There is, in fact, little in the way of single words that you can functionally use in Inupiaq, but rather verb and noun stems, infixes and endings which you have to learn to combine in strings of meaning which in mutual collaboration may be up to fifteen or twenty syllables long. Within the interior and at the ending of these blocks of meaning, noun and verb stems and suffixes change according to the nature of the sounds with which they are combined...

These represent the shallows. I have, this past week, been confronted by another feature. This involves the convergence of subject and object in one verbal ending. In such a construction 'I' and 'it' are combined into a single ending.

Imagine, given possible singular, dual and plural numbers for both subject and object ('We **two** eat **three** of them' or 'They **three** eat **two** of them') the dizzying multiplication of possible endings.

Given these complications, you might think that people would hesitate to open their mouths unless they had something important to say. But the effort involved in learning forms like this from birth is presumably no greater than it might be assimilating any other linguistic formula. Imagine ingesting sub-atomic physics at the breast! And how remarkable that people can chat casually in Inupiaq without having to search complicated tables of elision and assimilation! Oi!

My project here is to learn enough Inupiaq to communicate at a superficial level and show a willingness to integrate into a complexity that I could never do more than function in – like a sailor disembarking after a rough crossing on the coast of Coramandel and learning unsteadily to walk again in order to communicate in passable *Hobson Jobson*.[8]

---

[8] Hobson Jobson: Anglo-Indian jargon used by British soldiers in nineteenth century India. 'It is in fact an Anglo-Saxon version of the wailings of the

More to the point, I must accept the fact that I stand outside. Perhaps we're liminal in most things. Just as I hesitated on the threshold of Asatchaq's bedroom, so we avoid leaning too far into the field of other people's realities. Nor can we properly lean backwards, but live instead uncertainly in an attempt at balance.

Still, working in Inupiaq feels like swimming in French rivers, about which I composed this nostalgic poem:

The River Yonne in 1960.
Rushes green and intermittent
dragonfly reflections.
Black water on the surface lacquered.

*

from Letter to G. 9 November 1975

Dear G,

You won't have the card I mailed on Guy Fawkes day.

But meanwhile, I feel daily more like Turgenev's superfluous man. Fairbanks does business. And while the world's in action, I do little. Still, I'm due in Tikiġaq late December and next week fly to Anchorage to sign a contract with the Historical Commission in acknowledgement of project dollars. I'm grateful. But funds shame my laziness.

Now that hustling has realized four thousand, other terrors rear. As Pope wrote, 'Alps on endless alps arise...' My happy vision from a London vantage is hard to sustain. But as Harold Wilson proclaimed after his 1964 victory, 'We've got a job of work to do. And we're going to do it.'

Still, Tikiġaq may be easier than Fairbanks: the solitude more physically challenging and thus perhaps simpler to grapple with. In London I met a Buddhist teacher and when I confessed my fears, he replied: 'When you're afraid, you will scream. And when people hear you, they will understand.'

This, at the time, I thought wise. But he was wrong. In Tikiġaq it is essential to maintain control. Narcissistic self-expression's risible. And so for now I'll have to sublimate my terrors.

Mahommedans...', chanting 'Ya Hasan! Ya Hosain!' Henry Yule, *Hobson Jobson*, 1886.

Life here is lonely. My solitude is coordinated with a succubus that sits on my chest and all but chokes me. 'The mother', as Lear called it, rises in the thorax:

O, how this mother swells up toward my heart!
Hysterica passio, down, thou climbing sorrow...

But there's no mileage in a panic on the floor of JCPenney where, yesterday, as evening fell, I wandered, Virgil in my parka pocket.

I'd entered JCs without purpose. *Stamm* in Hebrew. I've joined the Israeli Leah as a sibling of the miscellaneous. Like many that converge on Pipeline City, we're deracinated wanderers. Human stuff, like things in their millions at JC Penney.

But this wasn't a movie, although somewhere, in the men's department, I thought I might find Jimmie Stewart rambling.

'I'll take,' he growls, 'a couple of these... *doohickies*.' He pats a jacket pocket, settles his fedora and we follow a view of his tweed receding.

JCPenney is a Fairbanks icon. I'll not impugn it. Nor am I deluded by imagined superiority. If I have a critique, it has to do with things unnatural.

First, JCs is a temple of the artificial and here in Alaska, an emporium of importation. Little at JC's has been manufactured in Alaska. Throughout the States, the flow of factory goods provides low income families with life-support and cheap materials: hardware, furnishings, doors and windows, bedding, bathroom and electrical appliances, chains for car wheels, Visqueen for window insulation, hand tools and machines for digging, chopping, work clothes, down-filled waistcoats, thermal underwear, hats, gloves, mittens. A downhome Aladdin's.

*

Nature and Manufacture

And just as manufacture predicates non-natural products, so the market generates unlovely essentials. You visit Penney's not to purchase pretty but for hard-wearing artefacts.

Just to get outside the oil-fired heating is a sweaty business. And while polyester house clothes creak and nylon sparkles, good, lasting, outdoor wear's constructed in the pioneer tradition: blue jeans with their hard, tight stitching, goose down, woollens, denims that old timers wore for panning, poling rivers, sawing down the forests, herding cattle.

Therefore while I mourn the handmade and the natural fibre (buy at Nordstroms), I acknowledge commerce and the inexpensive with its built-in obsolescence.

This has its contradiction in a hippy-fringe existence which practises self-help and wilderness subsistence and whose folk patch clothes, pick blueberries, cranberries, mushrooms and raise chard, beets, beans and carrots which they can and bottle, breed hens and rabbits, stack logs for stoves from Maine and Norway that they've bought with pipeline savings, have get-togethers in log cabins to holler Country Western and howl bluegrass and mush dogs they feed with moose they've shot illegally and get stoned on dope they cultivated in the summer.

The dominant demography at JCPenney lies with white folks: decent Christian people, albeit the miscellaneous collectivity is far more complicated. On the one hand there are sourdoughs, long-term residents, exercising capability and sustaining mainstream, often libertarian, survival, as though Alaska were the heart of what White America has been in essence: God's Wilderness with which to struggle and express enterprise, in opposition to DC: unloved object of derision that the far west pronounces scornfully as *Warshington*.

There are many others: black folks, Filipinos, Jews, Mexicans, Koreans, Japanese and South Americans who likewise have a stake in northernness as an inflection of America, virgin land in which to improvise a chance, away from roaring cities that consume your effort.

Reverting to Penney's, you'll find Jimmie Stewart sooner than you'll catch a hippy in the car park – a department in itself of JCPenney without which shopping below zero is difficult.

Another demographic split is metaphysical. Penney's represents the dollar side of Christianity. Alternative Fairbanks is yogic, Buddhist, eco-animist or into massage. That said, I've met communards who groove on *agape* with commitment to ecstatic self-extension.

'You can knock me down,' one love-stoned antinomial shoved in my face one night on Second Avenue, 'you can knock me down and wipe the floor with me. But I'll still **lerve** you.' This was funny and sincere. It also made me love him.

The Department Store

Thrift, hard work and modest living. These, especially for the poorer folk among the evangelicals, are Christian virtues. One difference in Fairbanks is that poor folk in Alaska earn inflated salaries, though everything here is also expensive.

JCPenney is a 'downscale' company which caters for the 'lower classes' and was founded in 1902 and grew up alongside other great department stores. An extract from a Wikipedia article gives this history:

> [JCs]...reached an audience... more interested in value than in upscale fashions and which de-emphasized the latest fashions in favor of practicality and durability. Its stores were oriented to motorists... [and] had ample, off-street parking...[9]

Purpose-built parking areas and department store architecture belong, in the service of commerce, to the same sphere of practicality. Penneys in Fairbanks is a single storey building whose interior is divided into departments regulated to customer pressure.

Less than a decade later, larger, more inclusive supermarkets, further from downtown and reachable by new road construction, have been sited to attract both value-dependent lower income customers and a wealthier middle class, and these market places combine value for money, choice-balanced upscale grocery options alongside household, hardware and clothing departments.

These new operations are larger, more opulent and luxurious than the more puritanical Penneys. They are lighter, roomier and more fun to visit. Children lark round the aisles and people have the space for conversation. Whereas in Penneys you tend to emerge with the pinched and driven pallor with which you entered, here you can fill your cart with tomato seedlings and European wine and cheeses, besides work boots and denims.

The department store and the supermarket have converged in these newer enterprises. You feel less that you are hunting simply to survive, than that you are participating in a ceremony of wellbeing in a fraternity of like-minded fellows.

---

[9] Zola's *Au Bonheur des Dames* (The Ladies' Paradise), records the creation of the first Paris department store. In this, the *doyenne* falls into the foundations of the new building which rises over her interment.

While the newer precincts are more humanistic in both feeling and environment, they are perhaps warehouses from which the fortunate, rather than those largely driven by need, visit to extract what they want as well as what they need and where spontaneously they have come to celebrate positive life ways.

Mahler's Fourth Symphony

Reverting to December 1975, I'm both trapped in and enchanted by orchestra rehearsals. We're doing Mahler's Fourth: a shortish Mahler symphony.

The *Adagio* is a quiet, almost passive composition, perhaps anticipating the Fifth Symphony's *Adagietto,* famous as the score used for *Death in Venice.*

Though the movement's introduced by the violas, these quickly sink below the second violins. And there's a third, inaudible part that lies within the viola harmonies, themselves muffled in the middle register. I wonder why I bother to try playing this as I sit at the back, until the two front desk girls turn to hiss that I'm spoiling it.

'It's like the rest of life,' I want to answer. 'Nothing ever makes much difference.' Still, I take my part home, a 1947 *Breitkopf* edition. It's nice to realise there were people in 1946 Leipzig preoccupied with music.

It's half-inert, this slow processional: the tiny Mahler dreaming he's a gentile, tall in long robes, with candles, crosses, chasubles and censers swaying down the nave of St. Steven's.

The orchestra holds back, until, dying, a clarinet translates the vision and we're in fourteenth century Friesland, virgins in white shifts announcing the angelic promise.

A woodland bird with slack-winged lift-off slips out to proclaim the final movement. It's a languid triplet. And then harp and cellos play together muted under woodwind. The bar that opens the *finale* initiates a quicker rhythm, artless as the text that follows.

All this is prelude to my hour in JCPenney. A meeting of mutually foreign worlds. But this music's entered, decorated my isolation. The lukewarm halo of the singer's dotted rhythm sinks through my hair and flaps round my worries.

Without further digression, I imagine that I might encounter here in JC's the beautiful soprano who's singing the *Finale.* She's a high school teacher. Undemonstrative and modest. She resembles Trudi, of Frith's Fossils, who hit the home run in September. Her pale, narrow voice adopts a light vibrato at the end of phrases, guileless as the text is primitively Christian.

I've tracked down the song words in the library. It's *Das Himmlische Leben*, 'The Heavenly Life', and imagines pleasures that the pious will enjoy in heaven:

> ...Everything lives in the gentlest peace! We lead an angelic life! Nevertheless we are very merry... Meanwhile, Saint Peter in the sky looks on. We lead a patient, innocent, dear little lamb to death! Wine costs not a penny; angels bake the bread.

> Good vegetables grow in Heaven's garden! Asparagus, beans and whatever we wish! Good apples, good pears and good grapes! Would you like roebuck, would you like hare? Should a fast-day arrive, all the fish swim up to us with joy! No music on earth can be compared to ours. Eleven thousand maidens dare to dance! The angelic voices rouse the senses so that everything awakens with joy.

And this, appropriately at JCs, sketches what the churches preach to poor folk and to Natives. With piety and church attendance, while you scrape to get what you need, you're promised an afterlife of plenty.

Mahler was a tyrant. And while his conversation and his letters expressed compulsive ambition, each movement's heading, as though borrowed from the *Tao te Ching*, is spiritually helpful:

1. *Bedaechtig, nicht eilen* – Thoughtfully, don't hurry.
2. *In gemaechlicher Bewegung, ohne Hast* – At a leisurely pace, without rushing
3. *Ruhevoll* (Poco Adagio) – Peaceful
4. *Sehr behaglich* – Comfortable, contented

I vowed, having read these musical directions, to calm down a little. How mad I'd been to rush round Tikiġaq last year, as though anyone cared about the timing of my visits. 'Taam Fast Walker,' one kid called me. Remedies lay, not least, in the scarcely audible violas.

Trudi

Rehearsing to myself some second movement notes as I wander between different strengths of Visqueen rolls and grades of tyre chain down an aisle of JCPenney hardware, I thought I sighted the soprano balancing an axe in one hand and a bag of curtain fabric.

Trembling, I approached, and had begun to introduce myself when suddenly, too late, I recognized a different person. This was Trudi, who had smacked the home run for Frith's Fossels in September.

'I'm frightfully sorry, I thought you were the *Das Himmlische Leben* soprano. I'm in the violas.'

Trudi skipped the small talk.

'Scram, buster. Or I'll call the store detective.'

She produced a whistle.

No point in bleating that I'd witnessed her September softball moment.

Part 4

Mrs Charlotte

Historical Note

Following the establishment of the Anvik Mission on the Yukon, the Episcopal church has been in Alaska since 1887. The missionary John Chapman built a school and a hospital at Anvik, in the course of which he mastered the Athabascan language. In 1890, Episcopalian elders dispatched two lay preachers to Alaska, one of whom was the medical missionary John Driggs who travelled through the Dakotas en route to Tikiġaq. In post, he learned fluent Inupiaq, opened a school and worked as a physician.

Driggs was deposed in 1907 and was replaced by Augustus Hoare who had previously worked in Anvik. In 1919, Hoare was shot dead by a teaching assistant. One of Hoare's acts, in 1909, was the removal of traditional grave relics to ground he had consecrated west of the village.

There was unspoken significance to the meeting in 1975 of Asatchaq and Mrs Charlotte. Asatchaq was born when the millenarian *uivvaqsaat* cult had already arrived in Tikiġaq in the 1880s. This syncretic religion promised, in the context of epidemics and game depletion, the return of ancestors and game animals. Driggs understood *uivvaqsaat* to have been a traditional religion.

There was real but geographically separated coincidence to Asatchaq's meeting with Mrs Charlotte, who had witnessed the aftermath of the Wounded Knee massacre in 1889. The Sioux uprising had been partly inspired by Ghost Dance teachings, which, like *uivaqsaaq,* promised the return of traditional harmonies.

Native revivalist thought had probably arisen in the American north-west in about 1877. Sioux emissaries travelled across the country to learn these doctrines, while similar ideas somehow travelled north, reaching Tikiġaq in the 1880s. Neither Asatchaq nor Mrs Charlotte was apparently aware that they had witnessed ideologies deriving from the same source in the Pacific northwest.

September 17, 1975 – At the Priest's House

Asatchaq was fond of women and one of his supporters was Elizabeth who visited him in the care home and bought him thrift store clothes. Gifts of other supplies – a crate of eggs, a dressing gown, a blanket – were welcome once Asatchaq was in Tikiġaq. But given that Tikiġaq lay within the Episcopalian diocese, the warmth of the relationship was also a formality.

It lay within Elizabeth's pastoral responsibility to minister to members of her husband's statewide congregation. Still, they loved each other. Asatchaq called her 'Lady Elizabeth' and he also saw an opportunity to propose marriage to Elizabeth's widowed mother who lived in the family house to which Asatchaq and I were invited for lunch. For much of that September afternoon, I lost sight of Asatchaq. The present section is dominated by Mrs Charlotte and the harangue she delivered in the garden.

The priest's house is a large clapboard building in a rustic spot in central Fairbanks. Elizabeth and her husband have lived here for ten years and she works the front garden where she grows vegetables and flowers. Now in mid-September, dahlias and chrysanthemums are still in bloom, sweet peas have dried, squash and tomatoes are ripe.

This is my first visit and the garden presents a quasi-English character. Straw hat, secateurs and wicker basket decorate an iron table. We might be at Vita's, Sissinghurst, in 1930 and I glance round for a typescript. Re-focussing on the present, I grind Asatchaq's wheelchair down a gravel path between the gate and veranda and haul the chair up. 'Lady Elizabeth' is in the kitchen moulding a piecrust from chocolate-chip cookies. Everything is tranquil. I'm entering one sanctuary of Christian Alaska.

'Hi *Jimmie!*' Elizabeth has a natural sweetness toughened by isolation on past Dakota missions. Her charm penetrates me and unsettles the anti-Christian arrogance on which I have sustained pre-contact history allegiance. The old man grapples the Priest Wife's long pale hand as she stoops to kiss him. 'You good to *in*-vite me,' he growls.

Elizabeth's mother, Mrs. Charlotte, comes in from the garden with a tray of tomatoes and her presence deepens suddenly the layers of time expressed by Asatchaq's association with both 'pagan' Tikiġaq and 1890 Christianity.

I'm young, a foreigner; also a non-Christian. And no doubt represent, as evoked by T.S. Eliot, a cosmopolitan freethinker alien to High Church tradition. My Berlin elders, born before Asatchaq, were a presence in my childhood.

Mrs Charlotte is of their generation. She is nearly one hundred and carries her century like a goddess. Straight-backed and grand, she enters as though sweeping back a curtain of the present to convey a hinterland of vaster moment. She was raised on a Mission within earshot of the Pine Ridge reservation where some three hundred Sioux were slaughtered by the US army in the Wounded Knee disaster.

That was December 1890 when Mrs Charlotte was about eleven and she hurried with her parents to the Holy Cross Chapel to serve in the makeshift hospital that the Rev. Cook had improvised. Straw lay on the church floor. Paper chains still decorated the chapel.

*

Mrs Charlotte, as she herself said, was 'a high toned old Christian woman'. But she was also a complex, divided, perhaps conflicted, individual. Having grown up on a Mission to the Sioux in the late 19th century, she escaped in her late teens, perhaps intending to put an end to the hardships of her upbringing, to study languages at Barnard College and had graduated when she took up with an old sweetheart who had travelled east to find her. Together they returned as missionaries to the Dakotas in the early twentieth century.

I'd read *Bury my Heart at Wounded Knee* and parts of Mooney's study of the Wounded Knee fight. Young Mrs Charlotte had adapted to the hardship of Mission life, spoke Lakota and understood the issues Mooney outlined in his study.[1]

In the course of our meeting, there followed two episodes when I found myself alone with Mrs Charlotte. And for two and then three hours she talked about her life.

I scribbled a few notes when I got home. But otherwise, my record consists of reimagined recollection. Her monologue was uninhibited, often caustic and judgmental. It was the 'old pagan', as she called Asatchaq, who'd brought us together. But Asatchaq, throughout, was upstairs in the house and I was left with Mrs Charlotte.

*

---

[1] Mrs Charlotte's sympathies were with Sioux people, but knowledgeable as she was, she wasn't acquainted with all the bands that made up the Teton Sioux nation – these included the Brule, Hunkpapa, Miniconjou and Oglala who lived on the five of the reservations. Pine Ridge was the scene of the Wounded Knee massacre on December 29 1890. Sitting Bull, one of the Ghost Dance leaders, had been killed on 15 December.

Mrs Charlotte's Harangue[2]

Once we had been introduced to one another, Mrs Charlotte launched her monologue. She didn't wait for an introduction, but diagnosed, with some impatience, my character and attitude to Native business. Impatient also, maybe, to unload the contents of a split mind to a likely fellow.

'I understand that you're not churched and you're against the churches. It's a justified opinion. What right has one view to impose itself on captive people?

And yes, they were captives in the country where they also exercised their freedom. It's contradictory, an injustice, in this land, America, proclaiming freedom.

'It's one thing to debate a notion. Another to send messengers of power to damaged villages. I can hear that plaint. I share the outrage. The Natives enjoyed freedom. Worried white folks on the east coast enjoy freedom. They exercise freedom to extend themselves. I appreciate that vision. We, after all, are also living by translation and have acculturated fragments of a Middle Eastern cult, imperfectly recorded, into domesticated, urban uniform. We have civilized a footloose sport of antinomial Aramaicism into an adjunct of the local government until it's an aspect of an urban uniform.

'Yes, look at how the church develops its self-government. And is an aspect of respectable self-governing society. We've become conventional. Independent spirits become prelates, dignitaries in church robes, who speak in studied ways, fund offices and manufacture ritual instruments, build careers, live by agenda and create a history. It's ghosts in uniform. They constitute an army fighting with historical imagination. Some Sinai desert visionary is made professor. A sage tamed to promote respectability. True up to a point. The church becomes a decency, retreat into gentility.

'Now your missionary's a part of that. But *he* – you have to marry one if you've ambitions – can revert to a Christ-like sort of disaffiliation. Yes, the churches allow, promote, require perhaps in order to refresh a fading

---

[2] I have reconstructed Mrs Charlotte's conversation after more than forty years and her views contain some of my own projected thoughts. Important nonetheless to remember that the Episcopalian communities in the Dakotas and Alaska embraced a number of Native ideas and incorporated them in Christian doctrine. Many Dakota missionaries became fluent in Siouan languages. While the representation of Wounded Knee and references to Driggs and Sheldon Jackson aspire to historical accuracy, Mrs Charlotte's views are semi-orthodox.

self-view of their sanctity, idiosyncratic, self-promoting lonely wanderers: Driggs, Edson, Stuck and Hoare,' she named Tikiġaq's missionaries.

'I'm not a sage. I'm not a saint or even much of an old sinner. A decent student if I'd stuck it. Though I might quite well have crashed once I'd finished my MA at Barnard. And now I'm just what Stevens called a High Toned Christian Woman. Exercising my *complacencies* to quote the poet.

'Most of what we need to know about this country's in Walt Whitman. That's who expresses and presents the textures, courage, brightness of America. It's agonising work that brings us through, that *makes* us. Though where we arrive remains ambiguous. Yes, incessant labour, raw noise, bodies, restless movement. Read Whitman and you're right there in that mish-mash. A society patched roughly, boldly, like our map between Atlantic and Pacific. Hard to keep track of and account for all the races, tribes, types, jobs, workshops, pioneers, professions, genders even. But one thing I noticed.

There ain't no Jews in Whitman's America…' she added in response to my Hebraic eyebrow.

Later I wrote her a piece in parody of Whitman but received no response. If ever an old buzzard deserved roosting with the angels it was Mrs Charlotte. Here's what I sent her:

I put on a dress and wash my beard. I light the Sabbath candles
And pray with cupped palms over weeping eyelids in the Hebrew.
I spoon out chicken broth and matzah balls to which I've added
    schmaltz and parsley.

I adjust, in comradeship, my circumcision and celebrate my
    host's exemplar.
It's a flower from the desert translated to the Bowery.
It gives him headway in the sex act. It inhibits prematurity.

I dance. There's a *frohlich*. Fiddle, trombone, clarinet, accordion.
I embrace each instrument. I embrace the rabbi.
I weep and laugh with grandmothers who have been widowed.
I throw high the children, catch them and return them to their
    older sisters.

I think that's something Mrs Charlotte would have smiled at. My own contact with Episcopalians was happy. These are the nicest Americans you could meet: selfless in their non-dogmatic character. In which connection I wrote:

> *I've met an Episcopal prig or two*
> *But these are relatively few.*

They were easier to be with than the edgy, creative crowd in which I numbered.

'What do you think of our Gospels, Tom?' asked one of my teachers at school in the 1950s. We'd been in Divinity, a non-exam lesson.

'I think they're jolly good, sir,' I replied, slightly forward. *Frech,* my grandma would have called it. 'But why should anyone believe them any more than they might the *Rig Veda*?' Which was probably rude.

'You're late coming to the field, young man,' continued Mrs Charlotte. 'Most of what you're looking for is finished on account of white men, never mind if they're scallywags or bishops. That includes the likes of Christian folks. Hare was bishop in the Dakotas, called it Niobrara, before 1880. The word Dakota followed. And me and my hubby, we followed like gun dogs, all the way from Princeton.

'You're going,' she continued mightily, 'where the native folks will view you as a random being. And you'll see them through the lens of ego. I know: you'll care for them and work hard.

'But remember, they're still people, not ethnic types, material you want to wrap up in a book. Yes, they're book material. But to themselves – they're not figures in a work. Their lives are real as yours and mine. Unpredictable, in constant movement.

'And here you are with this old pagan,' and she pointed with her chin towards the kitchen window.

'You see him as a sage and icon. Imagine, if you can, his day's experience. It's unknowable. As are fifty years of doings, thought, relationship and struggle. The details of which knowledge he'll impart to you in scraps and shadows. You'll note these down. You'll get high from that achievement. But they'll be shreds and tangles that mean one thing to him and another in your comprehension.

'Then there's his age,' continued Mrs Charlotte, 'How far will what he tells you be what he once knew? Could it ever be free of fifty years' of half-forgetting? What we old birds remember is a nest of what was criss-cross to start with and which over the decades gets stuff sticking to it every-which-way in a bird's nest of accumulations. The original disappears. We hear other versions and we get tangled.

'The issue's not which path to take. The old protagonists have gone their ways. Natives, traders, missionaries, BIA men, anthropologists, have clashed, accommodated, battened on each other. The white man saw some gains and natives suffered losses. The modernizing dispensation, in the Dakotas as here in Alaska, was settled eighty years ago. It was *Pax Americana*, and the Christian message was its escort, honey on the hard bone. A ghostly icing on the carbohydrate.

'There were native agnostics. Still, to accept Jesus was an aspect of a new belonging. You get preferential treatment and achieve the Christian heaven. The masks and puppets of the old tradition heaped in rotting tipis and abandoned *iglus*.'

Mrs Charlotte left the field which I'm about to enter. An inadequate explorer. I seek the Great All, its whale-shaped dimension. The world's enormous. Its old paths faint. I blunder forward. My surroundings wither.

The hinterland looks beautiful. I stride forward, in the tutelage of Whitman, to embrace the wholeness. A place in the sunset. Two half defunct traditions. The globe's circumference girdling my own uncertain stomach.

As for the crossroads where I meet Mrs Charlotte, we acknowledge that our paths are culturally coincident but historically, religiously, divided. She'd been present at an early, raw encounter: between 'savages and Christians', interpreting one tale from the vantage of another. From the depths of shambles emerged the Christian promise. Transubstantiation: wine and carbohydrate suited people whose own communion was with buffalo or whale meat. The converted knelt to take communion as they had bowed to Reservation Agents.

For meat-eating tribes, wine and biscuits offered parallels with transubstantiation. Both Sioux and Inupiat worshipped and consumed the animals they hunted. To eat Christ was a logical extension.

'What, anyway, do you think you're doing?' Mrs Charlotte asked sharply. 'You might be at home with Proust, Kafka and Heine. You're of their party. I can tell that. Those are oracles of self-division, torn between denial and devotion, ecstasy of *Heimat*, but still scratching at the stuff of exile.

'I can't believe they'll have much truck for you, in Tikiġaq, with your wilderness mysticism – a juvenile variety. I'll bet that while you're struggling with this old pagan's stories you'll be fingering your Virgil. Longing to be back with *As You Like It*. How long did Duke What's-his-Face stick it out in Arden?' She sat down, frowned and launched family history.

We'd been standing in the sunshine. You could hear the clink of cutlery from the upstairs kitchen. Someone nearby with an axe was splitting firewood.

'You know my father taught at Princeton before I lit out for the Dakotas? From Princeton Seminary, knew young Sheldon Jackson who evangelized Alaska. Jackson was a knuckleheaded zealot. Good career move, even while he was at Princeton. But he had no gift for contemplation.

'Hadn't got what Keats called negative capability: a mind flexible enough for passive receptivity. Those east coast Christians were worthy individuals, but they had no vision beyond a right-wrong dialectic.

'Now my professor father taught me to read widely. And there at your peril, in the literary classics, you ignore the inconvenient fact of relativity. Isn't everything ambiguous? My daughter Libby tells me not to say this. Still, Who was Jesus? What did his words mean, when and where he said them in what language? My daddy quoted Marvell:

The Pict no shelter now shall find
Within his party-coloured mind.
But from this Valour sad
Shrink underneath the Plad.

'Whatever Marvell thought of Cromwell, we can't but associate ourselves with parti-coloured mind's construction. Whatever that meant. Which might have been my dissertation topic, except that I got married. And since that time, both outside and within the church community, *parti-coloured* is the universal tartan. Your Asatchaq is Jimmie: shamanist and Christian. *Do I contradict myself? Very well I contradict myself,* said Whitman who embraced America and whose diversity he danced with.' She fingered the cross that paralleled her withered dewlaps and a pair of well-developed arteries.

'You'll wonder hearing all this in the High Priest's garden. I'm a strange old bird my daughter tells me. And I don't talk like this to everybody. You'll please forget it.' Which I couldn't.

'The world is such a pigsty and you, as I have been, will always be angry. How come I lived so many years out on a mission, you'll be asking? *Ich grolle nicht. Je ne regret rien,* as that little sparrow sang in Paris. No, my husband was a true believer and I submitted to his loyalty. Yes, I too, believe. But I'm also a sceptic. Like your old pagan. And no doubt you, too, if you're honest. Don't make sense, eh? Nothing much does.

'Whatever you think of the missionary business – and you'll have noticed that my mind, like yours, is parti-coloured – I think you'll concede the story is remarkable.

'You seen that photograph of Holy Cross Mission on the Pine Ridge Reservation? After that fight, those murders by the Seventh Army? The mission improvised a hospital. Mostly for the Indians. And a few US soldiers. They're moaning on the floor they've spread with grasses. There's snow out doors. Christmas decorations on the chapel walls, Indians and whites stand round in blankets. You'll find this hard to credit. I was a child. But I was right there with my future husband.

'Don't ask me his story – he'd been a junior officer in Forsyth's Cavalry. Somehow escaped court marshall for a near desertion. Refused to raise his weapon. He was twenty. Me, eleven. Waited a decade to marry. Hard to believe these stories, ain't it?

'You know I was there with Mammy and Pater. They tore up Union flags to bandage those heathens. The cavalry turned a blind eye to that sacrilege. And you know what I used to bandage one old feller? A Ghost Dance shirt. Blood soaked muslin. Those shifts that Kicking Bear had claimed would make the Miniconjou impervious to bullets. Sad magic.

'Yes, there I was cleaning a leg wound and then binding it up with this object of delusion. It breaks your heart. But that's what happened. Died of gangrene, the old heathen.'

*

She was almost a hundred, Mrs Charlotte. What if this had never happened and she was just projecting moral salve to mollify her recollection? No matter. I believed her.

'You don't need to read much to get some comprehension. I mean real understanding. Books are a blessing. But they're also just compendiums of what's out there: transcribed, dressed politely in civilian garments. It's the same with us Christians. Too much church. Too little loving.

'Your missionary Driggs, he had it right. When he got to Tikiġaq he just went on living as he wanted, maybe as he always had done. Yes, he opened a school. But otherwise he did what local men had never stopped doing. Hunted, socialized. And he learned the language. So they loved him. The next lot of preachers were over churchy. Edson in his cassock and his moralizing sermons. Obsessed with dirt and promiscuity. Hoare, boring, priggish. Missed the point of Christianity. All wrong. Just go and live there and show people what a Christian life is: loving and not dogma. Bad as the shamans' hocus-pocus.'

From the garden Elizabeth was visible still working in the kitchen. Asatchaq was sleeping in his wheelchair, an angle of his glasses glinting intermittently above the window sash.

'So what are you up to here in Fairbanks mixing with the Eskimos and Christians? Jewish ain't you?'

'Yes,' I said, anticipating something evangelical.

'I like you Jews,' Mrs Charlotte went on, without expressing the embarrassed hurried, tucking-things-away that one anticipates.

'They're our brethren and fathers,' said Mrs Charlotte. Then,

'You'll say *Kaddish* for the old man when he leaves us?'[3]

It was hard to believe I'd heard this. Stiff mannered from a nineteenth-century mission in Dakota, she, High Toned, Christian, moralizing and yet open minded, waspish, old world, hovering between the orthodox and the agnostic, not entirely non-judgemental.

'You can put this in a novel.' Mrs Charlotte's voice grew sharper. 'I met an old Jew at the market in Rapid City. Summer before 1900. My mother brought him home in our dog cart. He stayed through Jew's Sabbath and on Sunday sold my parents knives and skillets.' I watched this scene as though in newsreel. Ancient, scratchy. It was hard to imagine Mrs Charlotte as a bare-legged adolescent.

'He was peddler? German Jewish?'

'Something like it. His name was Isaac. Any rate, my father knew a bit of Hebrew and together they read aloud from Torah. Sounded mighty strange to *my* ears. That was the day my puppy got its head bit half off by coyotes. Came howling in till Daddy shot him...'

'The peddler said *Kaddish?*'

'Yes. Taught me a few Hebrew words. Or Aramaic. That Isaac was an unbeliever. A good man who'd say *Kaddish* for a little Christian's puppy.'

She spoke some words of *Kaddish* and we lapsed into silence, broken by the ring of nearby hatchets.

'What sort of logic brings all that together?' she went on, musing. 'An atheist. A man of learning. Homeless traveller. A Jew-man on the Christianising prairie. That, I never put together till I read Whitman. Take a look at his poems and then get into the fields and logging camps. Leave history in the school room. The present, it's chaotic. It's multiplicity

---

[3] *Kaddish,* or Mourner's *kaddish* is a magnification of God. In Hebrew and Aramaic, it is spoken in memory of relatives and friends.

is us. Multiply confusing.

'That incontinent old Whitman. "His *turbulent* embrace," my Grandaddy called it. As though America is hugging you. "And in return you get to be the continent that he's embracing." So said Grandad. Back in 1900.

'But now, young man, your opinion of the Ten Lost Tribes? Are you a Levi or a Cohen?'

'Those things are actually quite vague,' I mumbled. 'And folklore, maybe. Some people claim a tribe of priests, but not my family. My grandparents were nonbelievers.'

'Turned off by images by Blake of caterpillar priests, perhaps?' she asked shrewdly.

*

Her questions were uncomfortable. We had Levi relatives by marriage. And my surname is ambiguous. Its first syllable, with *umlaut,* almost sounded 'levi'. While on the other hand, the German 'lion rock', derived from non-Hebraic aristocracy, though this was resonant of Judah and its lion symbol. None of which was relevant to personal identity or tribal membership.

'My friend Polly,' Mrs C went on, 'was daughter in another Mission. This was 1892. And she told me that the Natives were descendents of the scattered remnant.'

'"People are saying,"' she quoted Polly, '"that the *Sioux* are *JEWS?*"' I asked her.

'But Polly, Goody Two Shoes, changed the subject. She was parroting some local gossip.' Mrs Charlotte took up Polly's history.

'I just now got a sudden hit of Polly. But she's long dead now, I reckon. She had a kind of indoors piety. The church she made into her bedroom. Quaint, pious, powder-featured Polly. Still, just like me I guess, she hauled in a preacher. Bedded down in chapel. Clean, decent couple. Not like us eccentrics who struck out for the wild as missionaries, strangers.

'The missionary will be always be a stranger. Removed from the centre and sent out to the *sticks*, the *boondogs*, as kids call it, to tell the unwashed and the marginal to take their lives into the centre. There's a paradox.

'But Polly, bless her, settled with her holy man in West Virginia. That was 1920. Bill and me were up Dakota way already. But we kept in touch at Christmas. And this bit, you'll appreciate. Polly sent me books to keep me current. Stop me going altogether *wild*, she called it.

'Then in 1934 she sent me a last parcel. That still rankles. Hurts because the wrong we did was mutual. She did wrong, and me responded, likewise.

'You've read the great panjandrum, the *Rev.* T.S. Eliot? My older brother was his Harvard classmate. They studied with Lanman, first steps in Sanskrit, round 1911. Great Tom! Pure Tom! I liked his early, weird, satirical, bad-tempered poems. Should have stopped with *Shantih*...

'But *landsakes*, in those lectures in Virginia, the *Reverend* Tom got Christianity muddled up with high and mighty culture. Oh Lordy, what a muddle. He never liked the Jews, my brother told me. Maybe that inspired his *very cultivated* Christianity. Belonged better to the seventeenth century. Cotton Mather and divine New England. Lancelot Andrewes: scourge of pamphleteers and cobblers.

'So Polly sent me old Tom's lectures (he was always *old* Tom even as a freshman). She went to hear him around 1934 and bought the published version.

'*After Strange Gods.* Mine-a-geedy, what a farrago! What pietistic nonsense! Pious Anglo-Christians of his stripe versus cosmopolitans, and bless me, stiff-necked Jews, who don't subscribe to wine and biscuits.

'These were the Jews – he can't personally have known 'em – were struggling to leave Europe, the successful ones, before the holocaust. I know you kids have learned to call it *Shoah.*

'You can guess what I did. We read it out one evening in the prairie thunder, my husband red-faced, stamping, out-shouting the Great Father. He took it worse than I did. I thought he'd bust with indignation.

"Impious!" he hollered. "Not in this house. Give me a Ghost Dance over that benighted, anti-Christian, misconstruction!"

'So I packed back the book in Polly's wrapping, drove to town and slipped it through the post box. I did write *Thank You.* Said,

"Thanks for ye book, Poll. But we don't need it out here in the Badlands. Not a syllable on Christian love there. Theologically irrelevant. Dangerous."'

Mrs C and I were both exhausted and sat down at the table. Bees on the rudbeckia. There were pumpkins, ripe tomatoes and some green ones. White pointed fence posts spoke America. I thought Tom Sawyer and Aunt Polly.

*

'I'll soon be done. But I might as well continue. It's to do with being strangers. Strangerhood. We laboured out there, all the way from "civilized" America. From Princeton and Barnard with our boxes packed with everything from prayerbooks to Goethe. From Europeanised America to an alien, heathen landscape, less American, it seemed, than France and Germany. And the Dakotas? Looked like nothing most have seen outside a photo. Boundaryless space with unchurched heathens, some still nomadic, scattered on infinity, others scattered in unhappy cabins.

'They have, the Sioux, their local ways, but are corrupted by the roustabouts that overran their hunting grounds and holy places. The Black Hills, sacred to them, that the miners have been excavating. It's Miltonic hell.

By Mammon first,' she raised her voice to round the cadence with its ponderous caesuras:

'Ransack'd the center, and with impious hands
Rifled the bowels of their mother earth
For treasures better hid.

'What does this imply for missionary enterprise? That we two little people, go in, uninvited, and tell the Natives that we're different from the drunken, cussin' element that's swarming on their *mother earth* – that's Milton's phrase which corresponds precisely with the local metaphysic?

'Those miners and rascals, they're the wrong sort of white man. That's what we tell the local Natives of the fifteen hundred scallywags rampaging through their territory. We two small Christians are decent representatives of white society. We're helpful Americans. Like my irony? We're not there to *ransack* the Black Hills. We're not here with gold pans. We're poor folk like you. I suppress the fact the church does hold a property portfolio.

'So by force of persistence and frugality we convene a Christian caucus. There are Sioux heads don't dislike us. Wise heads, equally, suspect the game that we're pursuing. We've intervened in history. And history is a run of interventions: trials, conflicts and migrations. Tried in our small way to divert its current. Leave smiling reflections on its surface. I'll grant our contribution might be cosy. We had our small successes. And because we took on board their version, the Sioux version, of Great Fatherhood, homologised his lore with gospel exposition, learned their language, prayed in Lakota, there were folks saw the point of our endeavour.

'Still, the less we talked up Christianity, the better we got on with people. But don't get me wrong. I was always a Christian. Always will be. Still don't presume the right to metaphysical superiority. Who am I to tell 'em that I've brought the Truth out here and that everything they think is plum misguided?' Mrs Charlotte went on:

'"You're telling us what's in your book," one woman challenged me. "I got a book too", she continued. Not on paper. It's sky, earth, animals and rivers." She came up to my shoulder at the picket and we gazed out on her Bible. Sun above us. Grass without horizon. Buttes, gullies, mountains. The odd prairie chicken. It was Monday on the Badlands. Sunday evening we'd near bust the windows with a lamp-lit psaltry. But what's Sunday in the Badlands? Only recently some gentleman had come out with the European calendar and chopped the days up into rows of sevens. I remember the first book of *Genesis*. When Elohim divided everything. Put some order to creation. That put an end to *tohu va bohu*, mish-mash, chaos.

'So one lives in strangerhood, in separation. "Alienation" in the current lingo. Strangers to a place and people, necessarily because we go where none of us belonging to the parent group that's bursting to spread itself, has been before. And you separate from home community. The likes of Polly and her husband in a comfortable parish repudiate the challenge. I don't criticize. God gives you one life. You must deploy it somewhere. And for your life to work out, you must trust your choice and be prepared to love the people you are moving in on.

'Mostly one suffers. You don't talk about it. But it hurt my husband. I could live with the wreckage of my education. I might have liked to sit with New York students contemplating ambiguity. I'd watched beautiful absurdities played out in books I'd read at Barnard. Montaigne, Flaubert, Goethe, Kafka. But the loneliness my husband suffered. And the shame of failure. Mission life implies complexity of failure.

*

'You don't create an undivided Christian parish on the prairie. You develop a relationship with God, lopsided and unrealised. And with yourself construe a sacrificial dedication that you give to God which outwardly returns you nothing. Maybe somewhere in the process you bring at least some happiness and comfort to the folks you've come to serve and learn from. Both those are few in my experience.

'But in solitary meditation, you realize you're enclosed, and in impenetrable company. Everyone that's both like you and unlike's suffering estrangement. Not your kind maybe. And that your parish is a wilderness bespeaks, necessitates, a solitude that's squalid as it's holy. The worthiness you represent, is shaming. Some want to be like you. While others turn away contemptuous. Pursue the path of contradiction. I don't blame them. Bless them in their determination.

'Thus you're branded. You are white *folk* which on the East Coast had never occurred to you. And from this category flow the mutually abrasive and abusive classes. We create communities of castes as Hindus call their palette... Full blood, half breed, white. As if these categories summed up identities to live by.

'I mentioned Kafka. Not so far fetched as you might imagine. Less *Trial* and *Castle*. More *Amerika* – your kind of story. Franz Kafka, the Czech surname means crow. Quite apposite as prairie resident. Master of Selfhood as Outsider. Separation as a sense of being that defines existence. One little text I turned up in the Badlands haunts me. Not many read K's *Meditations*. I didn't know those texts till I stumbled on this title:

Wuensch, Indianer zu werden – 'Wish: to be an Indian'. Here it is in its entirety:

If one were only an Indian. Alert. Ready. And on a running horse, leaning into wind and quivering across shaking earth. Till one let the spurs go. For there were no spurs. Till one threw aside the reins. For there were no reins. And one scarcely saw the plain in front of him. Without horse neck, without horse's head.

'Imagine my surprise in the Dakotas, to light on this. A magical coincidence. Or was it a given? How could I have not have this text engraved on consciousness? How Kafka understood and suffered a belonging to his separation! I knew this too and felt it with him. K an Indian! Big joke. It took him months before he'd book a train from Prague to see his sweetheart.

'Yes, I felt separate. Still I was connected by those Sioux wounds back in 1890 that fed my heart's blood. That day in December marked a nation's dispossession. When you look at the present, I mean now in 1976 on the eve of white America's two-hundred-year-old birthday, you understand a little all the teenage suicides and alcohol, despair and violence that have flowed from that occasion. That's how Wounded Knee continues bleeding.

'Reverting to Kafka – who imagined that the Indians were still as German comics showed them: unharnessed spirits, alive and freely travelling, at one with earth and animals that all belonged together in spontaneous reciprocity. That mutuality was reciprocal was K's ideal projection from the urbane suffocation choking him: his asphyxiated whimsy weirdly consonant with trammels that, unknown to him, were newly paralleled on a Dakota plain that he could not imagine. Yes, late 1890 was the moment when the Sioux that Kafka had imagined were cut down by the US Army and their liberated riding, reined and hobbled.[4]

'You've seen, some photos of that period? Two images have stayed with me. In one, the caption identifies 'hostile Indians'. You see tipis, fragile, out of date within an era cameras that portray them signify. You see people, women mostly, clustered inside tipi tent props, hunched under blankets. The plains round them. People and their places naked of each other, mutually alien. That's a strange thing, speaking of estrangement. These people have been herded into inactivity. They've become redundant. Their land's transformed into America and they're displaced within it. Now there's a transition.

'And the other photo is of General Miles on horseback in his uniform. He's with Buffalo Bill and a small group of Bluecoats in their riding outfits. The plains stretch round them. There they sit on horseback. Miles is pointing.

They're surveying the land they've galloped to appropriate and make *Amerika*. As German spells it.

And these same grasslands are now the possession of a uniformed authority. Those men themselves might well have been good fellows. They're caught up in events. Complexities beyond contemporary comprehension. It's history, unexplained and uninterpretable we're staring at. Momentous changes. Those acres will be parcelled out and mapped, then ploughed, fenced, grazed and some of it donated back to reservation Indians.

'Of course, the European cliché of the Indian derived from images of 'noble' horsemen: Plains Dakota, 'Red Indians' on horses (they'd learned to ride from colonists who sold them horses). Who in Kafka's 1913 Europe could have understood the ironies within the cliché whose metaphysic Kafka crucified himself with.'

---

[4] A romantic view of the American West was projected by the German novelist Karl May. Kafka, like many Europeans, absorbed May's version of Western history and folklore.

I thought of that manly human Kafka had imagined: masculine in power and self-determination. Brother, husband, son and father: the convergence rendering him an individual. Free and yet belonging to the group he represented. Representative of what the tribe, the man, was as a person. Kafka's sketch was a projection of his own half-seen-by-self, an uncoordinated sketch of body: how it felt to be a disaffiliated urban half-man, Czech, German-speaking Jew, lover, ailing, tolerantly loved, misunderstood, reclusive, as against this heedless and self-integrated horseman riding without tackle, without horse, in wind, at one with earth which shakes with the percussion of his travel.

'Maybe,' she continued, 'after all, you or folks like us, just belonged on the margin. So we stayed three decades as lookers on and when my husband understood we wanted an assimilation there, like Driggs in Tikiġaq, he reckoned we had best retreat and not deceive our masters. He was, like Driggs in Tikiġaq, a 'failure'. Loved the *Indianer* more than he loved Jesus. Half-compromised, half-scalped, half-disinherited, we high-tailed, drove our wagon back to Princeton. I mean this, dearie. Just imagine rumbling our dusty little Ford T back to campus. Had the urge to give it oats and water.

'Hard to comprehend this social isolation business. Though we're talking about everyone, world history. Home and prairie – which was home we understood far better than the university we rattled back to and sat round in for the next years, dreaming of ravines and grasslands. That's where Libby started reading Proust and Kafka. Whose writings spurred her, paradoxically, to travel back to the Dakotas. Can't remember if we'd read K's *Wuensch* together. She did however read me Rilke's first *Duino Elegy*:

'and the clever animals have already observed that we don't feel very at home in the interpreted world. There remains for us perhaps some tree on the slope that we see daily and yesterday's path also remains…'

'What her parents had loved but which stayed foreign and extrinsic, she'd assimilated and she never left it. A simpler girl than I was: but self-integrated, whole, spontaneous, natural.' Mrs Charlotte gestured to her daughter, now aged sixty, in the upstairs kitchen.

*

'But one's alone in these estrangements. Though everyone imagines they're uniquely isolated. All solitude's a shared thing, generally or ultimately. You *can* invite another isolate to share your isolation – that is, if you have the generosity to make it happen. I flatter myself that that's what I am doing now with you, young Jew, and you, perhaps, with me, a half-dead, Christian lady, teetering across the threshold of what H. James muttered at his dying moment. I like the nod of recognition that he paid the void before he entered what he called the final and "distinguished moment".

'But going back to separation. In the end it's *one thing* which is always part of two things. We become what Andrew Marvell casually described as *parti-coloured*. Self-contradictory, as Whitman boasted of his thinking. You, course, are one of the new pagans who'll ally themselves to any contradiction. Dabbling in every kind of half-baked spirituality. You're the jesters of the kingdom, clowning with the changing shapes of paradox. You think you've seen *the two* but fall between them.'

I suspected Mrs Charlotte and her tendency towards inclusivity would, with the smallest movement, find herself among agnostic cosmopolitans – the rootless freethinkers from whom Eliot estranged himself. She had set herself against the exclusivity of culture and 'tradition' that Eliot identified with Christianity. It was as though I'd sprung her on this. Because perhaps my cosmopolitan freethinking had survived Old Possum's posture.

The Photograph

'Imagine how we settled,' went on Mrs Charlotte. 'It was 1925. Brought up daughter Libby. Blossom of the Mission. Wordsworth's *Lucy* babbling Lakota. We were strangers. Elite Americans among pagans. Well, it took a photograph to teach us what our status there was.'

I'd prompted this digression, describing views I'd seen from the window of the twin-engined Otter as it banked round Tikiġaq. I'd been there some months and absorbed its day-to-dayness, had met people who disliked me: teachers, who'd initiated, so I thought, hostilities.

As from the air, the place, which seemed huge, shrank into focus. I could see in a glance the houses I had lived in, their proximity to friends and enemies. Saw paths of interaction I had tangled in, that linked the white man's houses and traders' cabins. Paths intersecting in faint sandy traces. Beaches. Meat racks. Tarped cabins. Village store. Two churches.

Episcopal, green painted clapboard. And the white, metallic, square Assemblies building.

All this I saw in its imagined tensions, wavering and incoherent. Striped surf motionless against the Point and driftwood piled on beaches. Sea ice. Outlines of the north and south sides slanting towards the point of the peninsula. The ridges that the point's composed of. How they stripe its movement as it stretches from the mainland. The community enclosed, supported by the symmetry the sea allows it.

Then the plane flies low along lagoons that lie between the south beach and the tundra. Marshland, sea and river. And I list the migrant birds that breed there. All this you survey in five minutes, details miniature and distanced. Every pain and fear you suffered diagrammed and harmless.

'Now, about the photograph I mentioned,' Mrs Charlotte went on, 'that showed us something that I hadn't thought of. A couple of boys from Rapid City flew in one summer. Corn-fed farm kids who could fly a Cessna.

'One of the lads had done a Geography MA and specialized in mapping. Knew more about our place than I did. He was junior in the Agriculture Census team – that dates it, 1925, that summer. County by county they surveyed South Dakota – so's to plot its yield potential. I never knew the counties named for farmers of the era: Ziebach, Shannon, Armstrong, Spink and Edmunds. Names come and go. Though some big names can stay longer – Custer, Dewey, Brule, Yankton.

'We fed 'em pie that Libby knocked up while they roamed round with their tripods. Nice kids. Called me 'Mrs Reverend,' which my husband borrowed when the mood came on him.

'Six weeks later sent a stack of photos, first from the air and then ground level. (Packed that pie away in good time, I remember. Libby also served them Skunk and Bobcat stories. I could read between the lines, all right. Libby married the tall, dark one and he passed out four years later as a preacher. "Just to hear more Bobcat stories," he whispered at the wedding. Close enough to truth, I reckoned.)

'But his photos from the air. Those put us in our place. Both geographically and metaphysically. Looked like a moon shot. Bare rock, striped grass, canyons, buttes and uninterpretable contours. Not an inch of animal or human. Grey, grizzled distances. And plum in the middle lay our Mission. Church beside it. Two grains of photochemicals, and the garden – a blur of nothing... Us and what we'd cultivated overwhelmed by nature.

'Where were the Yankton and Lakota? On a separate photo, a few tents standing every which way and at angles. Where was Jesus? What business had he in the Badlands? What business in this stony context? (I won't quote *The Waste Land.*) How did our home with prayer books, poetry and novels belong in these spaces? Unanswerable questions. Though those boys *did* measure 'em.

'Still, the photo taught us what we should have known if we'd been smarter. How small and separate our world was. Christians come to stick themselves on 'savages'. Not that the photo suggested we'd intruded. It was rather that we didn't matter. What if those boys flew in fifty years ago? Would their photograph look different? Not much. There would have been no church and mission house. Same clusters of tents, more widely scattered.

'My point will contradict this. (I learned Whitman's habit): we missionaries existed in a social quarantine. Looked after ourselves just so our Ministry could reach the other. We were aliens who'd landed from another planet and created a self-gratifying colony of fine intentions. That was the lesson that those photos taught us. As though God deflected how he viewed our self-regard to higher vision – that sent us to our knees, all right.

'"If that's how God sees us," said my husband, "then maybe the Lakota likewise view us." "And if nature has a vision, she too maybe wants to show us in our proper context."

'Still, we got excited by those pictures. My husband well nigh started dancing. "There's Sharp's Corner, Chimney Butt, White River, Cuny Table, Porcupine and Redwater! Those last were creeks we'd supped at. Trotted ponies all through Pine Ridge. Collected names, too. I've looked at today's maps. Much of the place in 1952, when the Army did its latest survey, is empty contour. As though no-one's ever been there.

'Your situation won't be compromised as ours was,' Mrs C assured me. 'You'll be there to learn not teach them anything. And you'll cocoon yourself with poetry... Now for my equivocation.'

*

The Wounded Knee Catastrophe

'I've described our realization: we'd brought Princeton to the Badlands. I read German of the evenings. My husband did his Greek and Hebrew. Folks now listen in to the wireless, bless 'em. My husband was an innocent. Doing good and studying were second nature. All he knew were love and service.

'But to the Wounded Knee fight. Late December. I was ten or eleven. Ain't many old folk still remember. That day still haunts me.

'It was Wounded Knee that pulled me to the Badlands back from university. I bludgeoned my husband with that ambition. Behind each syllable of Baudelaire and Kafka I'd read at university, I heard the cries of victims on the floor of Holy Cross Mission as mother plied the bandages and we breathed cordite that the army field guns left in flesh wounds. Gangrene and cordite. Combination that made history of America. A sacrifice I hope the good Lord's nostrils recognized, *not pleasing to Him.*

'Two things stay in memory. Two symbols of the confrontation. Natural man (that label) versus modernizing young America. Those two artefacts confront the contemplation.

'On the one hand, Ghost Shirts. Kicking Bear who'd travelled to Nevada to meet Wovoka, the Ghost Dance prophet, told those trusting warriors to put these shirts on against battle with the cavalry and which he taught them were impervious. I handled a ghost shirt – was it calico or muslin? – bloody tatters. The old man I sat with died in one and pressed it to him. At the other extreme, there's the Hotchkiss cannon. An early machine gun. What a confrontation!

'And this, exposed on grassland, shows how modern warfare's handled. Or non-handled. It's a casual transition from handcrafted weapons and takes little effort. That's been done already in the foundry.

That same Miles, in 1890, was Major General of the Seventh Cavalry. That's just detail. Returning to the gun. A two-wheeled carriage and the cannon. Transported to the front line – here's a point of interest – by two mules. Makes you think of Jesus riding to Jerusalem.

'Ironware, starting with Columbus, blew the white man's path across the continent and Wounded Knee was part of that old pattern. That's our history.

'I quoted Milton. Here's another outcome: "rifling the earth" to mould her effluent. Metals are power. The shamans knew this but they only used it amuletically. It was the Whites developed murdering technology.

'There were also wounded US soldiers. Boys, ignorant of what they'd done and what had happened. Certainly, the background's tangled. You can read it in James Mooney. Deep man, Mooney. Stayed at the Mission ten days on investigations. I'd sit on a trunk of notebooks that he carted with him while he told me stories from the Cherokee that he'd recorded.

"Those were peaceful southern evenings," he would mumble. "Those Indians developed their own writing. That levelled our communication."

'Yes, but as it happened,' went on Mrs Charlotte, 'before Mooney came, I'd travelled with my parents to the Pine Ridge reservation. The Holy Cross preacher, Oh yes, Cook or Cooper, did the church into a hospital. You'll have seen the photo. Spread grass on the church floor. Wet from snow melt. Paper chains still hanging from just four days previous. Next days were blizzards.

'Now two or three things not in Mooney. I've mentioned separation. That was painful. But separated as I may have been, I never recovered, and still haven't, from that Pine Ridge weeping. As my mother bound them, so those wounds attached me to them. And I prayed to Jesus. Helpless, weeping.

'Helpless. And the wounded perished. Children orphaned. I could only crouch there. One old man, he laid his hand across my forearm. I offered him my own hand, but he wouldn't. Died without comfort. Knew, still, a ten years' white kid was entangled with him. She, little white girl, thought she'd come to help him. He knew that she was product of the issues that the Ghost Dance had confronted. What did it matter which kind of white folk came here, gentle Christian or cussin' gold prospector? Both were new America.

'Those wounds and cries have never left me. I tried drowning them throughout my education. Flaubert and Goethe versus the Dakotas. But those wounds took me over. You understand the Ghost Dance story? Not many realize that the Sioux had borrowed the revival teachings Wovoka and other prophets been preaching since the 1870s.

'Promised the dance would bring the game back, restore land that settlers had taken, dance ancestors back into existence? Desperate people clutch at mysteries. Think of women in Naples who danced in 1944 to stop them getting typhus. Then hurled themselves on corpses for the US Army to dispose of.

'I can see how the Ghost Dance which was s'posed to save them, acted as a trigger to the Wounded Knee disaster. Forgetting land rights, bison slaughter, poverty and sickness, all of which are central, the conflict rose from cultural mismatch, distrust and misprision. While the Indians were threatened by the white invasion, there was nothing they could do to educate the white man in the value of their culture. Bits of education crossed the cultural boundaries half a century later when some missionaries incorporated bits of Sioux religious practice. Hope it made a difference.

'But look. Many of those army lads were raw recruits and farm kids or half-educated townsfolk. Not 'Indian fighters' or survivors of the Little Big Horn battle. And the Reservation Agents mostly frightened, helpless. How could they know anything? The successful ones – McLaughlin and McGillycuddy – worked hard by force of personality, made friends with leaders, tried to act with probity. But how could even well intentioned white men enter the mind of an Oglala dancer? I was a child and see now see how people shared the white child's lack of comprehension.

'Just focus on fear. The Dakota feared the white man and his army, hated settlers. What few people, whites, know is a fear of Indians. That otherness that repelled and mystified. I'm not talking about raids, wars, scalpings. That's another subject. It's enormous. I can't address that issue.

'Take the Ghost Dance. Just look at it from outside and imagine the strangeness. Indians in hundreds in a clearing. Four hundred tipis. The prayer tree set up in the dance ground. Sweat lodges and the skins draped round them, bison skulls, half-naked people crawling in and out of lodges. Painted faces. Ghost shirts. Everybody carrying eagle feathers.

'Imagine the leader shouting out instructions and the cries, prayers, ghost songs. Then the dancers drop down, roll and go through trances, screaming. Shamans run round. Dancers race and stagger, butt on tree trunks, run at horses, shouting up to Wakan Tanka that they'd entered spirit land.

'I've simplified it, narrowed the issue to a ten-year-old's focus, done a colour drawing. The complexities were socially enormous. But just enter that child's view, that the white man shared. And you understand the foreign seeming nature of what white Americans who wished to 'normalise' the land into a country, confronted. These were awe-inspiring aliens whose character denied the *normalcy* of civilized America.

'I've satirized the church and told you about separation. That's personal. Not bitter. What else was there to give these very different people? It was only churches had the conscience, energy and spare bucks to travel out there. What other powers were there in America to salvage something? The reservation Agencies – weak and corrupt or pointlessly effective in deceitful operation. Did they have the ointment Jesus offers? Agents didn't have it.

'And when you contemplate what's grown since 1890, it's not nothing. I honour the Missions. They've persisted. Jesuits and us Episcopalians. Mooney's book may help explain things. Still, positives are not abstractions. It all has to do with helping others. Look at earth from air and you wonder, given the dimension of most people's suffering, if anything's worth doing. Still, you work local. That's all you can do. That's all we aim at. We raised Libby to do likewise.

'She talks soft, Libby,' she continued. 'But that girl was raised hard. Walked to school across the prairie. Rattlesnakes and gulches, rogue dogs, wild Sioux children. Talked Lakota, told them stories. That was 1920. Spring, did the garden and inherited my husband's rifle. Walked out bare legged one night, shot coyotes had been digging at our food cache. Still, Sioux men called her "Flower". *Wanahca* in Lakota. Now she's more 'an sixty, no prospect of retirement and another winter coming. And she hasn't stopped her caring.

'I can see you have a taste for us old buzzards,' she continued. She was indeed, a wiry ancient critter. She too had walked the hard Dakotas, spoke the language, dug through prairie roots to make a garden and could fire a Browning.

'You've read the Renoir book?' she changed the subject. 'His son who made films wrote his father's life and sayings. A friend of mine in Paris met the old painter. He said, "You Yankees, what's the point of all your reading? Look how the Jews live. They read just one book."'

'He didn't know about the Talmud and the million other commentaries. Bit of an anti-semite, worth remembering. In love with flesh pots. I can't blame him. Half Paris was whoring. You've read Maupassant's stories. Put your face in a book and you're missing what the book emerged from. Life's hairy and misshapen.

'Look at old Whitman. My granddaddy knew him. Said to me one evening. "I've come from the old man's *turbulent embrace*." You'll understand that one day. Oh, I said that earlier. I repeat myself. Whitman also said it.

'So we left the prairie. Couldn't take the contradictions. Mine especially. Universalists we were, I reckon. Going back to John Driggs in Alaska. Driggs, bless him, came through the Dakotas on his way to missionise. My parents met him at some railroad station, spring of 1890. That Driggs, they told me, had an appetite. Put away two stacks of hot cakes, drank a pint of coffee, stashed corn pone and bacon in his satchel. He wasn't gonna stay, not even stop to visit. Couldn't wait to get to Frisco and the shipyards, buy his year's chow, measure lumber for a Mission, order slates and pencils, choose a shot gun, cold weather outfits. All bully six foot of him.

'Look at that old pagan Libby's brought here,' gesturing towards the window. 'Wants to set up house with me. Because I'm mobile and can operate a kitchen. And because I'm powerful. Family shaman.

'I can also tell you he's still thinking sex. There's still sex in his system. I left mine on the prairie. Makes life simpler. How come the good Lord put us to the trouble? I can imagine you're still in that line of behaviour. What, for land's sake, will you do there for comfort? Just don't mess around, if you want some advice from a dried old woman. But your interest's in the issues up there, ain't it?

'I can see you have a taste for us old buzzards,' she repeated. She was indeed the boniest old matron. Her harangue had been exhausting and she needed to lie down. I was aching to escape her.

'Your old Eskimo was here last Tuesday. Heard I was a widow. Said we should keep house together.' She laughed sarcastically. She reminded me of blind, sarcastic Ayagiiyaq. I sent her my Whitman parody. But that was the last I ever saw of Mrs Charlotte.

Still hungry, stuck in grammar, I was anxious to get back to homework. I loved the thorns the language shared with Hebrew's sweet ones: protracted diphthongs, humming consonants, dark throat stops, both languages germinated in hard, stony places, radiating blossom, tough systematic foliage.

The Episcopalian Connection

After the Alaska Purchase in 1867, four main populations lived in Alaska. There were Native people: northern Inupiat, Yup'iit and Chugach Eskimos; Aleut people who'd been near exterminated by the Russians; Tlingit Indians in southeast Alaska. And Athabascan Indians of the vast interior.

There were small numbers of Euro-Americans whose potential wealth creation was one *raison d'être* for the 1867 purchase. Third, was the US Army whose duties were replaced by the Coast Guard in the late 1870s.

Finally, there were missionaries. Russian Orthodox in the south-west; Christian Covenanters on the Bering Strait; Friends and Baptists in the lower Arctic, Presbyterians in Barrow and the Episcopalians on the Yukon and in 1890 at Tikiġaq. The Orthodox had arrived with Russian traders in the late eighteenth century. The 'Comity Agreement' of 1889–90 had, under the auspices of the Presbyterian Jackson, divided up Alaska almost at random.

The Lakota Ghost Dance and the Inupiaq *Uivvaqsaaq*

The historical head note touches on this connection, but omits a description of one crucial component: the history that linked Asatchaq and Mrs Charlotte. What both had observed was a revivalist religion. Asatchaq in north Alaska. Mrs Charlotte in the Dakotas.

Transmission, from the late 1870s and 1880s, of revivalist religions happened possibly at Celilo Falls on the Columbia River that Lewis and Clark visited in 1805, describing the Native meeting there as a 'great emporium… where neighbouring nations assemble,' and a large population density.

Native artefacts from the Great Plains, the southwest and also Alaska, mutually remote regions, have since been excavated at Celilo Falls. On the border between Sahaptian and Chinookan people, this meeting place on the Columbia River was also a centre for speakers of the Chinook Jargon. With this help, jargon speakers from different tribes could expound revivalist ideas, and transmit them to diverse people who were otherwise separated. Thus what became Dakota Ghost Dance ideology and *uivvaqsaaq* in north Alaska, may have been transmitted via a jargon otherwise used for trade. It is possible that the otherwise inexplicable presence of similar cults with virtually identical purposes and a uniformity of symbolism might have been distributed by jargon speakers to different and linguistically discrete societies.[5]

Postscript – Axe Percussion

I'd noticed, as Mrs Charlotte moved toward her peroration and I sensed a band of cold air layering mid-September warmth, that she'd grown aware of axe blows reaching us from nearby woodsheds and that this percussion took her back to South Dakota: winter firewood preparation, the feel in her hands of axe hafts, logs that sprang apart and smells of resin. Pine, alder, cottonwood that she and her husband humped monthly from a woodland.

Hands. Axes. Smells of burning. Back ache. Woodland, prairie, horse loads, sizing up next winter against supplies you've stacked in the

---

[5] With thanks to Prof. Bruce Ingham, Lakota language specialist and Jonathan King of the British Museum for help on this subject. For a longer discussion of *uivvaqsaat*, see *Ultimate Americans*, 2009.

summer. Local timber. Insects you disturbed and others that you burned to ashes.

(above) Tukummiq and the author at work in Tukummiq's home, winter 1976.

(below) Ataŋauraq's grave markers, whale jaw bones and a later cross.

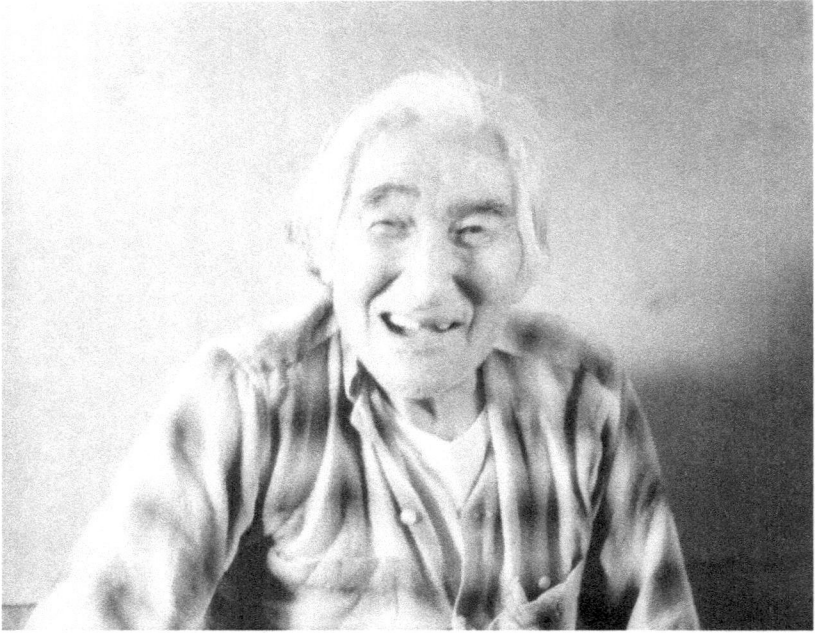

(above) Asatchaq, winter 1976.

(below) Asatchaq's cabin, looking north, winter 1976.

(above) Tikiġaq house following move to New Town Site, 1977.
(below) Margaret and Kool Daddy at cards in Piquk's house, winter 1976.

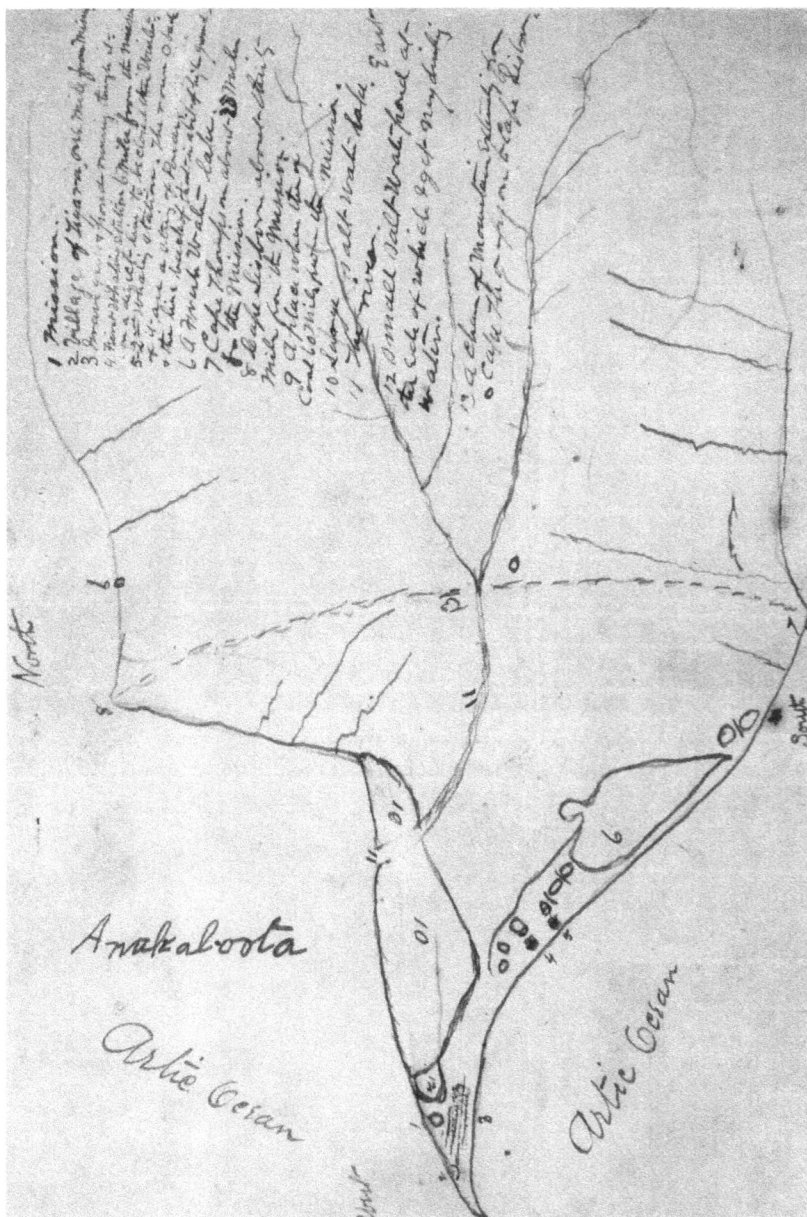

Tikiġaq map drawn for John Driggs by local man, perhaps Anaqulutuq,
with Tikiġaq by Driggs, ca. 1900

(above) Small crew whale hunt at the ice edge with skinboat
and windbreak, spring 1977

(below) South beach, summer 1977.
Cape Thompson on horizon and driftwood logs.

Part 5

The Gods of the Pipeline

They never allow themselves a day of quiet. Nothing can take their minds off figures; nothing of beauty can forget the export trade and market prices for a single moment. Knut Hamsun, *The Cultural Life of Modern America*, 1889

*

I recorded these conversation fragments during fifteen minutes in the cafeteria of the University of Alaska, Fairbanks, October 1977, three months after the oil began to flow:

- It'll be worth $2 million in a year.
- I'm asking twenty thousand for it.
- Fifteen hundred acres.
- How much did you try to get for it?
- He lives at 7.5 mile.
- 250 gallon capacity.
- We're pushing Title IV, though ARMB has asked for its consultant back.
- Reserves accumulating at the pump station.

Let the bastards freeze in the dark... Bumper sticker, Fairbanks, 1974.

'Mama asks if you would not cut down the orchard until she leaves.'
      Chekhov, The Cherry Orchard, Act IV

I first saw *The Cherry Orchard* at Sadlers Wells in about 1950. It was performed by the Russian Art Theatre and though I didn't understand the words, something non-verbal at the end of the play impressed itself on me. This was the off stage beat of axes that accompany the departure of the cherry orchard's ex-proprietors in Act IV and this percussion communicated a transition the audience might have anticipated but would not be witnessing: a process of economic and social development: a utilitarian separation from the foregoing spectacle of quiet familial disintegration.

The orchard also had its aesthetic component. The grace of the trees, and after a Russian winter, lovely blossom and finally the cherry harvest. The women would make jam, construct pies and pickle. The orchard would go into leaf and the family have picnics in its shade. There was continuity to this rhythm. The cherry orchard was an intimate space. The servants were not explicity excluded. They might enjoy it vicariously.

The message in Fairbanks coming from nearby axes reminded me of how old Russia went through transformation. Put more bleakly: parts of the Russian country were being hatcheted to oblivion. And while some characters in the drama would participate in the clearance process and the creation of new, small, neat environments that Chekhov satirised in short stories, other characters, in the grip of anxiety or in bewilderment and denial, drifted towards a future that would perhaps remain a vague, albeit temporary continuation of past certainties. There were, on the other hand, *ancien regime* victims such as Feers, the abandoned retainer, who is the last on-stage character. Feers is ancient and moribund. For Feers-like people, and those who were more active, there was apparently neither the possibility of life in the old, increasingly inaccessible world which had exploited them, nor participation in the new which would sweep them aside.

While the thud of axes heralded one aspect of old Russia's trans-formation, the wood chops punctuating Mrs Charlotte's conversation proclaimed something that was both parallel and different. The historical transitions suggested by axe percussion that Fairbanks afternoon both communicated subsistence continuities that were being partly superseded by the technologically dominant modern world but also, paradoxically, suggested the perseverance of continuing hands-on life ways. Certainly there would be changes in the Fairbanks sub-Arctic. There would be people affluent enough to do what they wanted, in which case the continuation of the handmade would become one of choice. Presumably they would be stocking their wood sheds long after oil started flowing. And there would also be poor people who would have no choice but to continue cutting firewood. There were also those for whom wood-burning stoves would become obsolete, or transformed to decorative features in a centrally heated, oil-fired domestic space.

In the silences surrounding Mrs Charlotte's conversation and its background ostinato, I became aware of two histories: one was ancient, vulnerable but not yet dead, the second was of the future, whose super-modernity was embodied by the construction of the Trans-Alaska pipeline that clattered, as Mrs Charlotte talked, in loading bays and railway sidings on the north side of town. Construction, organised from Fairbanks and in the twelve initial construction camps established along the pipeline's eight hundred mile trajectory, had started in 1974, and the last weld would be OK'd in summer 1977 when oil would begin flowing towards tankers in the Gulf of Alaska.

The two histories, ancient and super modern, were contiguous. But they coexisted in what was also an unspoken absence of mutual recognition. These coexistencies were also happening world wide, in Iran, Nigeria, Mexico, the US Gulf States, Venezuela. Here in Alaska, people continued felling trees, hollowing boats, cutting house posts with axes. There were, still here, in the Great Land, millions of previously scorned 'waste' acres purchased from the Russians for $7.2 million in 1867, and now the most virtuosic feat of engineering would be layering its presence from the north to the south of Alaska.[6]

The sound of axes that afternoon also expressed a melancholy timbre. Listening to Shakespeare's 'surly sullen bell', the surviving dedicatee was assumed to have life ahead of him. But the writer's imminent death was also implied. The Stratford bell, like Fairbanks axes, would ring into the future.

*

I imagined men and women in their sixties, Fairbanks sourdoughs who'd been cutting wood here since the nineteen twenties and who cultivated vegetables in downtown gardens. They hunted moose along the Tanana, went fishing and bartered surplus with their neighbours. Equally, they might be Brad and Darlene, Trudi, Kora, Ernie, or freaks on a mix of homegrown dope and Christianity. Yards down the track from Mrs Charlotte's, I coincided with an East Coast M.A., dropped out from Princeton: spotted bandana, with a necklace from which vaguely native amulets depended and who pressed his stubble on the axe shaft, quoting William Carlos Williams between whistled variations on a Dylan ballad. His hands were blistered, accustomed as they had been only to turning

---

[6] To build houses and boats, make weapons and stay warm, the axe had long been one of the mainstays in hard countries. Later in the season, I'd see Trudi in an aisle of JCPenney with an axe in one hand and in the other curtain fabric. The axes punctuating Mrs Charlotte's conversation proclaimed the perseverance of ancient lifeways that Trudi and Mrs Charlotte's neighbours continued to pursue. But there would be no stopping oil development.

pages. 'But this is real America', he told me, splitting an ambiguous division between worlds he'd studied in a classroom and now, as if it were a caged bird, let free a Williams poem to the evening:

The pure products of America

go crazy...

'I'm doin' it,' he growled. 'You're doin' it. It's the other way round from Williams' meaning. Ain't we both destroying it? Whitman saw it coming: manual work passed on to engineers and foundries. Williams handed down the old man's message.' He wrongly assumed I understood him.

*

There was also an irresistible momentum of technological advance that would render the hands-on way of life superfluous. It was this momentum that launched eight hundred miles of Japanese pipe from north Alaska. There seemed an ineluctability to this epic. I'd lived in Chicago, and it seemed natural that a 'completed' America should move northwest, and that the far north should take on the character of the lower forty-eight.

*

The impact of the pipeline in mid-1970s Alaska was unavoidable – except perhaps to someone like Mrs Charlotte who had removed herself from contemporary issues – though, Mrs C had memories of the Black Hills gold rush in the 1890s, and had she lived, would satirically be aware in 2018, of how parallel issues threatened Native people facing the Keystone XL project in the Dakotas. Asatchaq was also largely unaware of TAPS (the Trans-Alaska Pipeline System). And while Mrs Charlotte was semi-immobilised, Asatchaq was preoccupied with survival and with memories of a culture that were largely impossible to communicate. The 'line' was otherwise a daily feature of Fairbanks life.

Still, pipeline aside, Euro-American acquisition of minerals, fish, furs, timber and Arctic products such as ivory and baleen, had been a focus of Euro-American activity since the sixteenth century. TAPS was unique in that the complex nature of its construction transcended everything. The project of 'resource utilization' nonetheless also harmonized with previous acquisition initiatives.

But while TAPS touched almost everything in 1970s Fairbanks, one of its most curious aspects lay in its coexistence not only with the worlds of Mrs Charlotte and the tyro Trudi, but with the magical realm of Native vision. Discordant things have always coexisted. But in the coincidence of TAPS and the continuation of traditional Native belief systems lay a paradox which both touched and subverted my work.

*

The coexistence of these jarring milieux will mark the social and historical environment I shall try sketching. But to start with, this part of the narrative will open with a condensed outline of ways in which TAPS represented a climax to four hundred years of American exploration.

Eldorado

Gaily bedight,
  A gallant knight,
In sunshine and in shadow,
  Had journeyed long,
  Singing a song,
In search of Eldorado.
            Edgar Allan Poe

… 'the rapacious fury of the people of Europe, who have an unaccountable fondness for the pebbles and dirt of our land…'
            Voltaire, *Candide*

The dirt and pebbles lying round in Voltaire's legendary kingdom were what Europeans recognised as precious stones and gold. But these had economic value only to outsiders like Candide. The legend of El Dorado tantalised sixteenth century Spain and England equally. But the search for gold also came at the price of the decimation of many indigenous societies and the deaths of countless treasure hunters whose visions of lucre contrasted with those of American natives for whom luxury materials sought after by Europeans frequently held only ritual value.
To give just two examples. When in 1545 the Spanish part-drained Lake Guatavita in Columbia they retrieved gold figurines which had been tossed into the water during a king's initiation. Spanish gold-salvaging expeditions over the following three centuries were partially successful, but none met expectations raised by European recollection of perceived Native profligacy. Second, Walter Ralegh's pursuit of gold in Guiana in

1617 resulted both in the death of his son, and once Ralegh had returned to London, in his own execution. Insecure wealth acquisition and likely death were the reward of countless old world adventurers, and American resources, were viewed by Europeans as routinely available properties.

While part of Ralegh's purpose, as he wrote in *The Ocean to Cynthia*, was to re-secure Elizabeth's favour, one object in seeking Eldorado, was, in his words 'To seek new worlds, for gold, for fame, for glory...' The alternative was sterility: 'From fruitless trees I gather withered leaves,' he lamented.

The desire for possession in which male eroticism was homologised with New World exploration, the hypnotic movement in the direction of a desired object, was more explicitly expressed by John Donne some twenty years later:

> 'Oh my America! my new-found-land,/My kingdome.../My Myne of precious stones, My Emperie,/How blest am I in this discovering thee!'

Thus Donne in *To his Mistris Going to Bed*, homologising movement towards erotic possession with the acquisition of New World possessions. Quotations from Ralegh and Donne exemplify rather than explain the phenomenon of colonial appropriations. There were milder but no less explicit, contemporary voices such as Gonzalo's in *The Tempest*, who, paraphrasing Montaigne, declared, 'Had I plantation of this isle...All things in common nature should produce/Without sweat or endeavour,' and 'nature should bring forth/Of its own kind all foison, all abundance/ To feed my innocent people.'

Which expresses a similar, but more moderately considered vision of New World plenty available to European usufruct. Gonzalo, like most Renaissance folk, is represented as content to be the sort of European who assumed, in self-confident ethnic pre-eminence, that the globe beyond Europe was there to be exploited.

Fanciful excursions taking off from Renaissance poetics lead us directly to the cold fact of Old World/New World economies of transaction. From the moment that the American continent entered European history, whether in an eleventh century Norse view or in sixteenth century exploration, the New World represented an object of 'resource utilisation'. However Shakespeare may have represented Gonzalo, even his genteel sounding adventure would assume European-style consumption.

Bartolomé de las Casas

The Spanish in the Caribbean and Mesoamerica exemplify the most spectacular example of ethnic, national and religious self-justified appropriation, and the genocide perpetrated by sixteenth-century conquistadors in Hispaniola and Cuba was outlined by Bartolomé de las Casas in the mid-sixteenth century. He wrote:

> 'Nay dare we boldly affirm that in Forty Years space, wherein [the Spanish] exercised their sanguinary and detestable Tyranny, above Twelve Millions have undeservedly perished. Nor do I conceive that I should deviate from the Truth by saying that above Fifty Millions in all paid their last Debt to Nature.'

The horrifying details of de las Casas' descriptions of torture, enslavement and murder demand no reproduction. But despite all the wrongs done to American Natives, nothing on the scale outlined by de las Casas occurred in north America, even at Wounded Knee – which was disgraceful enough.

All of de las Casas's details 'for the Extirpation and Exterminating of this [Native] people' are important to acknowledge. But of most significance here is his affirmation that

> 'the ultimate end and scope that incited the Spaniards to endeavour the Extirpation... of this People was Gold only...'

*

Resource Exploration in North America

Nineteenth century North American sequillae to Spanish mining histories exposed by de las Casas are well known. And the phenomenon of gold prospecting, for example, runs parallel to north American industrialisation, urbanisation, employment crises, the land hunger of dispossessed Euro-Americans and the growth of immigrant populations. America-wide communications during the nineteenth century improved even for the poor, who could in some degree depend on the protection of the US army. The continent was being settled. White small holders and pioneer farmers continued to feel threatened by Indians whose lands they were entering; clear but uneasy patterns of division were being established.

Indians continued to represent an ownership and development challenge but Indians also could be defeated in war and displaced. Thus 'from sea to shining sea', the country moved into the control of federal and state authorities.

The continent during the sixteenth century 'discovery' period was viewed, as expressed by Ralegh, as a source of 'gold, fame and glory', North America being a barely inhabited wilderness with freely available resources. True, the Norse, in the eleventh century, limited their interest to timber and iron. And exceptionally, John Cabot, made American landfalls merely for water. That said, the Grand Banks south of Newfoundland had by the early sixteenth century become fishing grounds for Europeans. Basques, Portuguese, Bretons, Normans, English and Irish fishermen who rendered the Americas a prime source for what would end up as stockfish, thus competing with Norwegian cod as a staple. The seventeenth century next saw the French and the Dutch harvesting furs: marten, otter, ermine, fox, raccoon and lynx skins. And, given this animal's near extinction in Europe, competition for beaver. By the end of the seventeenth century, the British and the French became engaged in trading conflict in the northern USA and Canada, variously using Iroquois, Huron and Mohawk Indians for support.

Two main points arise. First, that the Americas, throughout, were regarded consistently, regardless of Native interests, as a food and wealth resource. Secondly, American abundance functioned to make up for scarcities in a Europe that itself was challenged by growing populations.

And while the histories of such utilization are too many to explore, there remains the single outstanding point that American land and water have represented to Euro-Americans, at least since the sixteenth century, a property resource. And while Native people have always themselves also utilised local resources, Euro-Americans have identified resources as means towards ends not associated with inherited local value.

This latter could not be. Euro-Americans were migratory and their interests derived not from inherited values but from extrinsic drives. The incomer need not in this respect be entirely discredited. The five big nineteenth century gold rushes exemplify material exploration by non-Natives in its crudest character: those, in the Midwest and West, starting with the 1849 California Rush and followed by the 1858 rush in Colorado, the Black Hills rush of 1874–77 and those of the Klondike in 1896 and Nome, Alaska in 1900. And just as Alaskan oil exploration in the mid-nineteen seventies was, in part, an American response to the 1973 oil crisis, so nineteenth century gold fever was tied to the global economy which was based on the gold standard – not a factor in the forefront of a prospector's thinking.

The Americas Viewed as a Resource

Given that today's North America is experienced as a nation among contemporaries, it takes imagination to conceive how it might have appeared to earlier people who viewed it, in contrast to an often agonisingly populated Europe, largely as a uninhabited space. Natives did exist and settlers had to compete with them. But there weren't many Natives and because they were unchurched 'savages', they were regarded as semi-human. Their interests like Caliban's, sometimes competing with those of incomers, didn't matter.

The Movement of People and their Land Use

The extraction of life-sustaining goods – timber, minerals, animal products, oil – depends today either on ownership of land or on the purchase of leasehold. As mentioned later, land since the federal Native Claims Settlement Act of 1971, is shared in Alaska by separate Native, federal and state owners. Companies like Atlantic Richfield, Exxon, Standard Oil, Shell and BP wishing, for example, to pursue oil extraction, have to buy or lease land.

At the beginning of the first European trips to north America, things were unregulated. When, for example, after a brief sojourn, the Norse finally abandoned Newfoundland in the eleventh century, they left, as the writer of *Erik the Red's Saga* remarked, 'a rich and fruitful land, but one we cannot safely inhabit.'[7] Given already small home populations in Greenland and Iceland from where Viking adventurers had sailed, there had never been many of them at the one site known to have been settled: this was L'anse aux Meadows, Newfoundland, and the cargoes of butternuts and wild grapes, which gave rise to the name 'Vinland', were luxuries harvested in New England during summer trips.

Long-term settlement was never a Viking option. Space was plentiful, but eleventh century Native people – ancestors of the Innu, Beothuk, the Micmac – already maintained land control within locally understood

---

[7] Thorfinn Karlsfni, in *Erik the Red's Saga*

borders. Norsemen certainly made trading expeditions into the high Arctic to barter with 'Dorset' Natives. Later pre-Inuit Thule Eskimos would travel from Alaska and displace the Dorset folk with whom Norse trading parties had had contact but among whom it was impossible to settle. As the author of the saga wrote, the settlement of small European groups would have been precarious.

Still, it is fascinating to speculate on the lives and motivations of the early Norse explorers. Archaeologists have excavated relatively little of cultural significance – suggesting that the Norse, who had otherwise developed rich technological and aesthetic cultures, didn't settle large numbers of people in North America. There were also very few women. Traces of Viking technology did endure. The Vikings built a long house at L'anse, cut wood to transport to tree-challenged Greenland or to rebuild ships for the journey home, and they smelted local bog iron ore in subterranean kilns of Norwegian origin for the manufacture of nails. In parallel, the TAPS project, conglomerated within Aleyaska, the controlling entity that incorporated the major TAPS oil companies, brought only a culture of extraction to the Great Land and left nothing but the pipeline and its dozen pump stations.

Innumerable publications detail post-1960 Viking American data. But there are admittedly no cultural or historical connections between eleventh century Viking iron workers and the makers of the steel-dependent Trans-Alaska pipeline two thousand years later. It is nonetheless interesting, as though looking down on the continent from an imaginary height, to view some of the uncannily similar ways in which both native people, Euro-Americans and Europeans have made use of land.

Native Consumption Patterns

American Natives have always made use of their home lands and their survival depended on the animals and plants with which they shared territories. Everyone must eat to live and almost all co-resident creatures have been prey animals to Native Americans. Natives, in this sense, like any human beings who pursue their livelihood, have always made a living from their territorial assets.

There is, nonetheless, a significant difference between resource utilisation by Natives and Euro-Americans. Native peoples have traditionally shared their territories with co-residential creatures. Native hunters never displaced a prey object. On the contrary, the pursuit of animals is in itself a reason for remaining in home territory. A subsistence dependent Native group will not make a capture and travel elsewhere. They will remain to repeat the experience.

This condition of residential/environmental balance, of long term subsistence-based residence, is different from the Euro-American activity for the purpose of deferred, out of territory, consumption. The two approaches are more than different. They are opposites.

The testimonies given in the following paragraphs eloquently express the importance of Native connections to inherited land and locally consumed goods.

Alaska Native Testimonies on Land Issues
Recorded by Thomas Berger [8]

Judge Thomas Berger was the Canadian on the Alaska Native Review Commission which toured Alaskan villages between 1983 and 1985 to record testimonies about the 1971 Alaska Native Claims Settlement Act and issues arising from commercial exploration.

'We live off the land and this is our garden,' as one Gwich'in woman testified. The garden image being a frequently used Native idiom for the local environment and for custodial Native utilisation which, in response to threats of oil exploration, I heard in Tikiġaq, where the garden includes the ocean.

What follows are verbatim transcripts published by Berger. Whatever their different landscapes, these witnesses express a unanimity of attachment to local life ways. Some of these people, such as Polly Koutchak and Ronald Brower, also discuss cultural losses since Euro-American contact. These feelings echo those quoted by Leona Okakoq's friend discussed later.

Testimonials Recorded by Thomas Berger

'We Yup'iks do not wish to lose the land. We would like to use the land as our ancestors did. We would like to use it without any problems. *Mike Angaiak, Tununak*

'I always feel deep within myself the urge to live a traditional way of life – the way of my ancestors. I feel I could speak my Native tongue, but

---

[8] Berger, *Village Journey* 1985

I was raised speaking the adopted tongue of my people, English. I feel I could dance to the songs of my people, but they were abolished when the White man came ... What I'm trying to say...is that I am... attempting to live a double life – and from that, my life is filled with confusion. I have a wanting deep within myself to live the life of my ancestors but the modernised world I was raised in is restricting me from doing so.' *Polly Koutchak, Unalakleet*

'Say a white man bought a license [limited entry permit] in Anchorage on this river, they figure they have a right to move into any spot in the country. *Bobby Kokrine, Tanana*

'We are dealing with the strong lies of the oil companies on [the Alaska north coast]. They are destructing the hunting grounds within Nuiqsut... Because of the oil companies, there is scarcity of fish and other game animals... But [these] have decreased because of the oil activities.' *Bessie Ericklook, Nuiqsut.*

'Oil development is a problem... We can anticipate that in a few years... the Arctic Slope... will have as many fields developed to the enormity of Prudhoe Bay. They're starting up in small areas, but cumulatively the total will have devastating impact on our culture... And that frame of mind has not left our people, even though we have been immersed into a cash economy...

'You see the oil-lease sales taking place in areas where our people have deep, sacred ancestral feelings. Oil development in the Arctic is destroying those feelings. You can see it in the loss of language that our younger generations are now experiencing... You'll find the eldest who may speak only Inupiaq and, on the other hand, their grandchildren speaking only English. So, we are presently experiencing a very different form of degeneration of our society, both physically, mentally, economically, spiritually, and culturally...' *Ronald Brower, Barrow*

The Paradox of ANCSA [Alaska Native Claims Settlement Act, 1971]

The extraction of oil and minerals in twentieth century Alaska became possible only after long negotiated agreements with different proprietors of land. Most of the vast Alaska territory, post-ANCSA, was owned variously and in a complicated jigsaw by Native corporations, Native individuals, the Federal government and the State of Alaska. There are also smaller privately owned holdings.

Since a near-disastrous plan of the US government and the Atomic Energy Commission in 1959 to detonate five atom bombs twenty-five miles south of Tikiġaq and the publication of environmental studies,[9] later statewide oil and mineral exploration likewise were to become hedged in with at least plausible ecological safeguards.

As Native people testified to Berger in the mid-eighties, some or many of these safeguards are optimistic, ineffectual or illusory. According to both Inupiaq and Gwich'in testimony, the movement of caribou and fish, among other species, were already endangered by commercial exploration. And the entire region is threatened by spills and environmental degradation.

Two points are worth discussion. With respect to ANCSA, it has been argued that Native lands were given new legally assigned Native ownership in 1971 partly to make way for negotiated commercial developments. Without these seemingly generous deals (the Native corporations established by the Act were given one ninth of state lands and $962 million were distributed both to the new corporations and to individual Natives, about half of this money coming from the federal treasury, half from oil sharing revenues) it would have been impossible, in the context of a late twentieth century climate of political and environmental awareness, simply to take over land as had been done in the lower 48 for corporate advantage. The quoted Native testimony expresses awareness of the tie between Native land ownership and development.

Berger emphasises another point. The ANCSA brought Alaska Natives into the sphere of property relations that Euro-Americans took for granted but which were foreign to traditional Native/land relationships. Post ANCSA, Alaska Natives became American land owners and if this were not in itself alienating, there remained the additional danger that individual Natives and/or village corporations could, given the temptation of short-term gain, cash in their holdings and thereby disinherit their descendants. Berger wrote:

> Under ANCSA's terms, on December 18, 1991, the Native corporations [set up by ANCSA] are required to call in all their shares... In every village I visited, Alaska Natives expressed fear that their ancestral lands will be lost after 1991...

---

[9] Ed. Wilimovsky, *The Environment of Cape Thompson 1966.* An account of the AEC's nuclear project, forestalled in part by publication of Wilimovsky's volume, follows later in this text.

But there is another view in Alaska. Many non-Native Alaskans believe that in 1971, ANCSA settled for ever the claims of Alaska Natives. The Natives received money and land, and legislation extinguished any further claims they might have had.

Along with this insight lies a danger just alluded to: that American enterprise would take advantage of the ANCSA deal as soon as land holdings became available for sale or lease. Prudhoe Bay oil development and oil explorations still closing in on Inupiaq and Gwich'in people, among other communities, were dependent on ANCSA, whose seemingly generous 'return' to Natives of Native land would quickly expose its availablility to sale and development. Berger continues:

> 'Now, the popular thinking goes, we [corporate interests] can get on with the business of developing Alaska, unimpeded by Native claims …There may be risks, but risk is in the nature of American enterprise… The Native peoples of Alaska want to hold their ancestral land in trust for future generations…
>
> 'In the Lower 48, generally, the federal government holds the land of Native Americans in trust for the benefit of the tribes on the reservations. In Alaska, state-chartered Native corporations now hold Native land as private land in fee simple… So long as a corporate model is the vehicle of holding Native lands, they will always be at risk… ANCSA has exposed the Natives' land to other risks, but here are the principal ones: corporate failure, takeover, and taxation.
>
> 'For Alaska Natives, the loss of their lands would be catastrophic. The severance of ties with traditional life and the foreclosure of any possibility that the villages might achieve a greater measure of self-sufficiency would have serious implications for non-Native Alaskans, as well. Without its Native villages, without the subsistence way of life, Alaska would not be Alaska'[10]

Opinions among north Alaska Natives remain, as Berger wrote, divided. There are those who have long foreseen nothing but environmental danger and economic exploitation, but there are also many, as voiced often by village corporations, whose post-ANCSA existence was to make Native communities financially independent, thus supporting development. Take the Arctic National Wildlife Refuge (ANWR) which comprises

---

[10] Berger, 1985: 96–7, 99, 101, 116e,

almost twenty million acres of Alaska's North Slope and which past and present Republican Administrations want to open to exploration:

> 'No one will be more affected by the opening of ANWR than Alaska's indigenous people, who will live among—and work on—the rigs, drills, and pipelines that would follow the discovery of any oil or gas reserve. The discovery of oil or gas in the region could bring an economic windfall to the subsistence tribes that live on Alaska's North Slope, the coastal plain that faces the Arctic Ocean. But if a major disaster… were to occur, it would devastate their homeland.'

The ambiguous status of such development is expressed powerfully in that statement. The speaker from a Gwich'in community, as paraphrased in *The Atlantic,* on the one hand expresses how employment, affluence and economic growth, all welcome, would come in the wake of development. On the other hand, with the advent of rigs and pipelines, the environment would be changed for ever.

But as one Inupiaq man, a geologist, commented in connection both to subsurface exploration and climate change on the North Slope:

> 'the reality is that our region depends on oil and gas development. If we stop exploration, our communities dry up. And [by stopping exploration] we don't change the climate one bit—it just means someone's gonna open up the valve somewhere else.[11]

'Wherever the valve is opened, the nature of the territory, its landscape and its people who will in future live with "rigs, drills, and pipelines", will change for ever, whether they support or oppose development.

*

On my last visit to Tikiġaq in 2009, public health, safety and comfort had been radically improved. There was a new clinic. Running water and flush toilets operated from a water tank. The north beach of Tikiġaq's old village had been fortified by the Army Corps of Engineers. A modern school building dominated the new town site. The public safety officer had

---

[11] This and the previous statement comes from the *Atlantic:* https://www. theatlantic.com/science/archive/2017/12/senate-tax-bill-indigenous-communities/547352/

been trained and was in communication with law enforcement colleagues. There were roads and trucks, though most people travelled on four wheeled Hondas. This modernizing environment had developed since the 1975–76 move. Most changes had been funded by oil revenue taxes paid to the North Slope Borough by the State of Alaska and through ANCSA moneys. No-one can deny people conveniences enjoyed by other Americans. Against these positives are the catastrophes of alienation from pre-contact values.

These existential agonies are shared by millions of people worldwide and also by culturally self-identifying groups who often live marginally and in poverty. The deficits of dispossession are impossible to ignore. Does the desire to give everyone as much as possible imply also taking something away and a process of alienation? As suggested in an earlier book, cultural alienation became a phenomenon of Tikiġaq's own experience of nineteenth century contact, when Inupiaq people, to survive economically, were forced to exchange local artefacts for manufactured goods. An animal skin, for example, with its complexities of social and subsistence implication, transformed from an artefact expressing traditional values into an object of exchange: a process of simplification of what previously had been local and complex.[12]

*

Fairbanks Journal, Autumn 1975

Late August. I've now been in Fairbanks twelve or fourteen days. I'd spent two months in Juneau, a smaller town: low mountain slopes lined with clapboard buildings: pretty houses with a smell of carpentry, whiffs, here and there, of marijuana. South east Alaska is damp and bountiful. There are lupin meadows by the water, walks into the foothills among wild flowers and berries. I went sailing with friends to fish halibut and browse samphire.

I'd arrived in Juneau after three months in the Arctic and settled on a quiet boardwalk house, with gardens, flowering bushes, humming birds at window shutters. The ambience, here in Fairbanks, harmonises with my rootless status. I'm living at the edge of downtown in a modest 1940s building. It's dark and unbeautiful. Still, the central heating is in working order. I've come to study Beginners Inupiaq at university and hadn't understood how far the pipeline's overwhelmed the city. It was here I learned that Asatchaq was in a local home.

---

[12] See *Ultimate Americans,* 2008:63ff.

*

Pipeline construction here, in the face of the 1973 oil crisis, during which America's pursuit of independent energy, is where the latest boom's in process. And here in Fairbanks, centre of construction planning, it's a mishmash of ethnicities and archetypes, a Rimbaud-esque procession of new homing-on-the-pipeline vagabonds, as I jotted ecstatically, the Princeton M.A.'s axe blows whistling behind me. Hence this other notebook entry in which pipeline aspirants are crowded:

There are hashishim from gumbo kitchens in the Louisiana bayous.

Dog mushing backwoods eco-warriors who drag the smell of dog shit through the Teamsters registration office. ('Sorry, feller. Try the Laborers.')

Quiet mid-western linesmen who follow the best dollar.

Yupiit from the Kuskokwim the Yukon rivers, forearms folded, in line to register at union offices.

North Slope Inupiat, equivalently patient.

Young white Alaskans in 50-below t-shirts.

Oklahoma pipeline techno-migrants tracking the pipe northward.

Cactus and honey Israeli princesses.

Survivors of resistance in Chile, Buenos Aires, Paraguay and Cuba.

Low in throat voices, and chisels hanging from their belts and pockets, young woman carpenters and tractor drivers.

Sadomasochists in leather gunned up from the lower states on Harley Davidsons.

Lieder aspirants who've come to earn their fare to Salzburg and Vienna.

Sun Dance ethno-groupy boys from drama colleges.

Past tense Beatniks burning to revive the Fifties.

White Sikhs in white *dastaars* here to start sub-Arctic ashrams.

Novel crazies pregnant with the 'Great American'. They plough through *Jaws* and *Shogun* in the union lobbies.

Astrophysics postgrads, here in flight from M.I.T and Berkeley.

Soloists from Juilliard burned out by Liszt and Czerny exercises.

New Yorker Essay junkies on research trips.

Bluesy cowgirls, studs and rhinestones in their denims.

Yelping bluegrass saints in hot bandanas.

Frowning Hassidim on mission weird to herd Jews towards a
Williamsburg *yeshiva*. At 3 a.m. they shout in Yiddish down
the wire from freezing phone booths.
Prostitutes from Salt Lake and Las Vegas who've dropped from
Mormon gene trees for Jack London-esque adventures.
Your down home roughneck US fucker travelled north to fuck
the last, inflated US dollar from the pipeline.

*

A part-paradigm of this convergence of the young Americas lay ready-
made on Nome's golden beaches, in the Klondike, the Black Hills of the
Dakotas. But while today's Alaska's population is cosmopolitan, last century's gold and oil adventurers were, as missionary writers called them,
'saloon bar sweepings': mainly white Americans, unchurched, drifting,
unemployed, albeit some were immigrants from Central Europe, Italy,
Ireland, China and less this gallery of opportunists, whose parallel, today,
lay tragically in young men taken into the conscription offices and wom-
en drawn to army hospitals by nursing adverts. It is sobering to com-
pare this influx of adventurers in Fairbanks with the conscripts recruited,
these same months, from farm communities, urban ghettoes, native villages, paid, as Kunak remarked later, 'to pay Natives to kill Natives'.

It was as though Fairbanks, which was the most efficient entry point
for line employment, represented the funnel top, capacious and broad-
lipped, for the process of suction into the economy. Like the vision in
the *Gita* of God's mouth, into which the armies of the warring kings are
sucked,

'They rush into your mouths, O Vishnu, you devour all people,
lighting up the universe and scorching worlds…'

Which, given the reality of the Vietnam war, was not a farfetched image
of Apocalypse. Just as armies flew through Vishnu's teeth, so folk are fed
into the Vietnam conflict. Or rush towards Alaska and are swallowed by
the line's intoxicating honey.

*

The demographic paradox represented by this community also had its
antecedent in the Whitman poems which Mrs Charlotte mentioned.

'I contain multitudes,' wrote Whitman in *Song of Myself*. But the cosmopolitan character of present multitudes lay even beyond what the poet might have imagined he could fold in his 'turbulent embrace', as Mrs C's grandfather called it.

Nor could Mrs Charlotte, herself, a grande dame of the contact period, relate knowledgeably to this new demography. She may not even have been aware of it. What she had known were earlier inter-relationships of white folks and Natives, and she thus surveyed, on visits with her daughter to Asatchaq's care home, the residents, with the eye of one who'd loved them as young people. And wept at their displacement.

There was a further, wider demographic discrepancy. Just as I'd viewed Tikiġaq from the air and Mrs Charlotte had seen her Mission as a chemical spot on a photo, so in reduction, I saw pipeline life in simplified reduction.

Gazing down in imagination on the pipeline population, this view was of people in vertically ordered assembly. Like blackfly on a bean stalk, they were organised in singular and linear disposition. Fed into the line, which as the word suggests, was linear, albeit it swelled into S-shapes, they queued up and were fed, or fed themselves, in a direction that took them to points along the single metallic thread that constituted a trajectory from which they were incapable of diverging.

Thus the population took on a pictographic disposition of the pipeline itself and became, in this vision, a partial version of its geometry. Once it had spent itself on the adventure, the population would scatter, as had Euro-Americans in earlier rushes, and the short-lived homogeneity of the pipeline community no longer existed. Still, for the period of its existence, while the line was being constructed, these thousands of individuals were, within the condensation of my vision, homogenised.

Looking, in imagination, down on the totality of the Alaska Native populations, the picture was very different. Here there was no single line of people clustered round a solitary metal conduit and clotted at its intersections in construction camps and pump stations. Instead, there was a panoply of peoples in mobile and self-organised patterns:

North Slope, Kobuk and Noatak River, King Island Inupiat, Yup'ik of the lower Kuskokwim and Yukon, St Lawrence Island Yup'ik, south western Eyak and the Chugach Eskimos, South Eastern Tlingit, Haida, Tsimsian people, Athabascans: Koyukon, Gwich'in, Holikachuk, Ingalik, Kolchan, Tanaina, Ahtna.

A minority queued at Fairbanks and Anchorage Union offices. For the most part, Natives pursued lifeways in their villages, travelling through snow and sea ice, negotiating rivers, hunting, setting fish nets, cutting timber, berry picking.

Otherwise, even for those city dwellers who were detached from the oil project, or 'skinny city', as line workers called it, ran like a vast umbilical through our houses, into sitting rooms and bedrooms, bathrooms, class-rooms, cafes, restaurants; it was present in the streets and bars, shops, motels and thrift stores. The concretion of everything that people talked about, our dreams projected on it, whether that be in ecologically informed opposition, on economic dependence or financial self-improvement. But somehow we were all there, whether or not we travelled north on the new Dalton Highway and took temporary root in work camps where construction happened: Five Mile, Deadwood, Galbraith, Dietrich, Atigun, Prudho – paradisos where the happy souls who got onto the union rotas worked and roistered, earned mega bucks with over time, plus restaurants where fresh vegetables were rarer goods than steak done how you like it, west coast king crab, lobster.

*

I'd walked round a freight yard several times on foggy autumn mornings and was dazzled in the twilight by flatbeds piled with lengths of pipeline, inert, looming through the frost haze. It was hard to credit that these glossy, chopped up macaroni, close-up, tangible, would soon be trundled north and welded to that big enormous everything, of engineering.

Still, here it lay in intimate and dislocated segments. You could raise a gloved hand, stroke it and go home to breakfast. Yet it stretched back through history and touched both future and the past where all development had started with the Spanish treasure hunters.

*

The pipeline was however a monumental artefact of commerce. And like the north-south, east-west Continental Divide, it separated 'for and against' opinions.

Given the political, logistical and financial clout of corporate intention and the support of Alaska state legislature, the environmental lobby was insufficient, even after exhaustive hearings, to block the construction initiative. Christo, at the cost of millions, might have negotiated rights to install his Running Fence across twenty-four miles of Marin and Sonoma Counties in summer 1976, and which would billow across the landscape for two weeks before being recycled,[13] but the Alaskan pipeline, to be completed twelve months later in summer '77, was being built on lands bought and leased from a dizzying variety of owners to endure indefinitely in an incalculable series of landscapes which, at vast expense and an unprecedented complexity of planning, had been designed to survive. TAPS did not pretend to the mind-expanding abstraction of art. Viewed imaginatively as though from the air – to repeat what we have already tried – the line might optically be construed as a mega-Christo: an emblem of human and mechanical intervention into the pressures of multiple environments of challenge. This was both paradoxical and impressive. A statement and a geste of human power in pursuit of the utilitarian. The virtuosic concretion of countless scientific calculations to project Alaska into the forefront of advanced engineering. And to accomplish the seemingly impossible in the face of almost insuperable obstacles that previous pioneers had confronted with their vulnerable bodies and their puny equipment. The gold panner, the fur trapper, the whale and bison hunter: those heroes of individualism and slaughter whose progenies now were corporate adventurers of unprecedented power to plan, employ and execute. Picks, pans, satchels, orts of sourdough, gold dust. These were the seeds, the germens and the embryos from which this land leviathan had risen. 'Crack nature's moulds,' as Lear shouted, 'All germens spill at once,' he cried. And in this least promising of hyperborean seedbeds, they were sown and nurtured with astonishing virtuosity.

*

During a conversation in *Jane Eyre*, the eighteen-year-old protagonist confronts her future husband with a subversive insight. 'The men in green,' says Jane of the spiritual beings of rural folklore, 'all forsook England a hundred years ago.' This was only slightly less true in late nineteenth

---

[13] "Photographs of the Fence's construction reveal the magnitude of the undertaking. Stunning photographs of the completed project enable us to see what [has been] described as a 'startling piece of calligraphy…' Running Fence may have stood for only two weeks, but its grandeur as an object and, moreover, as a testament to perseverance, courage, and belief, is enough to earn its permanence in our memories." *Journey to Running Fence*, University of California Press Blog 2010. Thus seduced, the art world's self-interest.

century Ireland, about which W.B. Yeats wrote[14]:

> 'There was an old man,' recalled Yeats, 'who lived near a bog a little out of Gort, who saw [faery people] often from his young days, and always towards the end of his life… His neighbours were not certain that he really saw anything in his old age, but they were all certain that he saw things when he was a young man. His brother said, "Old as he is, and it's all in his brain the things he sees. If he was a young man we might believe in him…" A neighbour said, "The poor man! They say they are mostly in his head now, but sure he was a fine fresh man twenty years ago the night he saw [the faeries] linked in two lots like young slips of girls walking together.'

A parallel here lies in the coexistence of the pipeline's fact world and the imagination of Native belief. The historical paradox in the mid-nineteen seventies of pipeline coexistence with the inner lives of Natives was a factor of one irresolvable clash. Another was peaceful coexistence of both with the Vietnam war, which still pursued its violence. As the Princeton axeman sang out, 'the pure products of America go crazy'. And this institutionalized insanity had the appearance of normality. Likewise, just as many Native people submitted to a 'heavenly father' while also retaining belief in local shamans, so lived Native tradition within twentieth century adventure.

*

I've alluded to gold and have marginalised the way oil has dominated the last two centuries. Oil has been described as black gold, and without displacing that metal as global currency, oil, in 'darker weeds' crept up to merge with her shining older sister. And while none of us can do without the oil towards which we feel an irreconcilable ambivalence, future centuries will presumably view oil as having acted as a temporary convenience, as obsolete as the micro-organisms from which it evolved. And while, again, it has kept modern society functioning, it will presumably kill us.

I repeat these easy thoughts because, in the context of the TAPS, the contrasts are bleak. In no other place and at no other time – the vast landscapes of mid-twentieth century Alaska and the minds of its older inhabitants – could oil's mismatch with the environment and with human

---

[14] 'The Friends and the People of Faery', in *Mythologies*, essays republished in 1959.

experience be starker. And the TAPS project, as experienced at the time, represented a remarkable climax. It was beautiful and barbaric, its virtuosity expressed perhaps most conspicuously by the completion of the Standard Oil Company tower ('Big Stan') in Chicago. This exquisite building was completed in 1974 just when the TAPS project went into operation. And just as the climactic importance of Alaskan oil, by 2015, had become dwarfed by oil production in the US Gulf States and California, so Big Stan was forced to shed its marble cladding and rebuild at the cost of its original construction.

Renaissance perceptions of 'gold, fame and glory' and the transience of heroic endeavours are, in comparison with the complexities of US economics, relatively uncomplicated. But they express a truth whose simplicity put Big Stan and the TAPS enterprise into the perspective of species survival.

It was climactic, and oil's sumptuous first upbursts after long, dry drilling was at each discovery (thousands of wells are drilled annually) followed by the happiness of achievement. 'What is all this juice and all this joy?' as Hopkins wrote in 1877, a hundred years before Alaskan oil began moving.

Alaskan optimism was natural and a relief to those in the state who had been disappointed by the failure in 1962 of Project Plowshare, or Chariot as it was renamed. Chariot had been a US Atomic Energy Commission project which in association with the Liveright Laboratories, had proposed detonating five atom bombs at the southern end of Cape Thompson. The intention supposedly had been the creation of a deep water harbour, but a number of factors, including opposition by Alaska Natives, university scientists and an American environmental lobby had discredited a plan so absorbing that few Chariot supporters publicly took note that sea ice would prohibit ship traffic for eight months of the year and so the commercial development of Alaska by 'peaceful nuclear excavation' was aborted, just three years after statehood in 1959.[15] See also later, the final section of this book.

*

There were an incalculable number of precedents, and it would be hard to enumerate American oil strikes. The oil industry itself is a vast world within our world. Briefly, in the USA, starting in 1859, there was the Drake Well, Pennsylvania, oil finds continuing into the Civil War that

[15] See https://en.wikipedia.org/wiki/Edward_Teller#Operation_Plowshare_ and_Project_Chariot for Plowshare map image.

spread to western Pennsylvania, New York state, Ohio, Kentucky, and West Virginia. Rockefeller, in New York and Massachusetts, consolidated oil production into Standard Oil in 1874. There were major discoveries in California and Colorado in the 1860s, while the 1890s saw oil strikes in Kansas, Oklahoma, Arkansas, Louisiana and Texas. The list is enormous and thousands of companies remain engaged in exploration, production and distribution.

A vast infrastructure of railroads, tankers, pipelines and trucking companies carried oil to every part of the nation. Alaska joined Texas, California and the Dakotas as one of the top oil producing states in the second half of the twentieth century. And while Alaskan production began dropping in the 2000s, Prudhoe Bay oil continued to represent a major state resource. Viewed as I'd visualized TAPS construction, it was as though the entire continent had been punctured and the subsurface spouted.

As Berger's informants recorded, the central issue was unitary and straight forward. Given the existential relationship of Native people and their lands, industrial development represented a threat to the entire structure of Native society and its cultures.

The complexities of development represented the assertion of a Euro-American way of life. Such was the process of modernization: the extension of what mainstream America perceived as civilized, normalizing. This, as compared to hunter-gatherer traditions, was unprecedented, and oil production was its major representation. Oil would, indeed, sustain modernized society for the time being. The future, however, looked much like the past: a wilderness derelict of the sort of macro-energy without which humans had subsisted in their pre-industrial generations. This latter was the alternative life way. But because it was represented by small societies which in themselves often lacked internal cohesion, Europeanising life ways would achieve dominance while the oil lasted.

*

This last section has been polemical and this I'd tried to avoid. There are books, papers and web pages devoted to details that would be out of place here. It remains to confess that both oil and pipeline culture have so far triumphed. But these victorious monuments, thrilling as they are, will eventually constitute earth's mausoleum. The present fount will swamp our coffins.

Part 6

The Snow Bunting and the Whale

'After the snowbird,' Aġniin murmurs through the Mission camp stove gas flare, 'after that snowbird... comes the whale.'

It's spring 1976. I watched snow buntings fly in last month: tiny sparrow-like creatures that migrate from south Alaska, Missouri and Nevada. The buntings swoop in low and at speed. They twitter as they land, revisiting cracks in old meat caches and iglus where their ancestors nested. The males arrive first and build nests of grass, moss, fur and feathers. The snow is receding. The air's clear and bright. At summer's end, they're gone. They migrate south, avoiding winter.

'Don't hurt the *avatiliguuraq*', warned the elders. The boys listened half ashamed of possible transgression. They learned hunting on the village outskirts: hunted squirrels, longspurs, snipe with children's bows and arrows. But hurting the bunting was forbidden. They understood the rightness, its symmetrical asymmetry. Protect one small and vulnerable species. Don't let children hurt it. Give the darkest being, whale, space to join the village. Protect *avatiliguuraq,* so move on to the whale hunt.

Ava-tili- guuraq is a word whose vowels are spread out in movement:

> *Ava:* two quick *a* sounds.
> *-tili:* the two short i's.
> *-guuraq*: the long *uu* balances the previously divided a.
> *–uuraq* is longest double syllable, denoting the diminutive.

But the final *a* of *-uuraq* lies deep in the throat. This is because of the *q*: a stop which drags the *a* down, creating a short variation on the first two *a* sounds.

'Snow birds', people started calling them in English. They're fleet, free spirits. Harbingers of spring arriving with the sun to nest in grass round iglu ruins.

'They come from above,' old people said, transposing spirit lore to Christianity. The bunting attends whale. It comes from the south as though drawing the whale with it, like the child in stories who executes the grandma's power. The bunting does the same for what's enormous.

Early this century, Christianised people called the buntings *Jiisiiraq* 'little Jesus'. Aġniin told me in English:

> 'My mother was sitting in front of her iglu when that bird landed right here.' Aġniin touches her head. 'It flew onto her head. My mother didn't move. She sat by her iglu and did nothing.'

*

This memory provided entry to an ancient story. The convergence each spring of small, never-to-be-hunted inland migrants and the whale swimming north that knew nothing of these symmetries.

In this convergence of the great and the small, of land and air migrant, non-utilitarian bird and the sea mammal that sustains life, there's symmetry and disproportion, divergence, sameness, opposition. A familiar fictional percussion. Wasn't this the great unspoken story come alive? Like fables about bear and lemming, peregrine and raven, owl and snow bird?

Avatiliguuraq birds are part of whaling lore. When buntings arrive, the people know the whales will follow. This parti-coloured bird heralds black-and-white streaked whale: land bird and sea beast, migrating for their separate purpose, bracketing our action.

*

I heard a version of this *avatiliguuraq* opposition on my first day in the village:

> 'A bunting sat on a tundra hummock and wept because her mate had been killed by a hunter. A snowy owl came up and sang:

> > Fool to mourn
> > that little husband
> > with his spears of grass!
> > I'll marry you!

> The bunting replied:

> > Marry an owl?
> > With those coarse feathers,

fat beak, thick legs,
bulging forehead,
no neck!

The owl stabbed the bunting's breast
and when she cried he taunted her:

There's women for you!
Sharp-tongued all right,
but one little poke
and she'll start whimpering!
And so they flew off separately.
Told by Qimmiuraq.

*

Journal, August 24 1973. Meeting Qimmiuraq and his wife Sunshine.

'This man wants you to tell stories, short ones for children,' says my translator. He speaks in Inupiaq and then translates. The old man sits on the big double bed. His wife's on the floor working on a seal skin.

The room contains a plywood table, chairs, bucket, basins, kitchen gear. A bearded Jesus in sou'wester at a boat helm hangs over the pillows. The ancient white-haired man in t-shirt, flannels, seal skin boots, breathes painfully. A cross hangs from string on his caved-in chest. My translator, explains that I will pay them. My presence is assimilated, not acknowledged.

The tiny woman sits with feet extended. Seal skin boot-soles under calf-length parka. She laughs as I unpack recorder. I'm tense and sweating. Qimmiuraq, Bob Tuckfield, named thus by Tikiġaq's first missionary, adjusts his torso so his voice can rise. His cross clicks on the fruit-can wrapper as he hawks. He's pale, slow, impersonal. Then comes a story. He speaks into the tape recorder. I'm not relevant. Stories flutter down to the recorder. The machine swallows words, but can't digest them.

The woman sets some fish and seal oil on the table. She laughs as I eat. But it's peaceful to sit without having to chatter. Her laughter's uncertain.

*

By the time I'd returned to Tikiġaq some twelve months later, both Qimmiuraq and his wife Sunshine were dead and for some reason I learned less about him than about his adoptive father.

When I met Qimmiuraq in 1973, he was almost ninety, the oldest person in the village. An orphan from the Kobuk, he was picked up, aged nine by a white whaler/trader. This was Joe Tuckfield, a Swansea man who'd travelled to the Western Arctic. On a separate trip north in 1888, he had discovered bowhead whales – made scarce in the southern Arctic ocean – 'thick as bees', as he said cheerfully, advancing towards their near extermination in the 1890s.

Tuckfield's discovery prompted a rush which led to the final blast of commercial whaling until baleen value fell at the turn of the century. About a year after his discovery, Joe Tuckfield set up as a shore-based whaler and married a shaman woman from the southern river people. When the whales grew scarce, Joe and his wife moved to the Kuukpak River estuary, where they lived in a boat which another American had abandoned. Joe died in the 1930s, and Bob grew up a Tikiġaq person.

All this is preamble to a story about whaling that Bob Qimmiuraq told:

> This story is about the whales. It's about how the whales behaved to whale-boats long ago.
>
> There was an *umialik* and his wife. They owned a whale boat. Now before the whales reached Tikiġaq, they would come together and talk. The whales said: 'There are some wives in that village who don't share out meat. We won't go near their boats and be caught by those people. But those who share our meat out equally, and give to the poor and the old people: those are the ones we will caught by. But people who don't share, we'll avoid.'
>
> And that's how the whale thinks. The whale favours women who share meat properly.
>
> And that's why Tikiġaq people are generous.

Such is courtesy, patterned on propriety and respectful relations between humans and whales and expressing the equivalence of people and their animals.

One might say further that the importance of the whale lies in an opportunity for people to share with each other. But how elegantly the storyteller balanced bunting and whale. And the symmetry exceeds the equipoise of large sea mammal versus small parti-coloured avian. All stories demand being told in twos. Otherwise, the first will fall over. This has the symmetry of a sacred pattern; thus, too, the storyteller's etiquette.

*

April 18 1976. Preparation of the umiaq

Yesterday I spent an hour in the National Guard Armoury, a long, corrugated shed where the women were sewing seal skins for an *umiaq*. The boat frame stood naked, a circle of men in the background as the women stitched the skins and oiled the gunwhales.

This is butchering in reverse. Last spring, these women skinned the seals their husbands killed and pegged out the hides to bleach above the south beach. Now they lay the same skins on the boat frame, as though reconstructing a living being: a transformation of the seal their men had taken.

The intensity of women's work. Skin-sewing, besides child-rearing, is a woman's most important project. It is birth in reverse. For sewing implies the construction of an interior warmth: the manipulation of skins for the human body to stay alive in.

Sewing, like a birth, is magical: it creates womb-space, empowering men to leave the *iglu* and to hunt animals needed for further warmth. The verb stem *ani-* means both 'leave the *iglu*' and 'to be born'.

It's freezing in the Armoury. The women talk quietly and run their fingers over the tight waterproof seams. The men breathe contemplatively through half-open mouths in the cold cigarette haze. Then they move in to lash the sewn-together skin to the gunwhales. They tap the boat's sides. It is supple and resonant. I help grasp the dry ribs, haul the boat outside. The skins are parchment-like, translucent; scattered blotches, hair-tufts. There are stories about singing, flying skinboats. Like sea birds, skinboats command the ocean.

*

April 1976. Whaling Preparations.

The whale hunt involves a transition from the long ordeal of winter: from hot rooms filled with tea-cups to a windswept plain, blue sky, blinding sea ice, birds migrating, wind cutting across sun and herds of white whales, the belugas, surging north through choppy water.

All this – plus shift from houses towards ice camp – people say is a 'change of view' (*aliqsigraq*): movement from closed boundaries to an endlessness, expansion of explosive thought and movement.

The village is transformed by the onset of this carnival. The wistful optimism of late winter – 'Whaling pretty soon, maybe' – the men whisper, transforms to machismo. Purpose gives our lives the shape of custom.

It's greater than this. The grandeur of the whale exalts both individual and the village. From the heart of one immensity, the sacred is conjured, to keep people's lifeblood circulating. Preparations start in March, though these are tentative. Skinboat owners muse on their equipment, visit sheds and cold-storage caches, check harpoons and meat they've stored to feed their crews with. Long-contemplated invitations to potential crew men are offered.

Then starts the gathering of camp stuff. A blubber-and-wood-burning stove is cut from an oil drum, chimney sections ordered. Skinboat owners need snow machines, Coleman camp stoves, gas, oil, Blazo, new sleds, axes, spades, picks, rope. Harpoons, grapples, flensing knives are whetted, shells and gunpowder are bought from the store or flown from Seattle. Caribou and bear skin blankets, sleeping bags and plywood tent floors are piled up in the storm shed, the wall-tent mended.

Umialik women also have to calculate. What will they need for their husbands' crews? Besides caribou, seal and last year's whale meat, they buy flour, rice, crackers, tea and coffee, dried milk, sugar and tobacco. Some wealthier *umialiks* order butter, jam, canned fruit, bacon, pancake mixture, Aunt Jemima's syrup. In previous days, the boat crews fasted: ate small amounts of frozen meat and sipped snow from skin containers carried underneath their parkas. Some days, today, on bigger camps, ranch-style breakfasts are cooked by women.

Hunt logistics are exhausting. The day we took the boat out. I ran beside the sled on which the skinboat, lashed with seal rope, stood. Suluk steered the snow machine between ice rocks. There were six of us to keep the sled upright and protect boat skins. Not even Suluk knew how far to go before we found a bay of open water.

Thus we ran, jumping, by turns, into the boat when we hit the flat. Recent old timers travelled light. They carried rifles, harpoons, stone points, knives, a drag-line, wound-plugs. Skinboats were kept empty: harpoons, knives, floats, amulets, a little frozen meat, a skin to sleep on. Today's equipment bulges mountainously above the gunwales.

Whaling eats us. In order to consume, we are consumed. Once it's started, nothing except whale matters, nothing besides whale, its journey towards us. Its grand nature has a tangible existence. Whaling is coordinated ferocity. The mind extending to the whale, pursuing its adopted kin, and cutting off the whale's migration.

Masks, tools and weapons are now museum artefacts. Thus we imagine through the masks that missionaries and travellers acquired, ways in which the whale and village in its whale mask moved towards each other.

*

Entry to the whale hunt's a collective enterprise. The village empties, moves out to the sea ice. A transformative event. And yet there's competition between whale boat owners and crews.

Like much in Tikiġaq, the collectivity is ambiguous. Very little remains entirely unified. A twoness, possibly a multiplicity, lies within convergence. The migration will happen and one of the whales will belong to her. Traditionally the female partner in a skinboat owning couple remains dominant. Her husband executes the hunt. But she remains the power.

Before the white man came, the woman sat at home, mimicking the whale's obedience. The whales came into *iglus* before they sacrificed their bodies, surfaced through the body of the primal whale, the Tikiġaq peninsula. It died in the water or the sea ice. Everybody understood this. But only once the animal had joined the women, breathed life into the *iglu* and unified itself with the mythological prototype. An uninterpretable convergence. Life and death were coexistent. Death implied birth. And birth incorporated death.

*

Land and sea in separation. Together they oppose each other. But as opposites, belong, embrace, complete a large part of the Land/Sea whole. The sea encloses the community. People occupy the land. But they sink their dwellings in an earth that in a myth was the sea beast. Thus they live whole, but still stretched between opposites. They're land/sea people. Paradoxically divided. Internally at peace with twoness.

The land meets the sea and this marks Tikiġaq. The way in which the land meets the sea's ambiguous, not dangerous. That moment of transition is a joyful moment.

Sometimes it's difficult to know the difference. The edge of the beach, the Point's hook – changing as the tide erodes and builds it – is frozen, sealed down, hard to distinguish from the inshore sea ice, the chaos of the inshore rubble. Transitional and scarcely noticed. 'Am I on the land or sea?' the hunter asks in crossing. Does it matter?

And yet transition implicates a powerful switching. The challenges of land were tangled. Family life, the growth of children, the old getting older, people dying, the presence of spirits, knowing who were shamans, singing, dancing, understanding clothes and tool deployment, labouring up hills, negotiating cliffs and beaches, skins, traps, driftwood, dogs and hunger, the individual in community. It was a labour. Responding always to environment. The ordeal of knowing, short life, death, life, eating, and not knowing.

Then suddenly complexities of land life drop behind them. Things that had been brown, black, green, grey, things that moved, grew, froze and melted. Density. Material. Now, suddenly a new environment, no less a challenge. Sudden freedom on the sea ice. The complexities of land transformed. Every challenge that all humans face was reproduced here.

*

Whale Hunt Journal, 1977

In 1977, twelve crews were spread along ten miles of ice edge. Most of this journal describes life with a small crew consisting of whale boat owners Umik and Sarah. Also their friend, the midwife, Aniqsuaq.

I was on my fourth field trip and this was the third whale hunt at which I had been present. For much of the time during a six week season, little happens.

Sometimes, in the distance, a whale appears, at other times it surfaces and vanishes. People otherwise hunt wildfowl, seals and beluga whales, a white dolphin-like species. There's also storytelling, gossip, competition. Mesmerized by constant daylight and fatigue, the mind drops its habits and enters states of being in which the hunt itself becomes a pretext.

May 12

Brilliant against low morning cloud, a single, sheer white ivory gull hovers and then glides towards us on short, stiff wings. The water's black and when the gull flies close, we see papery, transparent shadows.

I'm alone with Umik and Sarah. With no crew to help them, they're pleased with my company – inept as they know me to be. Umik and Sarah are a quiet couple who live outside the social hurly-burly, but who still efficiently pursue subsistence. Unblessed by wealth, noble in modesty, they might, in European folklore, be foresters or charcoal burners on whom for their inherent decency the gods bestow good fortune. Last year, for example, Umik caught a whale and the village gathered round him. Then, just as suddenly, he was again socially alone. Prompted by these thoughts, albeit not expressing them, I told a story Asatchaq recorded last summer:

'Here is a seagull with a song,' he started. But the song's in mystical and secret language contrived by shamans.

When, with the help of Tukummiq, I transcribed the gull's song and asked her what it meant. She closed her eyes and gently shook her head. My note reads 'This song is unintelligible.' Still I wrote out the song in its four groups of clusters. It may be satirical.

The story follows. (Also previously transcribed.) Unlike the other creatures who have met to play, the gull doesn't have a game. When all the others start playing, 'I won't be good at doing anything!' the gull says.

So the gull ties a stone round its neck and flies across river. When it reaches the far side, it looks for a bigger stone to take back with it. That's the gull's game, and it sings while it practises. Finally it flies across river, falls in the water, starts going under and then cries:

'Kayaks approaching! And two skinboats!' But the kayaks were his feet. And the skinboats his wings! So that was the end of him.

While the language of its song came from a lost shaman world, the song was later made accessible when someone created a dance to go with it. It's entrancing to imagine songs like this being repeated by children, who themselves often invented strange and original songs.

As I finish the story: 'Don't make us laugh too much,' Sarah murmurs. 'We want to catch a whale.' 'When you learn that story?' asks Umik.

'Last year. In May. When you were out whaling.' 'Maybe that was when I caught my whale,' he muses. 'That story could have been my lucky charm. Maybe that sea gull can still help us now...'

But the story isn't about success. The gull's an archetypal anti-hunter. 'That gull,' someone teased me last year, 'is *you!*' And yes: if I have a game, it's my incompetence. So far I haven't discovered a local term for this – beyond *kinnaq*, 'fool'. But the gull tale is one of several about *kinnaq* or 'lazy fellows' who are incapable of looking after themselves. Did such incompetence derive from my work in Tikiġaq, or did I bring it with me? Asatchaq was tickled by the fool's absurdity. (Kinnaq stories transcribed later.)

*

Last night ivory gulls wheeled overhead again. I called them *nauyaaluk* and Sarah corrected me. But because she originated in a river village, she didn't grow up knowing this high Arctic species and doesn't have its specific name. She did tell me that *nauyaaluk* is the term for both glaucous gull and a generalized word for the gull family. Umik once caught an ivory gull in his owl trap at the Point and took it home. The gull's leg was broken and Umik snapped it off and bandaged it with insulating tape. I asked him what he fed it. 'It ate anything. I called him Jerry,' he said in a matter of fact voice. 'I like those small ones. The big ones I don't like.' Umik kept Jerry for two weeks and then released him.

Umik, born in the early 1940s, operates in two languages. What he knows precisely in Inupiaq emerges less articulately in local English, and linguistic vagueness – as in 'big ones' – is what makes Inupiaq people occasionally appear simple to outsiders. The tragedy is that younger people inherit the non-precision of the village English and not the super-precision of Inupiaq. Thus perceptive sharpness can be blanketed in a new language which, at its present stage, isn't compendious enough to cope with environmental life.

Another double element in Umik: on the one hand compassion for the ivory gull, on the other the ferocity of the hunter who must make a thorough job of killing. When a 'big one' gets in his trap, he simply stamps on its head. This separation of species may come from an archaic system of classification in which considerations of both subsistence and aethetics play a part. Perceptions we observe thus diagrammed within the subsistence field are no doubt also visible within urbanised behaviour. We feed cats minced rabbit that may have been tortured by chemists in pursuit of a deodorant stick.

As I think of Umik and his owl traps, I remember my first visit to the village. It was a foggy autumn afternoon in 1973, and as I wandered the bluff, I saw a man on the beach who was walking to and fro in jerky concentration. His solitude appeared frantic; his movements disturbed. This may have been Umik moving between traps, whose delicate settings he was anxious to leave sprung for the owls that were hunting squirrels and lemmings. And that solitary figure reminds me now of the shaman Aquppak who stood dazed at the Point one autumn in the nineteenth century, as a party of spirits arrived in an *umiaq* and kidnapped him. Aquppak got home once he'd changed into a whale and his soul was released when a hunter had harpooned him.

But who was that figure silhouetted in the fog who seemed to live within this lonely culmination of the sand-spit, by some spiritual agreement or a shamanistic negotiation?

*

May 12 continued

A steep pressure-ridge of sea ice rises behind our canvas wind-break. We sit in the lee on a sled draped with caribou and bear skins. The skinboat, as though growing from a separate spine of ice to our south, points across the ocean whose surface, in sharp chunks, produces an occasional dull glitter. The horizon is dark blue, separated from the paler sky by the saw-tooth of the distant pack ice. Above this, mounds of cloud echo the ridge behind us. Recalling the reluctant Aquppak, I think in half-sleep:

Far off on the ice, a crew of spirits witnesses our materiality and is waiting to abduct our leader.

*

Glaucus gulls fly through to scavenge a carcass. They have grace and greed, are bigger than the ivory gull, which still glides alone like a disembodied spirit. The ivory gull casts no image on the water, but its shadow brushes the ice rocks: a white shadow, eerie. Blindingly white, as though fused from ice silk, the gull rises and evaporates. I'm dazzled by that sudden shadow.

The depths below the skinboat prow are green. The keel, just visible, has short blunt udders of ice that have been formed by the wash. These grow longer and drip with every backward motion of the swell. I'm entranced by the intensity of the projecting prow as it juts from the ice and threatens motionlessly to harpoon the water.

More than just a vehicle, the *umiaq* is a weapon and an animated hunting partner. Eight seal skins lashed across the open lattice of a driftwood carcass lend the boat dynamic character. This life was expressed in traditional times when the women ran ahead of the boat as it was being carried across the ice and who empowered it by having it brush against new garments which were still charged with animal soul life, thus transmitting both human and non-human energies to the new-clad *umiaq*. Even in these agnostic days, the skinboat radiates a life of its own, about which these other thoughts occur.

First, its tensions: in that the skins are stretched so tightly across the driftwood frame that they are united with it, while the skeletal structure is itself morticed and lashed into its own self-integrated and cylindrical configuration: ribs fixed to keel firmly but with sufficient give to maintain a shape which is flexible enough to bend slightly to ice pressure.

Second: the combination of materials. Like a drum, the *umiaq* is constructed with new skin and old driftwood, both of which are harvested on the south side of the peninsula where seal skins are taken after the whaling season and where also wood has drifted from southern rivers. The boat is thus a product of migratory movement from the south and it will be used to pursue the whale which migrates along the same path. While driftwood and seal both come from the sea, the skins are stitched together with sinew from caribou tendon. This latter gives the boat a third, land-derived, element; thus land and sea converge. Land dwellers who hunt both on land and at sea must bring sea creatures to land also. The stitches also harmonise with the new caribou skin clothes people wear at whaling and the raw caribou meat which constitutes much of their diet during the hunt. Men, wearing seal skin boots, and their boats are thus mutually adjusted.

Thirdly, the prow. To see the boat perched at the ice edge, the curve of its prow poised just above the water suggests movement and intentionality. While the prow expresses stillness, it gives the impression of wanting to take off: fly, swim, reenter the element from which the boat skins emerged. Some men lay harpoons along the forward gunwales, and these bristle from the prow, thus creating a composite projectile, as though the mechanism of the harpoon will be set off when it touches a whale and thus help propel the skinboat with which it is in partnership. Further, the prow, carved last century and smooth with long handling, has both thrust and sensitivity. While the keel absorbs vibrations from the ice and water, the prow stands in the wind aware, awake, alert. The boat points the way. Its sharp beak leads.
Back in the village lies my falling-to-pieces copy of Virgil with its images of ship's prows which subsume the world of ancient people's journeys:

Obvertunt pelago proras... et litora curvae praetexunt puppes...
they turn the prows seaward... and the round keels fringe the shores...

I think of the Inupiaq verb stem, *sulluqtut*: 'the sea travellers come ashore briefly' (Larry Kaplan's translation). What journeys across dangerous territory that term encapsulates! The hunter in his single mindedness. Men and boats, heroic self-interest coordinated with communality.

*

I've been on the sea ice for four days, sleeping in snatches, while the mind associatively shuttles between memories of childhood holidays on chilly English beaches. There is also an emptiness to this inactivity without bounds which opens like a colourless flower, while on that bitter English shingle, stiff wet towels chafe salt into the thighs, the teeth chatter, wind flings grit into fish-paste sandwiches and we drink diluted ersatz fruit juice. Time passes, changes and repeats in memory. Here on the ice, the emptiness is inhabited by scavenging sea birds, and the expectation of death to be followed by a rejoicing which is its contradiction.

*

Large white clouds whose darkened edges are like water stains on antique paper. Along with birds and mammals, hunters and the hunted, clouds migrate towards non-being.

*

The ice creaks.
Sikum inua atuqtuq:
'The ice spirit's singing.'
What does the ice say?
Like me, it's singing:
Aya-ya!
'I'm cold.
All the way to the heart!'
Aya-ya!
Oi vey!

*

The weather howls. In tents and village houses, the painful turbulence of men and women. There's rugged, formidable joking. Big Aniqsuaq says, '*Ariggaa!* Fred *qiaruaq*, (Great! Fred was crying!)' The poor inept fellow managing the store has been caught with his hand in the cash till.

Aniqsuaq mocks my Inupiaq and, baby-fashion, lisps my name, parodying my perfectly good pronunciation: '*Aniq-sua-yaaq uv-aŋ-a*, I am Aniqsuayaaq.' She tears up my muscles and returns them as jelly. The ability to joke is a species of power. The harsher the joking, the greater your unassailability. The young are taught both ridicule itself and obedience to it. On another level, they must heed their shame, living flayed until they stop making mistakes. Thus joking is action, a response to wrong action and a sign of action. Non-Inupiaq-speaking local children know the word for 'scold', and use it in English sentences. 'My mama sure *suak* (scolds) me!'

I must get used to *suak*-ing too. At last year's hunt, I was scolded by women till my ears bled for not keeping the blubber stove hot. This year I am scolded for using too much fuel. If I could reconcile these two extremes, I might achieve insight. Or perhaps just one hot ear and one cold ear.

*

Footnote on Aniqsuaq. She's a tribal healer, in training in Kotzebue with the celebrated Della Keats. Last year I sat on the floor of her house while she massaged my back. 'You got all this meat round your shoulders twisted,' she mumbled half-intelligibly. 'Put your teeth in when you massage your ethnographer,' I wanted to tell her.

The treatment was rough. Had Aniqsuaq lived last century, her amulet animal might have been brown bear. I thought of the story of the man who serially married a polar bear, a brown bear and a whale. When the couple quarrelled, the animal laid its skin on the floor and fought. The man was torn to pieces, died, rose to kill his wife and marry the next animal, thus in dismemberment/rebirth ordeals, he accumulated power.

The wisdom we derive from this perhaps lies in allowing ourselves to be taken apart and consumed: embracing totality with such thoroughness that we disintegrate in its embrace. Those who can reassemble themselves perhaps undergo the experience and live with reforged contact with arcane forces. Power deriving from such an ordeal is what Buddhists dismiss as *siddhi* (magical power). A higher path is to contemplate the absolute without desire, the object being to see and analyse; not to wield.

This is possible in post-neolithic societies. Shamans in hunting cultures both ingested and utilized power. There is a relationship between shamanism and both yoga and Buddhism. Yoga at its lowest is shamanism: the development of supranormal faculties, cataleptic dreaming, out of body soul flight. Shamanism, at its best, can bring enlightenment: what a Bering Sea man described as mind and body illumination (*qaumaniq*): an uprush of radiance flooding head and torso, just as summer fills the winter's body.

As I finish writing this impressive Note to Self, I hear Aniqsuaq mutter: 'Thank you, Jesus, for this doughnut…'

*

News on the radio of Carter and Mondale. Whales, bears and seagulls also bring news of their campaigns with happy but no less moribund, freedom. What, after all, can a shaman who marries into a polar bear family expect but be irritated by his wife, while she in turn will insist on fighting him?

*

There are two things in the tin: doughnuts fried in seal oil and pilot crackers. I reach for a doughnut. Aniqsuaq says, 'You're not supposed to eat that. *Qaqqualat* are for *naluaġmiut* (crackers are for white men), doughnuts for Eskimos.' Aniqsuaq is joking, but she also means what she says. And if I were silly enough to argue, we could have a devilish row, and I'd end up on the bearskin, my flayed meat steaming. Inupiaq people identify with what they eat: each village allying itself with the animals it loves and eats. Whale in Tikiġaq; fish, caribou and black bear in river villages.

It goes further than this. Hunting the whale and then ingesting it and storing its meat underground on the Point, people become whales. In which connection Kunak said to me as we watched a brown bear moving across Cape Dyer last year:

'When that bear sniffs me, he thinks "Ah, *maktak*! (whale skin)."

When he sniffs you, that bear smells hamburger…' 'But kosher,' I stopped myself from adding.

Likewise my joking partner, who soon will want to kill me, said:

'It's a good thing you like my food. If you didn't like it, you couldn't be my friend.'

Both physical and social survival are predicated on the meat-ceremony. The most basic human contact beyond language and sex lies in sharing food. In a hunting society where meat has a part in most activity, there can be no participation without happy commitment to this. My greed, which in my other life I might conceal, is here a mark of courtesy.

But Aniqsuaq is presumably aware of an irony in her remark about doughnuts. Certainly these treats are, on account of the oil they sizzle in, special to this locality. But the recipe is Euro-American, the first flour-based cooking having been introduced by whalers after 1880.

Asatchaq has told several stories in which flour soup and pancakes feature. The innovating shaman Ataŋauraq shattered whaling taboo in 1884 when he took women to his whaling camp so as to cook for his crew. And some new foods, eaten in combination with meat and oil, also entered the old taboo system. Thus in one of Asatchaq's stories, the ghost of a woman who, in about 1900, had fried pancakes with the wrong kind of fat appeared in a dream to Asatchaq's father-in-law to explain the consequences of the infraction. It should also be said in defence of two opposing points of view: pilot crackers entered the diet during the same decades, but that they seem not to have been incorporated into dietary regulations. There may thus be justice in Aniqsuaq's comment.

*

The lament of Sarah, a middle-aged skinboat owner, about the younger set and hard times in general. She says this at breakfast:

'Those boys never come to camp now. They're too lazy. The girls don't come either. They start coming at the beginning of whaling, but then they get bored. The teenagers aren't interested anymore. They want to go sleep in town. They don't do anything. Coal is so expensive. We're running out of *siqpan* (blubber) for the stove. Not much driftwood either, and the trail along the south beach is terrible...'

But there's a parallel between Sarah on driftwood and Aniqsuaq's observation about doughnuts. Carbohydrate entered the diet during same the years when Euro-American whalers plundered the south beach for their ship's furnaces. After they left ca.1910, the driftwood deposits grew again. But then Natives started to build European-style houses and abandoned seal-oil lamps in favour of wood-burning stoves in the 1920s, and the beach was again denuded. When imported stove oil became the heating staple of the mid-1960s, the driftwood piled up again and there's plenty now.

*

'Don't wake me in the morning!' said Umik only half-humorously last night. We all lay down on caribou skins, wrapped ourselves in old chicken-feather sleeping bags and slept till about 3.30. The stove went out at 2. I woke cold, grabbed my parka and had just warmed up when someone knocks on the tent frame. 'Whales out there! Two whales!' 'Let them go by,' I secretly plead. But Umik gets up. Sarah gets up. I pretend to sleep until someone pokes my leg. 'Whale. Get up!' I hunt for my socks. They're cold and wet. Umik is saying, 'Where's my hat? Where's my gloves? Where's my *kamikluks* (trousers)?' jabbing his voice good-humouredly but also in sleep-fuddled and disoriented imperative. Sarah is priming the Coleman for hot water.

I stumble outside. The ice hits my eyes painfully, but the wind's dropped. New arrivals are there, and we stagger round the skinboat, unloading caribou skins and rifles. We wrench the boat round on its sled till the prow faces the water and start pushing along the trail through a gap in the pressure ridge and so towards the ice edge.

There are four of us dragging. It's not far to the water, and although the trail's rough, the sled-runners move easily. Down by the lead, big new fissures in the ice have opened. There are gulches, ultramarine, immeasurably deep, into which the whole crew, boat and all, might be swallowed at a single ice pack shudder.

We fix our windbreak into ice rocks that I piled up yesterday. The invisible crack by the windbreak still creaks noisily. We stand in the tremendous silence which is broken only by the movement of this deep internal fault. 'It must need oiling,' says Umik. He chops a narrow gap in the ice as though starting to excavate the entire sea.

The sea is empty. After an hour, we see one whale to the north. Then one more. The wind is steady. A few gulls. Streaks of stratocumulus, white on blue sky, whiter above the horizon.

10 a.m. Eight whales cross the horizon. They blow triangles of vapour that collapse as suddenly as they rise. One whale travels closer. It breaches and we see the white blaze on its tail. 'Like waterproof boot' (with its white seal skin banding) one man murmurs.

<pre>
                    his-flippers-
    'Holy-cow-   I-see-'em...'
</pre>

murmurs Umik, his voice undulating with the whale's movement, the words 'his flippers' rising and falling like whale's breath.

*

Noon. I sleep for an hour. Dream: I'm with an Inupiaq woman who's complaining about the way John Arlott, recently dead, has been treated by the MCC. 'They shouldn't have done it to that man. They shoulda kept him on that programme!' Rising to close a window through which cold air pours, I explain to an American woman that English summers are flavoured by Arlott's cricket commentaries. 'His voice pours through the air like west country cider, mellow, with the bite of shrewdness.' My hand strays, by mistake, of course, to the woman's thigh, which is tight and brown under a floral miniskirt. I apologise. This is certainly not cricket.

*

Sarah came to the village in the 1960s from a river community to the south. Even Inupiaq outsiders have a hard time here. 'Times have changed since I first came,' she laments. 'They always used to dance when they caught a whale. Nowadays it's Bingo.' This is not true, but sufficiently to the point to preoccupy a semi-marginal resident's musing.

Sarah continues, 'Aniqsuaq is good, the way she comes to camp with us. She's a bit noisy sometimes.' Sarah wrinkles her nose. 'But she's tough. Not like me.' Two women more different would be hard to find. Aniqsuaq is bone-setter, masseuse and general healer, with lacerating female scorn whirling from her like whips. Sarah, by contrast, is vulnerable and nervous. Like many river people, she's soft-spoken, with a contemplative passivity that masks her tough-mindedness.

I respond to Sarah's remark with a sort of laughing assent. Laughter here is a concomitant of language and has a code of its own. There's the laugh of the skinboat owner which proclaims modesty and self-deprecation. There's the laughter of chagrin which acknowledges pain as a component of existence. There is laughter that rasps cruelly from the throat like knife blades. Wild laughter reels out of the chest in great ribbons of ectoplasm. (This in response to self-critical clowning, especially when there's death in the story, the fool-narrator having narrowly escaped being eaten.) There's also the empathic but self-protective laughter which says, 'I understand what you're saying, but factors too numerous and complicated to go into forbid me to take sides.' I'm hoping that Sarah has interpreted my laugh as such.

*

There's competition between younger men over sleep deprivation. 'I haven't slept for three days.' 'I haven't slept four days.' '*Saglu*! (lies). You slept two hours yesterday.' The importance of vigilance. We watch through one long skein of days, interspersed with speculation, stories and migration rhythm. The light suffuses memories of land and night, bleaching the negatives that lie packed in the unconscious… Sea, light, spirits. In myth-time: raven creator, the streaked peregrine and toccatas of mythologically charged life force.

*

'Those scientists up here counting the whales… They lie, their figures aren't correct. They try counting the caribou. How can they count every caribou in Alaska?' This is Inupiaq pragmatism: information authenticated by the senses. On the spot observation as measured against an accumulation of traditional knowledge.

*

I visited Kayuktuq's camp about half a mile north of us today. The trail along the ice rim is easy, but there are many rough patches where I fall into potholes.

Kayuktuq's is a prestigious, high-competence whale crew and I'm nervous. I've left two undermotivated and inexperienced people at Umik's. At Kayuktuq's, there are eight men by the boat, with others in the tent and in the village who'll come out as reinforcements. It isn't just the size of the crew that gives it status. Kayuktuq is a successful hunter who also prospers within the American economy on development projects, including our own village move. Kayuktuq flies regularly to Barrow for meetings and his prestige gives him the pick of the village for his crew, with a powerful balance of weathered older men and tough young hunters.

I approach from the south through the frozen carcasses of eight flayed belugas. Belugas yield a delicious white *maktaaq* (skin and blubber), but the meat is full of parasites and it's left out for the gulls and foxes. These great corpses lie in their frozen blood like rusted submarines or burned-out fuselages. One freshly caught beluga is still moist and gleaming. A slit is opened in the body and a greenish, transparent sack comes flopping out on a meat-hook. This was a pregnant female I realize with horror. The thin elastic tissue of the uterus is slashed with a knife, and the baby tumbles with a splash onto the ice: glistening, perfect, eyes blind behind their epicanthine folds. It has a delicate semitic nose, the whole creature curled like an ammonite or prawn, suspended between life and death and exposed now. The cord, thick as a hosepipe, is cut and blood gushes. The creature has a tiny penis. The skin is storm-cloud grey, delicate and silky. I'm aghast with terror.

*

Just south of Umik's camp is a bay with high cliffs of ice, flat on top and studded at the base where the water, lit by the ice to an intense ultra-marine, drips and washes. Within this bay, a small flock of old squaw duck float peacefully in mating pairs and call '*a-haa-lliq! a-haa-lliq!*' which is their name. These unpremeditated phonemes hit the ice and echo back in naked isness. Bird call and words travel, are deflected, snap in two, and drop in the sea.

*

Aniqsuaq responds to an ethnographic joke I make about no-longer-existent half-sibling partnerships. These are the brothers and sisters that people once acquired when their parents practised spouse-exchange with couples from another region to cement trade relations. Aniqsuaq's laughter blasted my joke away and I've forgotten what I said. It was probably something like 'Maybe she was my *qataŋun* (sister by trading-partner parents).'

Aniqsuaq was born about twenty years after the spouse exchange system was obliterated by the Christian marriage vow, but she knows all about it and her mind, so I imagine, fills with competing constructs: the ancestors as ideal figures pursuing lives that were whole and unspoiled but which were nonetheless discredited by missionaries. The fact that A's grandfather was a black whaler-trader who cohabited with an Inupiaq woman at the Jabbertown station in about 1910 lends the paradox a further complication. Every apparently simple phenomenon has internal paths that lead to yet more veils and layers.

'Taaa-aam!' Aniqsuaq's voice starts high, descends along the vowel and vibrates on the nasal before the hum is abruptly clipped. She is communing with my name: first ingesting it and then singing it through her body. What one needs for the soul to be evoked and stroked, is *atiq*, name; it was all right to entertain her with my allusion to the archaic but I probably trade too easily on this kind of saucy antiquarian privilege. But I can't help enjoying the flirtatious glee with which my older friends who know about the traditional world greet what must seem like bizarre pedantic episodes of mania and showing off. People who were born after 1930 both long for and abominate the dangerously rich textures of their grandparents' beliefs. I can move around in it because I'm immune. But sometimes I get the feeling that people are afraid that I'm dealing with contaminated matter.

*

8 p.m. I'm sitting on caribou skin high on a ridge. Sun bright on water, sea slapping the foot of an ice pile. Past and future surround this moment at its formless extremities. Pleasant vision! The past scavenges my years of wasted energy, its formless body a tangle of shadows in a dark corner of some university library where I failed to learn much. But I can scare that beast off. The past has happened. Each micro-second of its totality has led to this space/time, but time's atoms crumble as they come into being. The past's swallowed in the cold flame of the present. And the present is pleasant.

*

20 May, 12.30 a.m. At Kayuktuq's camp again. They know everything that's happened. Conversation in Inupiaq: 'Did Umik shoot a beluga?' 'Did you shoot a beluga?' 'No I don't know how to shoot!' Laughter. 'Your mustache is frozen.' 'More than my moustache is frozen.' Shouts of laughter. Then, 'Ssh-shh, you'll scare whale.'

The young men are playing pinochle. Their uncles make for the tent to sleep. I sit for an hour gazing at the pack ice which creeps towards us over the water. Silence vast as sea. A woman comes over the ridge carrying a large metal can. I stay for beluga skin soup and doughnuts fried in whale oil; tea.

I am transfixed by the beauty of Kayuktuq's skinboat. The low sides swell in two curves of parchment, meeting at each end in graceful uniformity. The two poles of the gunwales, their wood glossy, swell outward in a symmetrical convex. Flowing irregularly into the boat over the gunwales are the edges of the seal skins, drawn tight by thongs which are lashed to the frame. The boat covering is taut, smooth as a drum head, the eight skins meeting in fine sinew stitches like cranial sutures. Viewed from a distance, the surface of the skins appears unblemished, yellow in the sun and brown cream in twlight. Close up, they're lightly veined and studded here and there with tufts of bearded seal bristle. Next month the boat will be dismantled, its wooden skeleton hoisted onto a rack and a couple of the skins used in the skin toss game. The rest will be cut into useful objects such as boot soles and lashings, while some of it will be thrown away and will end up in the dogs.

*

Two short sleeps. The first was outside on the sled, after which I woke feeling ill. I staggered into the tent and lay down on a damp caribou skin, from which this nightmare reared: 'She raised her boot and kicked me in face.' "*Get out!*" I screamed. This perhaps suggested by a line in *King Lear*, 'She kicked the king her father.' But this, in my dream, was perhaps the opposite.

*

Back in the village for a day. Before returning to whale camp I walk round the lagoon and Ipiutak Pond. This was where whale boat owners used to cut the ice whose melt water the women took in ritual pots to whaling camp. They offered water to captured whales and similarly gave their skinboats a fresh water libation. A dead whale gets a drink because sea mammals are thirsty and its soul's thirst must be appeased. The skinboat gets a drink, because the water from Ipiutak has magical properties and will bring the boat to a condition of energetic desire.

I pick up a flint arrow-point which stuck up from the tundra that covers the last Ipiutak burials. At home on my table, I study the relief map. Ipiutak ('fishing line') pond is a speck of blue held in place by a narrow fishing-line-like thread of land that separates it from the lagoon and surrounding tundra. Everything is only one metre above seal level. Separately, I've sketched the layers of story and ritual associated with this speck on the map. Next to the lagoon, I pick through a top dressing of contemporary rubbish.

Using the raw evidence of our 'civilized' disjecta one might reconstruct a twentieth-century American subsistence-and-consumer economy. What does the wind sweep up on parallel beaches in Siberia? The US married to its Russian simulacra?

*

Midnight. I arrive back at Umik's camp after four miles over the sea. I'm frozen and sweating. The ancestors walked all day and night wearing caribou skins, indifferent to pain, complicit simply with collective need.

I've picked up some driftwood which has fallen off someone's sled. Aniqsuaq spies me through a burn-hole in the tent-wall and reels me in with, 'Bring it here!' – the Inupiaq sentence embedded in a long ribbon of semi-verbalised welcome noises. I stumble into the tent and start unpeeling sweat-drenched clothes. 'I didn't think we'd miss you today, but we did,' says Aniqsuaq. 'There's just two men down there,' indicating the boat with a sweep of her enormous arm. The women tell me to hang up my shirt and socks. There's tea on the stove. They're running out of supplies. I produce tea bags and canned meat. We fill the stove and eat.

In Aniqsuaq, ancient Tikiġaq woman still burns through the contemporary surface. I see and hear her in 1850 pouring instructions to children and dogs through the wind, her tongue like a whiplash over the distances, scooping stragglers into her wake. 'Who you been visiting town-site?' she enquires. I mention Qiliġniq. 'Getting old!' says Aniqsuaq as though inflicting a bruise to the old man's dignity.

Sarah is tired and in lamenting mood. She sits humbly, with her knees drawn up in front of her, smoking a Kool. She is both grateful to and afraid of Aniqsuaq, and as though to apologise for her own status as an outsider, she complains about the way southern Inupiat make fun of Tikiġaq dialect. Otherwise, she is preoccupied with the ridicule her own dialect attracts in the village. Last week she described to me how Pauluaġana, otherwise a kind man, mocks her. 'And all these new words I had to learn when I came to live here… *Arrii!*,' (alas) she sighed.

Aniqsuaq is in an indulgent mood and refrains from scolding me. Instead she praises me for being tough, 'because you sleep out on the ice'.

'I like it,' I reply.

'I like it too,' says Sarah. 'But I get tired.' And then adds:

'We shouldn't go whaling on Sunday.'

'Whales don't know Sunday,' growls Aniqsuaq.

Aniqsuaq starts to reminisce about three girls she knew and whose photographs she'd once had. 'I wonder where those' (pause) 'pictures are!' she muses, breaking the word *pictures* into two parts with a nostalgically musical push of her tongue. Partly perhaps because she's lost some of her teeth, the syllables emerge separately, though it is difficult precisely to locate the caesura. And because, in contemporary usage, 'picture' suggests photograph, the word takes on a peculiarly American character.

Aniqsuaq is talking about friends in an Oregon boarding school and there's a schoolgirl innocence to her attachment to that time and to the technology – Kodak Brownie – with which they were proud to have become associated. I'd expected the word 'girls' in the interrogative gap as she 'wondered'. The question was exquisite. It cast off intervening years and made her suddenly a careless child who'd lost 'those pictures' of girls half-remembered, and who used to live in her conversations each summer. The pictures remained with her, while the girls lived elsewhere.

I've seen snapshots like these. They show teenagers of the 1950s, girls with bobbed hair in frocks, boys in check shirts, blue jeans and black, shiny hair: smilingly optimistic, but slightly worried and disoriented, just back from their B.I.A. boarding schools. They write their old classmates warm, short letters. At Christmas and on July 4 they organize square dances in the community hall. Some of the boys play guitars and sing country western. But they are still hunters and *iglu* dwellers and while they are being democratically educated, their first language is Inupiaq. Umik is one of these. I've seen his picture.

*

3 a.m. I'm sitting on the sled by the water, Umik and Big R, a visitor, sleep next to me on skins. The wind cuts the back of my neck like cheese-wire. I'm waiting for my head to fall off. But then I won't be there to admire the perfection of the incision. My vigil's uneventful. Indifference grips me. I note changes in the sky and water. The sea is endless. I am nowhere and reduced to nothing.

4.30 a.m. A gigantic ice cliff heaves itself up with a rumbling sigh in front of the camp. At first I think 'Whale!'. Then I see colour, wet pearl-green, and imagine some outsized beluga. I wake Umik. He sits abruptly, staring ahead with a mask of astonishment. A second block explodes and shatters. Green and orange ice rocks wallow and jostle like vast blind mammals, sprawling, gasping, clambering on each other in the vortex. I've walked this stretch of ice ten times in the past hours. Now my footprints are dragged under.

The three of us rush guns and harpoons back to the security of the pressure ridge and drag the skinboat away from the water. Then silence again and nothing more to do. Coffee and frozen *maktak* in the tent. 'Praise the Lord!' says Umik wryly, with his mouth full of blubber. He means this sincerely.

Noon 24 May. 'I sure wanted to tell stories,' I murmured to myself in local dialect this morning. My feeling stems from three things: desire for activity; a sense of voidness that I want to fill with colour and our isolation on the sea and thus the need to provide continuity. Stories connect us to people and history; a fourth factor: a need to bind the present with the common dream. We'll have bonded with the past and gone through the narrative together; the event of the telling will in itself be our history.

'All right, white man, tell us a story,' says the young man who intermittently visits. I start with the history of Utuaġaaluk because this is an ancestor chronicle which reassuringly takes place inland and has the smell of grass, moss, caribou. No hint of exploding sea ice or marine catastrophe. The action takes place in the summer, ca. 1880. Umik says, 'Pretty soon we'll be up there (inland) looking round for caribou.'

'I'd be scared of those people, in those days,' Sarah comments. My sympathy is drawn to her premonitions.

*

26 May

Sarah said: 'I dreamt we had a new plywood floor for the tent. This one is sure difficult to keep clean. It's the first time I've dreamt for a long time. Whenever I visit, someone tells their dream to me. I never have a dream to tell.' Sarah's sense of double impoverishment is heartrending. I remember the sea gull without a game. A dream, a dance, a game, is self's self-presentation. Self says, 'Here I am. This is me flaring in the space my body fills for the time being!'

Thus it is with everyone. Simply to be here is the game I've chosen, and for now I'm content to just sit on the ice edge and do nothing. But I'm hungry and my mind flits restlessly between the ice floes as though to swallow with my eyes anything that moves.

*

Belugas in small herds pass closer than ever. I see their eyes and noses as they rise to breathe. Sometimes a delicate flipper appears as the body arches and rolls. One, bleeding profusely from gunshot, has a flower of scarlet on its glistening white skin. Still it keeps pace. These small whales have graceful, equine energy, and their arching rise and plunge express migratory purpose. There is ecstasy in their race north through the

212

waves. But their close-packed shining, pure white serpentining looping movement through the water is also disturbing. Their slick white skin, small eyes and the snaky rhythm of their swim has a nightmare quality.

Umik and his colleague Will poise themselves to shoot, but the belugas sense our presence and weave under the ice. One group seems to retreat, regroup and then swim out to sea before vanishing. I am happy for this.

But perhaps the belugas know us and anticipate their victimization? Belugas have been hunted on this run for two thousand years and they still appear innocent. Or do they, as local tradition suggests about the bowhead, have their own ancestor histories about the carnivorous bipeds who prey on them each spring, and for whom they graciously sacrifice some of their number?

With a whine and a thud, Will scores a hit. The beluga arches abruptly and sinks fifteen yards from camp. Blood and oil film the water. Moments later, a grey juvenile swims back and I realise that we've shot its mother. In the next half-hour, there are three more runs, but each time the belugas come within range, they disappear, alerted by blood in the water.

I lie down in an impotent depression and sleep for a few minutes on a skin. Umik wakes me. 'Drag the water with these *niksiks* (hooks)!' I take off my gloves, whirl the hooks and let fly. Pulling in is painful: ice forms on the rope and the slush runs up sleeves. Sometimes the hooks just drop at my feet. The two men laugh and make satirical remarks. After half-an-hour's effort, I take another minute's nap. I hear Umik murmur, 'Getting pretty hard, buddy.'

I get up to watch him whirling in a patient rhythm. A moment later he strikes. 'Get one of those!' he gestures, and I stumble for a pole hook. Turning, I see the beluga, tail up, dangling vertically: a carved white leaf in dead black water. The body swings against green under ice, its head in the darkness. I fix my hook in the tail and while Umik shouts for rope, we hold the body in the current. Umik then cuts a hole in one fluke and runs the line to one of the boat gunwales. 'Over there with that rope,' whispers Umik, and I climb the ridge to our north and hold the beluga while Umik paddles the boat after me and Will follows, pulling. We stumble along for thirty yards until we come to a crusted shambles of beluga carcasses. Aniqsuaq and Sarah – the one talking energetically, the other unsmiling but pleased – come over the ridge in their bright calico parkas, carrying their *ulus*. Umik attaches a line to the second fluke and for half an hour we heave and slither until the dead beast mounts the ice edge in a heavy, crawling and reluctant motion.

The butchering is less elegant than at Kayuktuq's camp. 'I don't give a shit how it's done,' says the otherwise mild Will. He comes from the south and perhaps feels he must adopt an element of local bravado. Recently, Q., who has promised to finish me off 'pretty soon', came to sit with us and asked, 'Are you going to church this morning?' Will replied, 'I don't believe in that horse-shit!' This plunged Q. into a profound silence, where bloody thoughts appeared to mingle indecisively with the wine-and-biscuits idea.

The butchering is painful. As Umik's blade strikes the creature's puckered, cross-shaped vagina, I feel a stab of sympathetic horror. 'Female, ah?' someone mutters. Junior, aged eleven, hovers to one side, spitting gouts of chewing tobacco into the blood. The flensing is quick and brutal. After we've dragged away the skin and blubber on hooks, I cut some meat. Only later, after I'd eaten some raw, I remember the flesh carries trichinosis. So much for my compassion and ambivalence.

Umik sends Junior for an axe to open the beluga's skull. The brain lobes are enormous: round, soft, grey-brown, veined with purple. He lifts them gently with his bare hands from the cranium. 'Brain soup tomorrow!' Aniqsuaq murmurs.

*

26 May

No sun all day. It's now so cold that eider ducks and murres have reversed their migration and are flying south again. I have two hours' sleep. I wake to find R sitting on the sled talking with Umik. He's had a radio message that his father's dying in hospital. R suddenly leans on his knees and vomits between his legs. I console myself for his misery by writing an imaginary letter.

9 p.m. A warmer evening, and the eiders are flying north again. Pleasant to be receiving the same atmospheric message as a quarter of a million ducks. I must remember to fly north when I have the impulse to sit on an egg.

3.30 a.m. Hundreds of belugas. Black sea checkered with vast beluga herd, surging, leaping. I hear their breath. It's hollow, whistling. They swarm past in the choppy water. Awe inspiring, terrible, creative divine energy. One female swims in mid-herd, a calf on her back. It lies balanced, curled against the mother. Mother and calf in mutuality and confidence, at peace with their instinct.

*

A dead twenty-four hours. We hear Kunuk's caught a whale. A few old squaw ducks float around and dive. They are frightful gossips and solipsistically call out their identity: '*Ahaalliq! Ahaalliq!*' If they uttered their scientific name – *Clangula Hymenalis* – I would join them making hymeneal clangour.

We feel small and alone. Cheeks smart in wind. Ash-coloured clouds on the horizon, sea unreflecting. Sarah has sliced up the beluga brains and we eat them in soup.

'*Alappaa* (cold) that weather!' says Umik as we nibble and sip. Each fragment of brain is a soft curly paste. Presumably nutritious but psychologically unsettling. What dolphin dreams of sea, migration rites, marine agility have I ingested?

Midnight, May 27

I walk to Kayuktuq's camp. His oldest son Milliq has built a nine-foot arch from blue pressure-ridge ice, with steps up one side. It lends a bizarre, metropolitan flourish to this most imperial of wilderness camps. As I arrive, the emperor *umialik* emerges from his tent wearing polar bear-skin boots, his face circled by a bear ruff. He joins his brother Red Fox who's been watching at the skinboat. Kayuktuq is a large man and has a still, but powerful presence. His brother is square-set, silent, energetic. He is Kayuktuq's harpooner. In contrast to Kayuktuq's flamboyance, he is one of the quiet men of the village. Wise people like him do not strain to be conspicuous. They perform their part, but their role never takes them over. Imperial spirits seldom express this perspective, but we depend on their initiative. And the emperor needs a reliable shadow; as often, the shadow carries his wisdom. The brothers stand with two young crewmen, balancing their knowledge against the young men's energy.

Suddenly the four scatter along the edge of the bay. A herd of belugas is swirling towards us. There's a burst of rifle-fire and all but one vanishes. A wounded beluga sounds, its tail beating the water. Piquk whirls hook and line. His second throw connects. I run along the ice feeding back rope, but the beluga snaps free, taking the grapple with it. Minutes later there's a second run. A volley of shots. Piquk hooks the wounded animal with his first throw as it rolls. 'Don't go too close!' shouts Kayuktuq. But it's too late. Piquk falls in the water. Everyone laughs as he heaves himself out, his bare hands secure on the crumbling ice bank. 'At least I *niksik*-ed (hooked) it,' he uncharacteristically mumbles in self-justification, without bothering to fetch dry clothing.

Margaret has meanwhile appeared, looking sunburnt, wild and magnificently pretty. She joins the men on the beluga-line and works alongside them. Her face emerges in flashes behind flying hair and the wolf ruff of her open parka. Then she stands with the hook-line, undoing a tangle. When she looks up and sees me, she clownishly slips on the ice and pretends to fall over. 'Hey, when did you arrive?!' she shouts. Her great heart-shaped face sends out solar pulses. Beaming radiantly, it sweeps across the ice at me. The wind carries off her next exclamation whose current, switching between me and Piquk, jolts my circulation. 'And then suddenly he's here!' she explodes in laughter. The sea ice starts to rock below me.

'Shazam!' I shout back, brazenly unzipping my down-stuffed parka as though to expose to her alone the god I cultivate in my thermals. 'You're like...' The wind rips off her satirical volley, cracking the ice ridge with her laughter.

2 a.m. Grey sky, dull water, nothing, fog. Past a small ice cape, in the middle distance, a skinboat emerges. It moves slowly from the south, with silent caution following a bowhead sighting. Umik drops his hooks by the sled and gestures us over. We stand by our skinboat. The travellers approach, anonymously cowled in white cotton drill snowshirts which the fog dims further. The boat moves past without acknowledging our presence. To speak is forbidden, a gesture interrrupts the rhythm of their paddles. Immobile in the prow, the harpooner sits; the north wind cuts around his weapon. At back, the steersman on a raised bench, stirs the current. They round the next ice point and we're alone again.

There are many qualities of silence, and several come with their own peculiar quality of light. There's the silence suspended in sky-and-water. This has a rarified, musical character. It changes with the separation of its parts, like notes which break silence only to intensify their context in the disappearing chord of which they are part, and which leave no stain on the stillness they've touched. The light in which this occurs is refined and ethereal. The sky is huge and soft, with thin tones of blue and small, high clouds. This is *endlessness silence*.

This morning's silence is muffled, heavy and inert: *cloud/fog silence*, the light uniformly grey, as though the world's enclosed in stone. Oppressed by the fog and from below by the sea, I lie down, lonely and exhausted. It's futile to hang on here with this demoralised crew. We are not even a skeleton. We're just dislocated, separated, arbitrary vertebrae.

I close my eyes and contemplate our little crew, the pathos of its disconnection from bigger village business. Lost here in this shifting-around no-place, perhaps we're closer to a global somewhere than to Tikiġaq which is, after all, just a mile behind us. It is relatively simple up here when you close your eyes to locate yourself on the planet – an imaginative plotting which to newcomers at extreme parts of the world such as the poles and the equator must come easily. In London or Chicago we locate ourselves within streets and transportation systems. Where does the sun rise relative to Greek Street in London or North Clark in Chicago? But at the 0 degree meridian, you can lay the body precisely along that faint straight black line and your sweat will trickle across it into the southern hemisphere or percolate towards the north as you feel the two halves of the globe boundlessly curving outward towards its diminishing polar culmination.

So too it is here, as though we're at the edge of some ultimate geographic crust: extended to the sky on the hemispheric curve, the whole globe below us, with a feel of the sea, the sea ice and mainland geology representatively extended: the activities and people and whales in rhythmic flow, encased and controlled by winds and currents, their local dialects and meanings offered to the totality of which we proclaim our inconspicuous special identity. The polar moon, inhabited by a Tikiġaq spirit, is also a close neighbour. It knows this district by echo location – the same radar used by whales.

My dream moves into silent comedy. Our bodies jig on puppet strings over the New World. There hangs Umik effortlessly flinging hooks across the Arctic. He strikes the edge of Greenland and starts gently to pull it towards him. Next come Kayuktuq and his crew. They stand by the water carving slabs of blubber from between the dry ribs of their skinboat which has turned into the whale they were chasing. The moon bends towards them and its mouth receives its portion.

Time flows backward down a longitudinal hairline. My body is whisked to a Chicago suburb. It's late spring and I'm in a warm room playing string quartets with university physicists. While this is a political moment – we're on strike against the bombing of Hanoi – we have just finished Haydn's *Sunrise* and have embarked on Mozart, when our leader's wife enters with a tray. She's baked butter cookies which we eat with tea. *Alles gemütlich.*

I go to wash my hands before picking up my bow, when the scene shifts abruptly. I'm walking barefoot over the Ipiutak graves which bristle with the scapulae and jawbones of the two-thousand-year-old dead. The tundra unrolls to reveal Umik and Sarah wreathed in chains of ivory and swivels. They're embracing a dog and a half dead gull. Its feathers are inturned, tangled in its skeleton. A broken claw stirs the bony rubble. I lie down with them and the turf flaps closed. 'Warm down here, ah?' Umik smiles. But I am cold and want urgently to urinate. I push on the earth, and my fingers are stalled by sharp grass roots and torn trouser zippers.

30 May

A giant suddenly inhales. A giant sighs. Or a cavernous engine releases clouds of steam. …Ahhhhhh… The steam turns to a cold, brackish spray. I raise my head to find Umik nine foot tall above me, his harpoon leaning like a tree across the water. Below him, with the skinboat toppling on a whale's head, black and huge, a bowhead rises. Another plume of spray shoots up, and showers us in salty rain. Suddenly there's blood. Rope speeds across the gunwale. The float jams on a bench and capsizes the skinboat. The whale dives. A hollow in the water opens, rocks, and the sea regains its level. In the silence that follows, water piles across the ice then surges violently back. Twenty yards out, the seal skin harpoon float rockets to the surface and dances. A flipper rises, spirals. The whale sounds and the sea is empty.

Umik rushes to the skinboat with a grapple and heaves it upright. It's shipped some water. We tumble in, bale frantically, then paddle. We pass a man whirling hooks on the ice edge. We take him aboard and make for Kayuktuq's. Umik raises his paddle, swaying it left and right over his head and Kayuktuq's crew shoots its boat onto the water. At Kayuktuq's signal, we stand in to them and take a man on board. There are now six in Kayuktuq's and five in our boat. We pass Kunuk's and he launches behind us. No tents, camps, boats and people humanize the ice edge. We're in primeval water.

We paddle slowly out to sea. The further we move, the heavier the water. The landfast ice recedes. The ice pack lies on the grey horizon. A vast space surrounds us. I'm frightened by the cold dead water. Our boat is fragile, my companions taciturn. We strain grimly through flint. The wind blazes in our faces. Soaked gloves freeze. We stop now and then and flatten our paddles against boat skins. Blades pressed in, retracted into idle floating, we deny our own presence, silent, immobile. For the whale we're not here. The current drifts us north. This is the stream the bowhead travels.

Paddling becomes painful. Each thrust brings me to my limit. These are new sensations. The intense relief, when we stop, is followed by a rush of heat, as though the body, long smouldering, had burst into flames. Strange to sit burning in the middle of the Arctic Ocean. Yet the cold still imposes its dull and stony grip, reaching through the muscles and groping at the skeleton.

We stop and gaze round. Kayuktuq idles in a bay where whales rest and feed. Across the sea, small men appear like carved ivory shapes precariously balanced on skin and driftwood.

Umik starts singing:

> *Yaa-ŋaa -ngaa -ŋaa*
> *Yaa -aa yaaŋaa -yaa*

Words without meaning, syllables on rhythm, float into the wind and the wind disperses them. If the song found its way to the whale, perhaps it would be deflected back to him, and Umik might hear its echo. Or if the whale heard the song, as Umik intends, perhaps it would respond in the language of whales.

'You know that language?' Umik whispers from his bench in the stern. 'The old man tell you *aġviqsiun* (whaling song)?' I shake my head. I've recorded such songs, but do not know them. Silence. Umik starts singing in a quicker rhythm to entice the whale, speed the song further. By now we're north of the Tikiġaq point. Cape Lisburne's cliffs are blue, streaked with white, on the horizon. We paddle towards the landfast ice. We've lost Umik's whale, his harpoon point and the seal skin float. The whale has swum on. Or it's dived beneath the ice to die. Umik's overwhelmed with disappointment. 'Too bad, too bad!' he mutters. We paddle slowly past the other skinboat. Kayuktuq's six men, saturnine and burly, are crammed on their benches. Kayuktuq stirs the current, his quietness balancing their ferocity. Q sits poised in the prow, his thunderous face surmounting a wolf ruff.

Place, Time, Light. Kaleidoscope

How well one gets to know one's place on the ice. The little cliffs and jutty friezes, views from pressure ridges, paths and shortcuts, snowdrifts, potholes, cracks, trails, snowmachine's and men's tracks. And then all the marks, once a camp place is abandoned, of previous habitation: bald plywood-stained squares which once held tent floors, still circled by ice rocks where the tent ropes were tethered. These sites are littered with an astonishing variety of stuff: driftwood, cinders, blackened chimney sections, seal skins, seal heads, carcasses with no heads, blubber, intestines, old sacks, tea bags, shell cases, pages of comics, caribou hoofs and caribou antlers, coffee grounds, butter cans, torn children's jackets, single mittens, old boots, dead dogs… And everywhere, the broad swirl of sled tracks leading to the open water, or where the water was before the ice moved.

These words attempt a kind of verbal archaeology of what can never be recovered. A surface excavation of contemporary surfaces-in-motion, recorded in words arranged in one of an infinite number of possible combinations. Language springs to the page from silent layers of sub-verbal unconsciousness. Or perhaps a silence identified – as in a library with its humming tubes of light – by the white noise of prelinguistic activity. The words appear obediently as though of their own volition in response to things seen and heard. But they are arbitrary noises. Their correlative tissue must, in any language, be likewise arbitrary. But perhaps there is a correspondence between sound-signs and these tea bags, antlers, intestines and comics. Words, like garbage, exist in transit. This garbage will disintegrate, be scavenged and eaten, wash up on beaches. Words get lost in the air or in a swamp of other words. What holds these scratches?

Yet each vantage of the sea ice, transient as may be, has its character, and the moment of arrival always marks a fresh perspective. Dependent as spacial identity may be on fluctuating patterns of sea and light, impermanence and the particularities thereof are coextensive and simultaneous. It is as though a speeded up succession of geological eras took place every day here. This vertical dimension of time/space is compounded by the temporally horizontal: the presence of specific people, foods, equipment, animals. The two dimensions of identity intersect to create place out of space. Space, here, may be defined as the totality of a continual flux. Within this, *place* finds its temporary coordinates. Place thus has only relative value, and it is at once genuine and unreal. We may recall last week's or last year's places on the ice, but we can never revisit them. Hunters of the past thirteen hundred years no doubt chose their points of vantage in relation to recurring and roughly predictable ice conditions and even perhaps according to some of the same procedures. But no 'present' camp inhabits the precise spot of an ancestor camp, and the ice 'here' can neither reproduce its forms nor repeat the components of its shifting materiality.

1 June, 1.30 p.m.

The light has been softer since it started getting warmer. Dark purple-and-white, then smoke-grey clouds stretch from north through west to south. Sky between clouds in varying intensities of blue. A mirage to the northwest: ice hovers above the sea, with a polished concentration of gunmetal blue light separating the ice from the water.

Icebergs in slow procession like ruined Gothic cities. Thrones, towers, buttresses, heroic escarpments of masonry. Black as bombed Berlin and Dresden, unmoored, floating helpless among the seabirds.

5.10 p.m.

I sit on the pressure ridge between Kayuktuq's camp and ours. Mist gathers in little pockets of air and disperses – as a ghost manifests here and there and dematerialises. Small crystalline particles of ice clink and whisper on the water surface. Ducks gossip in the bay. They dive successively. The last old squaw looks round, sees it's alone and goes under. A piece of bloodstained ice floats by. Then a jellyfish, lavender-coloured, rises to the surface against pale green ice rocks, an inverted marine parachute, with the most delicate longitudinal radials.

2 a.m. Intense orange sun in green dawn mist. Two chimneys gush blubber and driftwood smoke in the distance. Blue and white hills beyond the village like whales rising out of tundra.

4.15 a.m.

A vertical megalith of yellow-and-pink light on the horizon. It stands opposite the sun which has risen behind us. Now the column rises to meet a rainbow in the clear blue sky. It attenuates before plunging down, about fifteen miles from its first foot, to join a second column. Framed by this arch lie the dark sea and a single, castellated iceberg. The rainbow dissolves, and the columns retract into two luminous stumps which a bank of plum-red stratocumulus creeps through like a predator.

5 p.m.

The sun hits the ice edge. Pink salmon-tinted clouds fill the bay with their reflection. Eider duck fly south again, low. The ducks are a chain of light points against the red and grey sea. A spindle of light connects each point to its reflection, creating of each bird a double quintessence. Sometimes the line arches and descends like a whale. Sometimes they're a thread of silver shaken over velvet.

End of Journal

Suluk and his Wife Harpoon a Whale.

Suluk and Artemis, a couple in their thirties, catch a bowhead and Suluk's crew brings it to be cut up on the landfast sea ice and distributed. The Three Muses are teenaged girls who work as ice camp cooks.

After the harpooning, there is an interlude of dazed anticipation. We stand through the small hours gazing from the landfast ice until finally a smudge appears on the western horizon and twelve hours later four skinboats labour to the ice edge dragging towards us thirty tons of Suluk's bowhead. I had witnessed last week a scene of even more intensity, when three whales north of us were harpooned in brutal, quick succession. It was twilight when the news came and I sledded to the site, arriving one hour later, my bones in a jumble, three miles from Suluk's camp.

A vast plateau of ice had been marked out by four tents, their chimneys smoking in a light north wind. It was three in the morning, and sloping across a pale grey sky were banks of dishevelled stratocirrus. Silently moving across the snowfield came women and children who had left the village in the early morning to take part in the butchering. Fixed aloft to jointed harpoon shafts, streamed three Old Glories, one for each whale, in faded cotton, kept by whale boat owning families from the patriotic 1950s. The scene was unearthly, pregnant with apocalypse, and as though emerging from some battle at the end of time,

the folke stoode amayzed this glouryous morninge, wayting for their captaine's signalle...

We idled dreamily till the women had lit fires and boiled *tirragiik*: a large slab from the whale's back which we ate in violent quantities, plastering each segment of floppy black skin and its grey wad of fat with mustard or ketchup. I spent forty hours that followed with my gloves half-frozen to the oil and salt drenched ropes with which we winched the three whales from the sea and hacked up the meat into blubber-cased parcels for transport to the village.

Back at Suluk's we stand peering at our fish. Suluk is stunned by light reflected from the ice and long hours on the water. But now he must determine where to do the butchering. He wants also get to help from other crews and assemble equipment: block and tackle, flensing knives and ropes and sleds. He also needs an older man to supervise the distribution.

Suluk's sudden and imperative solemnity is frightening. As he limps up the ice towards the tent, he emanates a weary and unwilling heroism. He walks with his head down. He can not, for the moment, in the light of high good fortune, look at us. We are too far removed from the realm he's entered. But modesty requires, at the same time, that he struggle with hubris.

The hunters in old stories radiated this same mix of pride and self-effacement. Success brings dilemmas. To bring in a whale is the sublime achievement: but it makes you vulnerable to rival whale boat owners, jealous shamans. To counter this exposure, traditional *umialiks* affected modesty and reticence. They moved slowly, spoke little. From season to season, and with each new whale, their reserve grew more imposing. This tension between suddenly acquired power and self-governing humility generated two ecstatic moments. The first came after the harpooning. Alone with his skinboat crew, the *umialik* was allowed a shout of triumph, a whooping diphthong, '*Ui! Ui!*', in the manner of a seal's bark, clipped off at the teeth a fifth higher than its starting register. Insolently belched, with no audience beyond the crewmen, he addresses the dead whale's soul and the spirit of the moon which made the whale's capture possible – and likewise to the cosmos which the moon controls, and in which the *umialik* has established a new position. Further exalting his triumph, the *umialik* took a raven skin from an amulet bag he kept beneath his *umiaq* bench, and opening the wings, laid it round his shoulders so head and beak were nodding on his forehead. Thus becoming the Raven Trickster, who created the village from the mythological Ur-whale.

The joy-shout is repeated in the skin-toss game that marks the end of whaling season. This is the *umialik's* second moment, soaring with his wife on the seal skin blanket unwrapped from his whaleboat. Again transformed into the Raven, the *umialik* flies to proclaim the same ascendance. Exuberance must otherwise drum on the inner mind mask's tissue, as he bends his persona, season by season, to further depths of gravity.

Suluk's limp reinforces my sense of his ambivalence. I am familiar with his arthritis; any moment now, he'll ask me for paracetamol. Now as he walks towards us, I'm aware of another wound. Suluk has killed a whale. But he, too, is wounded, and our happiness for him is clouded with protectiveness and terror. Having gone out humbly in his skinboat, Suluk has returned with a semi-divine aura which he and his wife must extend with generosity.

How vulnerable Suluk therefore seems as he limps towards us: as though balancing the filament of light that surrounds him over a vacuum which separates it from the body, and to which, as the community projects it, it should cling. One false move, and this gilding will slip into the air, leaving the *umialik* naked. Like his skinboat, minus skins, and skeletal.

Suluk reaches the sled and rummages for a pole knife. He murmurs a self deprecating joke. We, uncelebrated, smaller people, maintain our silence as he limps back to the water to mark the whale's skin for the extraction of *tirragiik*.

The whale lolls flexibly in the current, awaiting dismemberment. The grind of Suluk's one boot, and the drag of the other, suggests how painfully he is tethered to the creature he's brought in. The whale is his, his wife's, his crew's, his *qalgi's* and the village's. It has left its own tribe and agreed to enter the world of the human. But Suluk must mediate these connections: and this other-species-brotherhood, that ties him to the whale and demands that their connection flow through every branch of Tikiġaq village, is awe inspiring and oppressive.

I glance at the tent we've set up and filled with floorboards, boxes, skins, stoves, bags of clothing. One of the Three Muses lights moss and spindrift and starts feeding blubber into the half barrel camp stove I'd helped Suluk cut last February. As Suluk passes, he turns, and with an ambiguous gesture, calls out, 'Move the tent!' His voice is toneless; it comes from a strange distance, capricious but urgent. For the next two hours we sullenly drag camp thirty paces south. I'm hungry, sweat soaked, freezing. When someone offers me a swig of Pepsi, it cascades down the throat in a glacier of caramel.

A long wait follows while Suluk's news travels to the other whaling camps. This is a time of suspended action, as when the storyteller says of time long passed: *They did nothing.* A gap opens in the hurly burly. On the margins of sleep or soul death, the characters hang in a void of non action. Whether what they've done is praiseworthy or wicked, the reflex generates inevitable responses. The past converges with the present and we watch what's happened. It's simply what it was. Everything is simply action. The specifics dissolve as we watch these recede towards non existence.

By now the sun is high and even in the wind it's warmer and some ten of us juniors dawdle round the tent, just waiting. The Muses sit smoking on the sled, creating a small, closed, female *qalgi*. Men arrive. Their snow machines roar to the pressure ridge behind us and they appear quietly on foot, dragging their sleds. The younger men walk down to inspect the whale, talk among themselves and deferentially avoid Suluk. Suluk's contemporaries thrust their faces into his, gripping his shoulders, laughing with happiness. Suluk softly talks logistics, deflecting praise. It will take time, but looks straightforward. All we can see at its tether at the ice edge is the dull black shine of the bowhead's torso like a huge slice of aubergine.

Suluk had stood by his whale, earlier, with a couple of young crewmen, contemplating how to lift it from the water. He caught a whale two years ago, but lacks long experience and needs the advice of an older man for both this and the butchering. He can't afford to lose this whale or cut it in the wrong proportions. The village would lose tons of meat and he his reputation. There are a number of older men, non-*umialiks*, to whom he can turn, and now he must make sure he gets one of them quickly. Men from other crews have arrived; they're waiting to start, and they want their shares. Latent in this interlude, there's quiet urgency. The ice may shift and the whale go under. The whale must be butchered before its innards rot. Besides, we're expecting a final run of whales. Everyone wants to be at their camps before the ice breaks and forces them back into the village. Once the ice starts moving, the hunt will be over.

'Go get Uqpik,' Suluk murmurs, extrapolating his decision from where, in his pain, it had slowly shaped itself.

Suddenly, as though he knew he was expected, Uqpik materializes. He is wearing a denim covered sheepskin parka with a wolverine ruff and a blue woolen hat. Suspended from a broad belt round his waist a buck-knife hangs. Uqpik, the Trickster who lives in Max Lieb's nineteenth-century trading cabin, is transformed from joker to a categorical, quasi-military figure, with disciplined step, decisive gestures, an authoritative manner.

Uqpik has come to supervise. Cavities are chopped in the ice underfoot to form holding spars, and with block and tackle in place, it takes fifty of us, fuelled with skin and blubber, a mere six hours to winch the whale up. And while Suluk hangs back in the wake of Uqpik's authority, a day and night's labour starts.

Before long, like a goddess in a masque, Artemis enters, transported in a quaint vehicle. The snow machine behind which she is travelling stops at the crest of the path through the pressure ridge, and the female *umialik*, who has been sitting in the shelter of the basket sled, descends. Artemis is wearing a parka cover of shattering brilliance, its pattern of yellow, orange and green angles interpenetrating against an electric blue ground. No Fauve could have designed an outfit more rebarbatively apt for a harpooner's spouse, nor one that could so outshine the sea ice. It is a dazzling sight, this meticulous woman, her parka ruff high, stepping down to the water to inspect her behemoth.

As Artemis stands on the ice above the whale, her parka clashing with the snow and water, the whale's power cascades through her body. The tension is terrific and her facial muscles, dancing behind a contemplative frown, to which tinted glasses lend a dark, divine complexion, show its play. But Artemis must not reveal what triumph does and she's controlled superbly. Rictus flickers just once at the corner of her mouth, and is banished. Composure reestablished, Artemis walks slowly to the tent to supervise the cooking. A cosmopolitan Inupiaq, as familiar with town life as she is with sea ice, she's at the summit of what it is to be *umialik*. And when she emerges from the tent – that Yankee whalers' innovation – she has regained her lovely, hard-edged multivalency. It's right there in her language, logistically focused, always generous:

'We have *yuukaq* (hot drink),'she calls across the ice, the *k* and *q* snapped off by incisors, 'but no *cups!*' – the syllable articulated as though to conjure, from the valley between consonants, what must be gathered. The Muses cringe as she walks round camp, snapping mugs from the snow and returning to the tent with them bunched round her fingers.

We eat, and I notice that Artemis has brought not just breakfast, but also a culture, and for the period that she is with us, we dwell partly in the clock's sphere which she's brought from the village. There is home baked bread and a can of marmalade. The coffee, brewed in sea ice water from a nearly salt-free pressure ridge, suggests chicory or dandelion. It is sublime and frightening, the coffee and marmalade lending a heraldic touch which parallels the black-and-white slices of whale skin that we gild with mustard as it flops on our knives from saucepan water. When I look up sleepily, I see our ten-year-old boy helper, perfecting his own sliding yoga (the *parama-sisu-asana*). 'Cheap ice!' he murmurs when he loses his balance.

We start butchering the whale and almost all I know is labour, dragging meat and blubber on a long hook to the sleds where each share's trussed and carted to the village. Occasionally, someone hands me a pole blade, and while he pulls with a hook, I work the knife through the blubber, which makes a gradual crepitation, as though stitches in some tightly sewn satin are torn shivering from one another. Sometimes the section I'm working on pulls away and whacks back in place across the meat, or else it peels off with a grinding, bloody slam and lands trembling on my boots.

The whale is dismembered with a kind of sagacious brutalism that Uqpik supervises gravely. 'Cut here, ah?' young men deferentially ask him. Uqpik peers down his nose through dark glasses, as though absorbing information through his slightly pendulous lower lip, and breathes '*Ii*' in assent. Or he adjusts someone's knife along a line scored on the whale skin, murmuring, 'Cut here… to here….' Then he climbs back on the whale to study a new section.

Suluk works by us. We talk quietly in English and Inupiaq. Then Uqpik – as though Raven, from the whale's back, through its throat to stomach – is deep within the carcass which has been opened for his descent, and conducts the operation from its centre, moving quietly with raised eyebrows and mouth half open, among the viscera where the whale's souls dwelt. Sunk in this complex of ganglia – a vast, webbed, polychromatic rigging of filaments and glandular purple and white tissue – Uqpik labours, brushing off spent souls flocking to his snowshirt and animating its ribcage till the body is half empty and he emerges over the puddle of microfauna in its stomach contents which he himself spilled, flicking blood from his glasses.

Except for the pounding of meat and blubber and the slapping of the liver as it finally emerges and the membrane's peeled off for an old man's drum head, it's been peaceful in the body. And thus all the more perfect, as he straightens and finishes, is Uqpik's long, concluding polymorpheme: a musical line whose strange, inflected endnote modulates, through a complicated flourish of laughter, back into silence where its impress shimmers. Work stops as the joke goes round the remains of whale, and Uqpik's *mot* is answered with an improvised counter subject from a visiting *umialik*.

An exercise, it's been of gynaecology, by these midwives of the ocean. A medicine of death to One is reborn in the life of Many: the whale joining the community in resolute and violent sacrament.

Now the whale's skull, streaked with flesh and sinew tatters, is rolled to the water where it hangs, dips, falls against the soft crust of the ice edge and collapses finally. Among the scarlet bubbles blasting to the surface, is the head-soul which the atlas vertebra had stoppered. Now this emerges through the skull's base and starts travelling south to be reborn in *agviġum nunaŋa*, the whales' country. Then another cry goes up, and the men shout 'Come back when you're ready!' – as though this whale's dispatch already coincides with its rebirth as another.

By now the senior personnel have sorted out their shares and sledded to the village to pave their caches in the permafrost with meat and *maktak*. Uqpik, a widower, whose children live outside the village, is joined by S., his older brother, who has materialized as though by soul flight from a southern township. Together, like shaman and assistant spirit, the brothers exit, Uqpik kneeling nonchalantly with one leg bent on his worn-out skiddoo seat, while S., with a pirouette, jumps on the projecting runners, and with one hand on the stanchion and one boot lifted, echoes Uqpik's imbalance as though casually sealing with his own seniority his brother's authority. So they whistle off their meat, leaving us to plod round with the coarser ruck of Suluk's blubber.

228

Part 7

The Traditional,
the Transitional, Social Change

Tulugaq walks out to his Father's Whale Camp,
Spring 1976

When, following a stroke, Asatchaq disappeared for three weeks, I was both relieved and upset. Relieved that I was implicitly freed from the responsibility of recording his stories with the devotion he expected and upset both for him and the prospect of pushing our work forward. His absence also encouraged me to broaden my knowledge of Tikiġaq society and visit the old people I had neglected. The following interlude emerges from the time of the old man's disappearance.

Because I was in Tikiġaq to record an old and sacred tradition, I was confused to be living in a society that had been moving towards commercializing America since the late nineteenth century and unnerved also to realize that Tikiġaq was a minority culture like countless others, not every one of whose components had been dissolved or made democratically equivalent.

But things were changing. And there was no resolution to the ambiguous and often invisible interaction between an archaic culture that had more or less been swept away and the mobile, transformative cultures of modernity. The people born within these interactions live in an intermediate history. This is a bewildering environment in which past culture looms indistinctly while many people wanted to identify with that culture without being able to touch it. This is the experience of intermediacy: an environment to which I also still belong and whose frequent unpleasantness is difficult to define.

Just as in Fairbanks I had divided my time between visits to Asatchaq and my life as a Euro-American, so now I associated both with Asatchaq's generation and younger people who scarcely knew of the old man's existence.

In imagination I had plunged into a myth world, whose 'truth', as Asatchaq described it, filled both my waking time and sometimes dream life, while I lived much of each day with young people who had been disinherited from the traditions to which Asatchaq clung. These parts were incongruous but in some degree I colluded with both.

Part of present reality lay in this very separation of the generations. Nor was Asatchaq the only elder. But apart from him, his sister Uyatauna and the solitary George Omnik, other elders lived within extended families. These were sociable and mutually supportive kin groups. As in the traditional period, old people quietly provided advice, while younger women ran the household, young men hunted and dealt with stove oil and water supplies.

Cultural separation was nonetheless marked. The elders spoke Inupiaq, younger folk talked English. One man, the seventy-year-old Umigluk, was demonstrating for me a string game and singing the song that accompanied it while his granddaughter, aged ten, who was hanging on his chair back watched. At which the old man stopped and told her to go away.

'You don't have to see this,' he said roughly, and so communicated to the ethnographer who was paying him for an hour's worth of information, a component of his own childhood. The girl took the incident in good heart, but it also illustrated ways in which she continued to be cut off.

On another occasion Umigluk remarked, 'We're not Eskimos any longer. Our ancestors. They were Eskimos.' He made this observation in the context of several narratives which he'd spoken in mixed Inupiaq and English. Witty, cynical and insightful in the face of a modernization he observed with ironic wisdom, Umigluk was also quite painfully conflicted. He was a leading dancer and was affiliated to traditions that dance perhaps represented. It must have been difficult for him to recognize, as clear-sightedly he did, deceptions both in a shamanistic system about which he was dismissive and a Christianity that he regarded as a convention. 'The shaman Asatchaq, great uncle of the living Asatchaq', said Umigluk, 'hadn't really travelled to the moon. He said he had. And people believed him. But he imagined it. Or believed in stories.'

And in connection with Christianity: 'I didn't agree with the missionary. He made things up to keep control. Threatened he'd confiscate the crosses that he'd given people if they went hunting on a Sunday. Well, I went hunting. And he took my cross back. I didn't agree with him.' Umigluk colluded with the Christian dispensation but he looked at it coolly and perceived ways in which it had been introduced for the sake of social control and what he experienced as amelioration.

The confiscation episode, enacted by the temporary missionary Goodman, which had shaken other converts, happened more than forty years previously and still it shook Umigluk's confidence in church authority. The incident also highlights a fundamental discord between the nature of Christian symbolism and the function of Inupiaq amulets that people still carried in the 1930s. Whereas the cross was taught to be both a sign of faith and protection against the Adversary, an Inupiaq amulet was functional and of the present moment.

But disjunction and sometimes discord between mid twentieth-century generations was something that I had no right to disparage and I attempted to weave the contradiction into my experience of the archaic. I was forced to accept that the archaic was transmitted through a medium that had been transformed, as things began changing in the late nineteenth century. Niġuvana's family had delivered Asatchaq into a construction of a traditional environment. It was important nonetheless to remember that in July 1890, one year before Asatchaq's birth, the missionary had arrived. And while Dr Driggs assimilated more successfully into Inupiaq life than the Inupiat initially absorbed Christianity, his very presence was a symptom of change.

*

Given that I was in search of a version of Urtime, this historical limitation was disappointing. But however much the remote past penetrated present reality, I could not renounce the present. I might not like it, but *today* was here. This was something that teenagers taught me. My 1976 journal reads:

'Am I in Tikiġaq to deploy an otherwise threadbare talent? Isn't this work in in the service of my own writing?

Or

'Am I deploying my literary inclination in the service of the community and perhaps especially the semi-disinherited children?

Or both in some measure?'

Later, when I worked on a history of Inupiaq contact with Euro-Americans, I came more fully to understand how Asatchaq himself had been born into a time of change: and that while he identified with Tikiġaq tradition, he had always made use of anything that the white man provided to make existence productive – tools, cloth, firearms, carbohydrate and other imports.

And change during the early twentieth century was as unsystematic as it appeared, now in 1976, to be haphazard – when now, following the Native Land Claims settlement (1971) and Pipeline construction, a new affluence filtered, albeit patchily, into the village. From the earliest moments of contact in the nineteenth century, people had adapted, in varying degrees, to anything that happened to come in. Such things could be concrete. Or they might be ideas, the dominance of English or elements of Christianity learned from missionaries or evangelizing Inupiat.

Nor was it a case of one thing simply taking over from another as might happen in replacing a machine part. This is how sometimes we imagine the process of evangelism. But it wasn't a question of one thing coming in with finality as a functional replacement. Conversion to Christianity happened to individuals in different and often unaccountable ways. Nor can intangible elements of intellectual life and affiliation ever be given an interpretably absolute identity.

In which connection, Rainey asked Dives Qukuq in 1940: 'Why did you change religions?' Qukuq replied through a translator:

> Because though at first he believed the shamans and they helped him, his brother told him about Christianity, and when he and his wife capsized on their way from Kivalina to Kotzebue they were able to swim (for the first time). He believed after that in the power of Christianity. He thinks that other people changed over because they were afraid their shamans would prevent them from going to heaven…

Both the material and intellectual phenomena that came from America arrived in the Arctic in a condition that was deformed and displaced from its previous environment. Every Tikiġaq individual utilized these phenomena in their own way and at different *tempi*. And in this respect the old timers of 1976 were comparable to today's youth whose expectations were similarly in transition. Here I will adduce some changes that followed Euro-American contact. The following section is in two parts. First, testimony of elders born in the 1870s recorded by Rainey in 1940. Second, extracts from my own interviews, 1976–7.

*

Changes, Concrete and Non-material – from Rainey's field notes

In contrast to the six weeks of the spring whale hunt, seal hunting remained a central activity and from October onward it was men's work to bring home the seals to fulfil subsistence needs. These were roughly as follows:

Seal meat and blubber	human diet
Seal meat and blubber	dog food
Blubber	rendered for lamp oil and medicinal use
Seal skin	material for footwear
Seal skin	material for lashings
Seal bone, teeth, claws	tool and amulet construction

With the arrival of technology based on metal, traditional dietary and heating needs remained. But guns and ammunition smashed a hole in pre-contact practice which depended on harpoons, spears and arrows. And while the gun offered a quick and accurate kill, harpoons and floats made for more secure retrieval. That said, some hunters born in the 1870s continued to use harpoons. As Qukuq told Rainey, 'some men used harpoons after they had guns – safer – might lose [seals] when shot'. Qukuq continued:

> Some rifles in village when Qukuq was a child in the late 1870s. Most men had guns when the Mission came, 1890. Then flint locks, shot shells, long shells whose iron fittings could be adapted .45 and .70 rifles with 'no hammer'. .45 and .60 with big iron fittings.

With the arrival of manufactured hunting equipment came a parallel change in human behaviour during the hunt. This change involved both men and women and also signified a new relationship with both seals and other animals. Qukuq and Rainey set out the *Before* and *After* as follows:

Before Contact in the 1880s

A hunter used harpoon, arrows, drag lines and bindings to secure prey. He returned from the sea ice, called down the *iglu* skylight and his wife came out to give the seal a drink of fresh water. After the woman had taken the seal into the house, the man entered, changed his boots, cleaned the harpoon head, returned to the ice, shook his clothing into a shore ice crack and said that while he had taken a seal, he hoped it would soon return [reincarnated].

Before the hunt, a man sat at the *iglu* entrance hole, sang, lifted his right foot and stepped inside. Every hunter knew hunting songs. Dogs were forbidden on the sea ice in case they got stranded except on the more stable north side.

Post Contact

The technology became semi-mechanized. Giving seals a drink and shaking off clothes stopped after the missionary came. Dogs were used pragmatically. Qukuq said in 1940 that no hunting songs were now used. Many people once had them, and he himself sang whaling songs after he was married ca. 1900. Some missionaries said it was all right to keep good luck songs. Others that it was against religion.

While mechanisation, whether it was the rifle or the sewing machine, often boosted domestic and community economy, it was more significantly a factor in dismantling the relationship between humans and animals, and the complicated structure of belief systems. For when animals were no longer spiritual beings and became, more materially, a source of food, then the intangible, shamanistic component of human/ animal coexistence was compromised. Christianity played a part in this. For as Driggs, who evangelized in the 1890s, told his flock, 'giving seals a drink of water is giving a drink to the devil.' Some desisted. Others maintained old practices. The most enthusiastic converts were relieved to be entering a place of new safety. Shamanism was frightening and taboo observation a burden. Christianity may not have made absolute sense. But to move into the fold represented a departure from anxieties attached to the old dispensation.

*

Here we move from Rainey's notes to passages derived from my own work which focus on contact relationships, ca. 1880–1910.[1]

Important here to remember that five miles south of the village, commercial whalers and traders established a community in 1897. This was the Jabbertown shore station whose mixed race residents were joined by Inupiat from communities who travelled to Tikiġaq in pursuit of employment. This, paradoxically, at a time when the Tikiġaq remnant was also afflicted by hunger and disease and some local people travelled to Barrow and the Mackenzie River in the north east.

---

[1] Extracts that follow are from my *Ultimate Americans*, 2009

Inter-cultural Assimilation – Joe Tuckfield and Nuvuk Koenig

The hunting, socialising, fuel gathering, gold prospecting and goods exchange in which Inupiat and white men were often equally involved are recorded in accounts of deals, routines and mishaps. Some of this interaction can be appreciated most vividly against the backdrop of new settlement topography.

In addition to the Jabbertown trading station, there were white men living on the north side, extending from the Mission House, Marryat Inlet and the coal bearing cliffs beyond Cape Lisburne. But this was fluid. The traders Kelly and Nelson who ran a station on a bluff called Pingutchiaq were both itinerants. And while Kelly employed southern Inupiat who travelled in search of subsistence, at Pingutchiaq he attracted Tikiġaq people to his northerly Barrow operation. The Swansea born Joe Tuckfield, on the other hand, had started his early career at Barrow and then moved to Jabbertown. From there he decamped to live for part of each year on a boat at Marryat Inlet.

Tuckfield was perhaps the white man who most successfully assimilated into Native society. While remaining close to the Jabbertown-based Heinrich Koenig, he married a shaman woman from the Kobuk and also entered local custom by adopting an Inupiaq immigrant and naming him Bob Tuckfield. The stories of Bob and of Joe offer a diagrammatic picture of uprooted mid-1890s life in the northwest Arctic.

Born in 1884 on the Kobuk, Bob's Inupiaq name was Qimmiuraq. (He gave the stories recorded above and died soon after my 1973 visit.) In the diseases and famines that claimed many in the lower Arctic, Qimiuraq lost his family, and in 1893 the boy and his aunt Avagruaq walked to Tikiġaq in search of shelter. Stumbling up the beach from Cape Thompson, the two migrants found shelter at Jabbertown, and within a few months they were living as a family with the Swansea man.

'Little Joe' Tuckfield had worked for Charles Brower in Barrow in the late 1880s and had travelled for Brower to the mouth of the Mackenzie River where he discovered new bowhead feeding grounds. Tuckfield's find initiated the rush to Herschel Island from where the final bowhead whale hunt was launched by steam whalers at the turn of the century.

Like the adventurers in Joseph Conrad's stories of the same period, Tuckfield lived in a world of traders gone Native and Natives who frequented white 'outposts of progress'. On his schooner *Emily Schroeder*, Tuckfield and his wife provided frequent refuge for travellers at the mouth of the Kuukpak River. One story, evoking the mix of travellers and residents at this point in local geography, describes how the Irishman Jim O'Hare perished near Tuckfield's home:

Jim O'Hare dragged down by Giant Mollusc

One summer 'Little Jim' took off with Peter Pigaaluk, a 'coloured man' and who also worked at Jabbertown. They sailed to Corwin to fetch coal and to gather eggs from Cape Lisburne. On return, their boat was sighted by Tuckfield's wife and another Tikiġaq woman. It was a clear day, and the two women had a good view of the boat.

After they had watched it for a while, they went back to their work and forgot about the boat. Then they remembered Little Jim again. Perhaps the boat travellers had landed? But they never showed up. Boats went up coast to look for them but found nothing. Capsized. Sunk. People said the boat must have been swallowed by an *aqalugluk* (giant shellfish). This was an area where those shells were found.

An American world of schooner and coal mine, assimilated here with local folklore, provides a richly textured backdrop to Tikiġaq, African American and European individuals, while the story itself is seen through the eyes of a local shaman married to a Welshman. Two years later, a letter from Jim's brother in Ireland gives us a flavour of the late Jim's own dialect. Likewise, we can eavesdrop through Tuckfield's letters, on his own Swansea idiom: 'We are all well and happy', 'The old woman's pleased with the sewing machine', and 'The trader is leaving yere [sic]' and 'with love to hall [sic]'. By 1907 there are 'byckles' at Jabbertown, albeit 'on the shelf....' In this audibly Celtic music of comradeship, some of Jabbertown's chatter survives.

Tuckfield's 'old woman' at her sewing machine provides another kind of vignette. In addition to wood-burning stoves and metal kitchen equipment, the sewing machine was a significant addition to women's domestic technology. It was a superb new tool. With a mechanism of visible parts for which some replacements could be improvised, the machine complemented, but did not displace, the arduous process of skin sewing which was still done by hand. The machine was perfect for making calico and cotton drill clothes. But it also gave women the opportunity for creating outfits for Europeans, and this brought women into the new economy. Unlike those early bicycles, which would, if they materialized, have been only practical on flat parts of the south beach before the autumn snow, the sewing machine was there to stay, and it remains an important item in women's working inventory.

Another of Tuckfield's friends was 'Nuvuk' Koenig, the Westphalian Heinrich Koenig's brother-in-law through his wife Pausana. Before Koenig went south in 1907, Nuvuk had adopted that surname and with Tuckfield took over the management of Koenig's Jabbertown station. Nuvuk became literate as an adult at the government school established at Jabbertown in 1904 and his letters reveal something of a twentieth century Native who has converted to Christianity and who, like everyone in Tikiġaq, continued to struggle with imported diseases. Nuvuk was perhaps the most economically successful Tikiġaq man of his generation, and we may assume that Heinrich Koenig had married into a prominent family. Here, in 1907, after Heinrich Koenig had removed to Washington State, Nuvuk writes from Jabbertown:

> 'My dear Nephew Fred Koenig: Are you good? Me speak to you mama all time of Blessed Jesus. All people Eskimo Blessed Jesus come. And Bertha, Dredrich [Hachmann], Charly Marlin me give you best greeting. [Tikiġaq] men shot 4 white Bear... a Kobuk man shot other man dead. I go after fish come back quick. Me go to sled Kobuk. I will write to you letter. You write to letter come back. My baby boy... she is a little sick... Kakoon baby girl she is 3 day sick.'

It might be easy to smile at Nuvuk's grammar. But given the circumstances in which his generation adapted, Nuvuk's writing is accomplished.

*

Language Change, late Nineteenth and early Twentieth Centuries

Many Euro-American goods entered early twentieth century Tikiġaq and acquired Inupiaq terminologies that described them in coexistence with a local language that remained healthy, albeit in a retreat.

Such imported goods became part of Inupiaq reality. The many kinds of animal oil on which Tikiġaq diet and economy depended were supplemented by new kinds of oil for heating and lubrication – kerosene, gasoline, motor oil, grease, gun oil. The Inupiaq language was accordingly bent to these innovations. Here is an account of this process from my earlier study:

'Inupiaq and English were the main languages of the peninsula, and these were criss-crossed, modified, sometimes enlarged, and at other times submerged by a trading jargon based on both languages, along with smatterings of Russian and Hawaian. It is unclear who spoke the trading lingo, how it fitted into Inupiaq and English and how often it was used. Since the jargon developed as a tool of barter, it operated mostly in conversations between Inupiat and non-Natives. But a large number of new jargon-derived nouns to cater for imported items entered Inupiaq. If there was a grammatical system to the dialect, it was rudimentary, and took two forms: a simplified, pidgin-style English and a reduced Inupiaq. Because English is easier to break down than the polysynthetic Inupiaq language, some sort of English was usually the vehicle of any complex utterance spoken by Euro-Americans. To denote local things such types of ice and Eskimo equipment for which there was no English equivalent, Inupiaq nouns and a few simple verb forms were used. Similarly, within a short period, Inupiaq people coined terms for many imported goods, and some these neologisms are discussed below.

'Neither the Jabbertown trading station nor Tikiġaq village itself were linguistically unique. In the early twentieth century, Vilhalmur Stefansson recorded a trading jargon on Herschel Island and along the Mackenzie River. Stefansson notes a three-way contact between Eskimos, white men and Kutchin Indians, the Indians sometimes adopting the lingo for trade or when they interpreted for Inupiat and white men. Stefansson does not mention Tikiġaq refugees at these outposts, but he presumably knew of them, and the jargon spoken in the eastern Arctic no doubt resembled the Tikiġaq-Jabbertown dialect.

'Stefansson recorded both grammar and vocabulary. In the case of non-Natives, some individuals used simplified Eskimo structures to express subject-object needs ('He wants to go aboard ship', 'I am hungry', 'Give me meat'). But the dialect seems mostly to have consisted of nouns, pronouns, demonstratives and a few verbs such as 'want', 'eat', 'break' and 'die'. These dialect words were mainly based on Eskimo terms. But there was also a growing vocabulary of Inupiaq neologisms generated through a correct use of Eskimo modifiers. For example, through the addition of –hluk or –qluk (strange, bad):

Jargon term	Literal meaning	English meaning
kam'mik-hluk	strange trousers	cloth trousers
oktcuk-hluk	strange or spoilt oil	kerosene
tuk-tu-qluk	strange deer meat	pork, bacon
tan-a-qluk[2]	strange alcoholic drink	molasses

'Some categories might be represented, according to who was speaking, by different but mutually intelligible words. The Inupiaq word *nuliaq* (wife), as adopted in trade jargon by a Kutchin Indian for use in conversation with both whites and Eskimos, corresponded to the Euro-American jargon *kuna*, probably from the Danish *kone* – a word whose consonants are found in the Inupiaq which lacks the 'w' and the 'f' of *wife*. Stefansson also recorded the way Euro-Americans learned some Eskimo suffixes then misapplied them, but then generated new words from the confusion: *nunamun*, 'towards land' being translated as 'on shore'. *Nunamun* (grammatically the dative 'towards land', but in jargon, the locative 'on land'), transforming to 'tent'.

Local Jargon

Jargon is not quite the word to describe the lexicon for the new artefacts that entered early twentieth century Tikiġaq. Jabbertown came and went. But manufactured goods arrived to stay and new words entered the language and were absorbed into Inupiaq. Some of the new vocabulary came from English, when the English word fitted Inupiaq phonology. Words such as gasoline (*gasaulik*), molasses (*milaasiq*), and tea (*tii*) easily slipped

---

[2] The root here is tanaq which was already a mid-nineteenth century loan word from 'tonic'= liquor, as in 'here's my tonic'. Dr. Irving Rosse of the Revenue Cutter Corwin wrote that the word 'tanuk' originated 'with an old Eskimo employed by [Captain T.E.L.] Moore...in Plover Bay [1848]. Every day about noon that personage was in the habit of taking his appetiser, and usually said to 'the Eskimo, "Come Joe, let's take our tonic'.

into verbal compounds such as *tii-tu[g]-niaq-tunga*: 'I'm going to drink tea'. Dr. Irving Rosse of the Revenue Cutter *Corwin* gives a good example of how Inupiaq compounds evolved to describe American phenomena: 'Canoe is *umiaq;* ship is *umiaq+pak* [big ship]; steamer, *umiaq+pak+ignirlik* [big ship with fire].

'In the absence of precise phonological equivalents, a word such as 'flour' could be spread into *palau*. There were also imitative words such as *qaqqaulaq* whose guttural q sounds convey the crackle of pilot bread being eaten. Some manufactured goods corresponded to Inupiaq words and things. Different kinds of imported oil and fuel lubricated or burned in some of the same ways as did animal and fish oils. Inupiaq coinages for each of these used a common noun stem (*ugruq*, 'oil') plus a suffix to create a new lexical idea. Thus kerosene was 'like oil', motor oil was 'old oil', grease was 'thick oil'. New terms for stoves and stove parts such as chimneys and ventilators could likewise be improvised from words for traditional lamp, fire and *iglu* features.

'Food provided an even richer field for invention. Some rare items such as oranges (*asiaq*, 'berry') might be somewhat vaguely assimilated into the language. But the colours, shapes and functions of foods were often conveyed vividly and with a sense of fun. Rainey compiled a list of terms, some which would have been coined in the lifetimes of informants born in the 1870s:

Imported Item	Inupiaq term	Literal rendering by Rainey/Ivrulik
Bananas	usuuŋnaq	like a penis
Beans	kumaurat	caribou droppings
Beans	niliġuaq	something that makes you fart
Rice	uraaq	adaptation of 'rice'
Oatmeal	sirri	ear dandruff [Rainey gives ear wax]
Sugar	avu	something you mix in
Mustard	ililgaam anaŋa	baby shit
Cheese	tchi	adaptation of 'cheese'
Liquor	taanŋaq 'tonic'	– see footnote above
Tobacco	taugaaqiq	adaptation of 'tobacco'
Coffee	kuukpiaq	genuine river

'Whole new terminologies were also generated for culturally powerful and elaborately differentiated word groups such as pipe, pipe deposit, cigarette, chewing tobacco and snuff (chewing tobacco). New coinages for household goods and other imports flowed into the language almost as quickly as the materials they signified: fork, spoon, bread pan, muffin pan, dish, basin, sugar bowl, coffee pot, flour sifter, scissors, camera, telescope, clock [small sun], wrist watch, looking glass, tea strainer, flashlight. Some of these words were shared by other Inupiat, others were specific to Tikiġaq. A number of deformed Polynesian words, such as *kow-kow*, 'food' and *pani-pani*, 'sexual intercourse', also entered the jargon. This transitional lexicon became for Asatchaq's generation part of Tikiġaq tradition.

'The fact that Inupiaq took in these new phenomena reflects both the wit of the people and the lively, accumulative nature of the language. Like any unwritten language with an elaborately differentiated vocabulary for all the features of an environment within which it worked and whose dynamics it must describe, Inupiaq continued to express the relationship of people to Arctic conditions. Species, places and, not least, a minutely discriminated terminology for subsistence equipment and the scrupulously anatomised parts that went into composite tools, represented just a fraction of the linguistic assemblage.

'Inupiaq was a language of both tradition and uncertainty, with a subtle and elastic syntax that generated new forms efficiently. As changes within the tradition occurred, the language adapted. It grasped what came in and fashioned new terms from existing phonology so that new technologies were linguistically put to work. When the white man came, the language was already well-exercised in the unforeseen. Terms for new domestic and subsistence equipment were needed if these goods were to be integrated effectively. Many such terms would enter twentieth-century Inupiaq language and survive for the life of the things they described. And while some of the terminology assimilated by pre-contact Inupiaq had fallen away by the mid-twentieth century, the process of language change continues both among Inupiaq speakers and in the dialects of English that have since evolved.'[3]

---

[3] Edited from Lowenstein 2008: 92–95

Language Loss

Immersed as I was in the local, I later understood that language loss was both a local and a global issue. Tikiġaq belonged to the Native majority whose languages had been marginalised by English – an outcome of indifference, positive suppression or other historical circumstances.

As Michael Kraus shows below, this is also a worldwide phenomenon parallel to environmental degradation and the depletion of species. In America, the loss of tribal languages is part of the twentieth century process of homogenization in which minority cultures cling, at best, to an insecure status, and at worst have a minor place in the majority discourse.

Much, even with Alaskan state support, has been attempted to revive Inupiaq. And it is never too late. But having listened to just one Inupiaq ten-year-old talking fluently to his monolingual grandfather, it was also later a pleasure to hear many San Francisco children chattering in Chinese.

Michael Krauss has written extensively on this subject. And there are linguists and educationalists who support indigenous languages. None claim they will restore fluency in the use of some of the world's most complicated grammars. Such might be dreamed by Indo-European language speakers. One might perhaps revive French if it were to be wiped out. But Inupiaq is not French. And even French is a challenge to children brought up in an Anglophone world that tacitly reassures them that they only need English.

The following extracts from a paper by Krauss summarise the global language crisis and the relation of this to Native American language loss:[4]

'The Eyak language of Alaska now has two aged speakers; Mandan has 6, Osage 5, Abenaki-Penobscot 20, and Iowa has 5 fluent speakers. According to counts in 1977…Coeur d'Alene had fewer than 20, Tuscarora fewer than 30, Menomini fewer than 50, Yokuts fewer than 10…

'Language endangerment is significantly comparable to – and related to – endangerment of biological species in the natural

---

[4] Krauss, *The World's Languages in Crisis*, *Language*, Volume 68.1, 1992. Krauss In 1972, by state legislation, Krauss established the University of Alaska's Alaska Native Language Center whose mission remains 'the documentation and cultivation of the state's twenty Native languages'. The Inupiaq specialist Lawrence Kaplan succeeded Krauss as director of the ANLC in 1994.

world. The term is presumably drawn from biological usage. …
Languages no longer being learned as mother-tongue by children
are beyond mere endangerment, for unless the course is somehow
dramatically reversed, they are already doomed to extinction,
like species lacking reproductive capacity. Such languages I shall
define as 'moribund'…

'In Alaska now only 2 of the 20 Native languages – Central
Yupi'k Eskimo and Siberian Yupi'k Eskimo on St. Lawrence
Island – are still being learned by children. For the languages
of the small Soviet northern minorities it is much the same:
only 3 of about 30 are generally being learned by children. Thus
in Alaska and the Soviet North together, about 45 of the 50
indigenous languages, 90% are moribund. For the whole USA
and Canada together, a similar count is only a little less alarming:
of 187 languages, I calculate that 149 are no longer being learned
by children: that is, of the Native North American languages still
spoken, 80% are moribund…'

Krauss proceeds to survey mortality among the world's languages and
concludes that 'mortality is already [likely to be] 50%… He continues:

'The circumstances that have led to the present language mortality
known to us range from outright genocide, social or economic
or habitat destruction, displacement, demographic submersion,
language suppression in forced assimilation or assimilatory
education, to electronic media bombardment…

Concluding the first part of the article, Krauss writes:
'Therefore, I consider it a plausible calculation that… the coming
century will see either the death or the doom of 90% of mankind's languages.'

Finally, Krauss addresses some of the remedies available to communities
seeking language preservation:

'We should not only be documenting these languages, but also
working educationally, culturally, and politically to increase their
chances of survival. This means working with members of the
relevant communities to help produce pedagogical materials and

literature and to promote language development in the necessary domains…'

And he quotes federal and state law whose purpose was

'to preserve and enhance the ability of Alaska Natives to speak and understand their native languages…'[5]

Here, extending the same theme, are extracts from Lawrence Kaplan's *Inupiaq and the Schools* which provides an overview of how Inupiaq has coexisted with English in north Alaska.[6]

'The new [Christian] religion profoundly disrupted traditional Eskimo culture as missionaries introduced foreign ideas and values, presenting them as universal truths when they were actually artifacts of European cultures. They encouraged people to adopt European-American life style, including dress, table manners, and other kinds of behavior which the newcomers admired in themselves and wished to see mirrored in the people they encountered…

'The Native language was another target of those who thought they would 'improve' the Native people of Alaska. Education was to move Native people into the mainstream of American society; this was of course not the traditional sort of education by which Native people trained their children… The teachers were White people and the language of instruction was English. The first students came to school speaking only the language of their home… Many people who went to school in the early days report that… they did not learn much…

'No schools in Alaska under the Territorial administration [up to 1959] encouraged the use of any Native language. Most, in fact, discouraged it by punishing children for speaking their own languages…Not only did these attacks on their language strike at the foundations of the children's identity, but the forms the punishment took were violently at odds with accepted behavior in their culture…

[5] The Native American Languages Act, 1990 and the Alaska Native Languages Preservation and Enhancement Act of 1991
[6] http://www.alaskool.org/language/inupiaqhb/Inupiaq_Handbook.htm

'Another factor which has affected the viability of the Inupiaq language is boarding schools to which many children were sent, especially during their teen years. Since village high schools did not exist until recently, children were often sent out of state to Bureau of Indian Affairs high schools and later to BIA schools in Alaska, located at White Mountain, Eklutna and later Mount Edgecumbe in Sitka... Many young people barely spoke their native language while they were away from home, so that they got into the habit of conversing mostly in English... Boarding schools must be considered as an additional force of acculturation.

'Leona Okakok of Barrow... spoke about the effect that boarding schools have had on the passing on of traditional skills and knowledge: "One of the young ladies I knew at the University said that she went home one summer, after having been away at school for what seemed like forever. She had all this education and brought it back home and was confronted with having to butcher her first seal, and she didn't know one thing to do. She said, "What did I go to school for? I've come home and I don't know how to do a very elementary thing that young ladies know, how to prepare an animal for consumption."

'It was the intent of the educational system to convince Native people that English was superior to their own languages... The effect was indeed profound. As the school and other mainstream institutions have taken over the roles that traditionally belonged to the family and community, traditional activities and customs yielded to foreign ones. Thus children have come to know less and less about the culture of their ancestors...

'There are in fact few children and teenagers anywhere in Alaska who can speak fluent Inupiaq. At Wainright, south of Barrow, there are small children who speak it, and in the villages of the upper Kobuk River some high-school-age children still converse in it... A language with few or no children who speak it is called a moribund language, and if this situation is not changed, it will be a dead language, one with no native speakers...

'Language death is tragic. People whose language is being lost may feel this loss very strongly. The last speakers of a language experience great loneliness... Members of an ethnic group who have not learned the old language often feel deprived of their tradition and feel alienated from their community. People outside the group who appreciate its culture regret the loss of a unique treasure... which thereby takes another step toward "monoculture," the prevalence of one dominant language and culture where once there were many.'

These excerpts are from an Alaska State publication, and Kaplan, director of the Alaska Native Language Center, is not just expressing a personal view. As Krauss wrote, language reclamation demands educational input, and since the early 1970s, Kaplan has supported the production of written and electronic learning materials, trained teachers in bilingual education and held workshops that promote the Native language. The North Slope Borough Education Department itself has joined the initiative and students increasingly are being encouraged to learn Inupiaq.[7]

*

Leona Okakok's Story

Ms Okakok's story is representative. And it constitutes a microcosm of an unlearning process endemic in Native American societies.

We have seen how seal hunting constituted Tikiġaq's central subsistence activity. Meat, fat and skins provided nourishment and heat, while the logistics of preparation were also a focus of domestic cooperation. There was division of labour between the sexes. Hunting was men's work. The role of women was to perform ritual that acknowledged the seal's sacrifice.

Also important were skinning, butchering and division. These were tasks that women learned in childhood. While her husband plied the harpoon, the woman's tool was the *ulu* whose slate blade she used both for meat preparation and clothes making.

Ulu-s of different sizes remain the central component of women's equipment. In the past it was logistically crucial and its semi-lunar form connected it to the Moon Man who controlled game animals. And although the moon spirit was acknowledged as a sexual criminal, it was women who supplicated him, shouting into the sky on winter nights to encourage his generosity. When the spirit responded, it was to drop figments of animals into water pots that the women raised to him

---

7 http://www.nsbsd.org/domain/44

'through the sky hole' – sometimes in the hope of splashing him with the same source of water they offered seals.

In February 1976, I witnessed a scene almost identical to the one in Ms Okakok's narrative. It was early evening in Piquk's house and K, Piquk's youngest son, had come home with a seal which lay now in the centre of the cabin. I had been on the sea ice several times with K. We'd leave in morning twilight, a strip of sun briefly visible on the sea ice horizon behind us and I sat on the sled as the dogs rattled across the landfast ice, jumping narrow channels till we reached open water.

This was half a mile off the Point where southern and northern currents sweep together the fish, krill and crustaceans that seals feed on. They jerk up, spotted seals, interrogatively, look round with their slick heads turning as though in expectation of a cheerful conversation, to get smacked in the face by a hunter's bullet and then, half-drowned and angled clumsily, hang until the hunter's grapple reaches them. It's a brutal encounter for which traditional Inupiat apologized by way of ritual propitiation. I too was brutalized in collusion.

As K dropped the dead seal in the family kitchen, I shared the limits of our empathy. The notion of a seal's soul had become an irrelevance. Did seals indeed have spirits when past people believed this? And was the present animal perhaps an incarnation of some individual taken by an ancestor who'd sent his victim's spirit home with a view to rebirth?

For now, given that we were modern people, the dead seal had become an eating object. All we needed was someone to cut it up and cook or freeze it. Like K's dog team beside the house, I'd snap up my share to assuage my hunger. The spirit life of previous seals had become irrelevant. Reverting to Leona Okakok's narrative, I wrote this short description:

> K had spread some cardboard boxes to catch the seal's bloomade, an initial first incision in the seal's belly with her *ulu*. As the seal came apart, instead of blood, there was a glistening white inch of fat between the guts and hide, which peeled off leaving the seal in four parts: guts, meat, blubber, hide – not to forget the head and bloodstained whiskers which the dogs ate... Surveying the pink-grey packed together labyrinth of seal intestines Margaret plunged one hand among them and asks, 'Hey, K, where should I put these deals, ah?'

Margaret was of Leona Okakok's generation and like Ms Okakok's friend, had been away at boarding school. She was a clever, charismatic woman in her twenties, and like Tulugaq, could understand but speak rather little Inupiaq. Like most young people, Margaret sprinkled her English with Inupiaq expressions. But her use of the word 'deals' suggested that she was unfamiliar with anatomical vocabulary.

'*Arrii,*' she exclaimed,' as she bent across the seal, 'that eye *katak* in the blood already.' And to one of her daughters, 'Hey baby, don't you go in there, you'll *katak.*' And 'Baby, don't you *pakak* in that *natchiq*. You kids, you're always *pakak*-ing'.

Katak-, a verb stem meaning 'fall', is one of the words most commonly inserted into English. *Pakak-,* 'rummage', is also common in child-directed speech. Everyone says *arrii,* an expression of dismay. While *natchiq,* 'seal' is also in general usage. The same goes for Inupiaq terms for whale, walrus, seal and bearded seal, Old Squaw duck and Eider duck, fish (generic), beluga, red fox, wolf, gull, guillemot, polar bear and brown bear. But knowledge of anatomy in its complexity is limited. Hence Margaret's distance from the term and use for a seal's intestine (*ingaluk*) previously transformed into rainwear.

These changes came in the wake of a long historical process and language moribundity was not in local control. And while language education offered contact with Inupiaq, it did not propose fluency. Language death remains a tragedy both for those who have lost it, and the world is thereby poorer.

*

Margaret. RIP 2015

I didn't know her well. She was a beautiful young woman who confronted the world with witty self-confidence and a satirical independence. Margaret's father Kayuktuq, was a public man, successful both as hunter and, in the American economy. Margaret's Inupiaq speaking mother had brought up seven children. Tulugaq was a younger brother.

I was too timid to establish many personal friendships. And so I remember Margaret from encounters in which I was usually a spectator. Perhaps it was this third party status that magnified my impression of her high octane power. Tulugaq expressed some of the same dynamism. And it was partly on this account that I associated him with the god Siva/Sharva.

Realizing only vaguely that he whom I called Sharva and Margaret were siblings, I homologised Margaret with *Kali Durga*, the Mother goddess who was also a version of the *Kali Ma*, the creative deity who was Siva's consort. The myths are complex and express the ambiguity of female divine nature. A hunting society version of the Indian narratives lay in Inupiaq stories, which themselves were variants of mythology shared by Siberian and north American peoples.

Inuit myth as expressed in Central Canada and Greenland, is dominated by the figure of Sedna or *Nuliayuq*, the Mistress of the Sea Beasts. Nuliayuq is an abused young woman but who reaches the seabed to become the mistress of marine animals. Not unlike Tikiġaq's Moon Man, she is both angry and creative and it was the role of shamans to placate her. But Tikiġaq's most powerful version of the Nuliayuq deity is the 'woman who won't marry' (*uiluaqtaq*) with whom the Trickster Raven creator allies himself. Another parallel version of Nuliayuq is Tikiġaq's sun deity, the abused sister of the Moon Spirit. These are the women who shout into the night sky in pursuit both of a spiritual connection and to assuage their families' hunger. Perhaps *Durga*'s best known story has her mounted on a lion or tiger which carries her to fight the Buffalo Demon which she destroys.

But Margaret was a real person and while these mythological interconnections harmonise with Tikiġaq stories, they are, in relation to Margaret and Tulugaq, largely associative.

Later, I learned the Sanskrit words *tejas* and *tapas*. *Tejas* is splendour. *Tapas* is burning spiritual energy. Durga had both. And I associated these attributes with Margaret – most particularly when she entered Tikiġaq's annual dog sled race. The temperature in March 1976 was thirty below zero and while the men dressed in parkas, Margaret roared home in a T-shirt. The fact that she'd won was just part of the mystery of how her *tejas* or her *tapas* warmed her.

Margaret also hunted, fished for sea trout in the summer and worked in her father's whaling crew. Just as Ataŋauraq broke taboo by taking women on the sea ice to reinforce his crew in 1884, so Kayuktuq, like everyone, inherited his ancestor's boldness.

It would have been dangerous to pursue infatuation. And I grieved helplessly for her fifteen years later when she lost her daughters in an accident from which she can scarcely have recovered until her own death.

If there was anyone who made me weep, it was Margaret – which she did, both later for her bereavement, and also when she attacked me one evening during the period of her seal flensing episode. It was a flamboyant shaft she let fly. And I felt I had been wounded by Durga or an Amazon, as though she had galloped past and casually discharged an arrow.

A propos of nothing much, and in the middle of a card game at which I was a spectator, Margaret shouted at me after somewhat feebly I'd said something in Inupiaq:

'I know. You've come here to steal our language!' And not having the sense to receive this is as nonsense I went out to weep. I was wounded, I suppose, because I both repudiated Margaret's accusation, and also because I believed in the partial truth of her anger.

It would have been useless to try parrying Margaret's accusation. I made the same mistake when Q wanted to beat me up and tried to get me to fight. I, on the other hand, wanted to talk our problem through as though in a Big Sur encounter group. The problem lay, however, in an insoluble combination of Q's anger and his disdain for my ethnicity.

'Don't smile at me, white man,' he muttered audibly in the post office queue a few days later. 'I shall always hate you.' Inupiaq friends of mine overheard this remark and shifted uneasily. The corrugated iron walls of the post office would have enclosed an uncomfortable place to stage a dialogue.

Similarly Margaret's awareness of historical injustice must have been what burned her. Yes, the white man had, in a sense, stolen Inupiaq. Or rather, people, in response to a hundred years of culture contact, had started giving up their language. And while Margaret inherited the burden of this, she perceived me as a representative of accumulated forces. I was here, after all, as a post-contact outsider. However benign my motive, I wouldn't have been in the village if traders and missionaries hadn't blazed the trail.

Both of us were older when I visited Margaret and an adopted daughter on my final trip to the village in 2009. She had spent many years assembling artefacts. Much of Margaret's collection was from nineteenth-century *iglu* ruins. But she'd also dug up older, Ipiutak relics. She laid one heavy piece along her palm. It was the effigy of a seal in fossil ivory, and together we admired its tranquil beauty.

Seal Meat, Seal Souls and the Souls of People

A few days after the flensing episode and during a visit to Kayuktuq's house, I was offered meat from the seal that Margaret had worked on and which had been distributed between the hunter's household and relatives. Several of the elders were given shares. Given that I'd participated in the original hunt, I was offered a portion. Traditional proprieties of distribution continued to be the way people looked after each other.

As I sat at Kayuktuq's and ate a seal rib, I remembered what the shaman Aua had told Rasmussen in the Canadian Arctic. 'The greatest peril in life lies in the fact that human food consists entirely of souls. All the creatures that we have to kill and eat have souls... which must therefore be propitiated lest they take revenge on us for taking away their bodies...' (Rasmussen 1929:56)

'What's happened to this seal's soul?' I wanted to ask Kayuktuq. And I heard in his imagined reply an agnostic or perhaps Christianised silence. We ate quiet. And the meat we consumed was as material as the chickens for which my mother used to pay the postman to strangle for us after the war.

The vast apparatus of pre-contact human and animal soul theory had, at the latest by 1960, become a thing of the past. The old ways were beautiful and complex and had informed life for hundreds of years. But as both Christianity and materialist relativism took root, it became underminingly apparent that most of the pre-contact spiritual order was an illusion. Promoted by the shamans, who themselves represented an orthodoxy of believers, spirit world metaphysics were a deception which in Tikiġaq more or less collapsed with the arrival of the missionaries and the 'Heavenly Father''s afterlife.

But there was no more reason to believe in these latter day propositions than there had been to credit the existence of a moon spirit. And while the church functioned to promote social order, it had, by the 1970s, become difficult for younger people to take its teachings any more seriously than they did ancestral beliefs about which they knew no more than they did Episcopalian theology. There continued to be church stalwarts but the majority lived in an agnostic medium. The consequent emptiness was familiar to me who lived within the same relativistic order.

Christianity and secularity developed in parallel and one was a version of the other in that both obliterated the processes that connected people to life forms. Christianity was an enclosing system. It took place at church and in the presence of priest and congregation. A convert could leave church filled with optimism and a sense of having been blessed. Such feelings might be lifelong and infuse someone with the experience of grace. The convert might thus also become liberated from taboo anxieties and withdraw from complex soul theory. The important thing now was the integrity of the Christian soul and avoidance of behaviours forbidden by the new orthodoxy. But animals and things no longer had souls. Christianity had de-animated the environment.

The new religion was also an ambiguous good. On the one hand it homologised the risk of departure from inherited standards, whatever inherent dangers these implied. On the other, it offered a benign spirituality and a structure to replace what had started falling away. The church was safe, and remains today a place of good works in which the worth of an individual is validated by standards of personal virtue, respectability and commitment to ecclesiastical activities. From the outset, it offered a haven from the uncertainties of animism and also suggested positive things to do. To attend church advanced the assurance that you were a worthwhile person.

To a population remote from centres of political power, the church was also a manifestation of national government. Traditional practice involved continual adjustment to uncertain regulations, part of whose rationale was to work within an environment of instability. Church attendance was relatively simple. It involved a series of actions taken in the course of a well-defined schedule. And to 'believe' was to say and think in ways that were less trouble than the performance of the myriad actions demanded by taboo.

During the period of my work in Tikiġaq, I became a typical liberal leaning supporter of inherited ways. And, as Mrs Charlotte suspected, an opponent of the evangelists. Such was my somewhat crude position, but it was unspoken and I was always on friendly terms with Christians, albeit white people knew that I was a free-thinking Jew and Inupiat assumed that I was a loosely affiliated Christian. Whenever I attended church in Tikiġaq I was given to understand that I was being a good boy and getting back on the rails after semi-involvement with archaic doings represented by what one of the shamanistically informed elders was telling me.

In an earlier section I have reproduced the account of Asatchaq's birth. My tendency as Asatchaq's student was implicitly to applaud his parents' conservatism and the implication that the baby's family had distanced itself from the village in an act of resistance to modernisation. And this was in order to initiate Asatchaq into the old dispensation, a gesture that might have been difficult within the intercultural cross-currents of nineteenth century life. But it would be simplistic to adopt a judgemental position from which to condemn the Inupiaq/American compromise. The old ways were of value but they did not represent an absolute good; nor, *de facto*, is modernism an evil. The truth is more complicated: partly, taking the issue of religion as a measure, because Christianity, by the mid-twentieth century, had lost the hold it had established by 1920.

By the 1970s, in the face of alcohol and drug abuse, the church also functioned as a haven. It also offered careers, ritual paraphernalia, and a secure place in which to pursue virtuous conduct. And as in the aftermath of Daisy's death, it offered consoling support and a means of retreating somewhere that people could both reveal their hurt and draw on the comfort of belonging.

The Traditional Dispensation and its Ambiguities

It was partly because the church offered comparatively little to people under forty, that pre-modern and pre-Christian lifeways appeared attractive. I was, in this connection, encouraged in the work of trying to 'save the culture'. 'We've lost our heritage,' was another frequently expressed opinion. 'We don't know where we come from. We've lost touch with how our ancestors lived.' Q who later threatened me with violence, expressed a similar opinion: 'Carry on, you're doing a good job. The old man will tell you what we want to know,' he said.

I was both encouraged and depressed by comments like these. Many came from teenagers. And it was helpful to have my efforts reinforced by younger people whom I felt I was working for. I believed in what I was trying to do and idealistic about a project that Asatchaq himself was promoting. (Asatchaq would retire that summer, and he died in his carehome in 1980.)

Rather like a child who grows up in the care of a healthy adult generation and who takes for granted its own longevity, I assumed that the village I knew in the mid-1970s represented an enduring reality. I took for granted the continuing existence of Asatchaq's generation and of those born before 1920. These tradition bearers would be here for ever and I valued them. Their lives would, however, in reality, be limited and I was lucky to have arrived in time. Thirty years later most of them would have joined the ancestors to whom they had introduced me.

Local opinion was both personal and generational. But degrees of cultural identification were mixed and indefinable. What young people meant by the 'old ways' was often vague and represented dissatisfaction with the present. Rainey and Dives Qukuq, in 1940, drew up a partial list of pre- and post-contact activities and the same could perhaps be attempted over later generations. Neither Krauss nor Kaplan assume that education programmes promote linguistic fluency. What they can provide is familiarity and a feeling of connection. The Inupiaq language belongs after all to specific places and describes them in detail impossible in English. And today's people who grow up in such places are entitled to be in touch with lapsed speech patterns. It is the same with the rest of the old order. The alternative is to be born into a condition of rootlessness in the very place to which one belongs and where the ancestors put down roots they were incapable of protecting and extending.

But those ancestors were themselves transitional people. Their lives, beliefs and habits were changing all the time. Such changes were often imperceptible: there existed frameworks of practice which, given the old world's slower pace of change, could be identified as orthodoxies. Once Euro-Americans arrived, changes accelerated. Still, one characteristic of the fast changing modern age is the desire to be in touch with the 'traditional' world and the increasingly inaccessible identity of what appear to be stable forms.

Past and Present. Time and Change

Margaret's artefact collection was beautiful but not unique. In June 1977, on the day that two RCA engineers activated a TV satellite dish, I was mortified to discover that large numbers of people owned collections they'd excavated. Having thrown the TV switch, the operatives toured the village, mopped up private collections and flew out with full shoe boxes.

I spent long hours beach combing, and would have been a collector if I hadn't been shy of obtruding an apparent financial interest into sub-surface Tikiġaq. I was already paying my informants for verbal *navraat* (old things) and was embarrassed by the prospect of appearing to be a greedy tourist. I was, in fact, involved in a long-term collecting activity. And however idealistically I might frame the project as an act of reclamation, it predicated a process of hoarding.

On the floor of my cabin lay the floppy compartmentalised canvas holdall that I'd bought in Chicago to take on holiday and into this I threw the cassettes on which Asatchaq and other informants had recorded songs and stories. Logistically I was a beginner, operationally a buffoon. Tukummiq would talk about the old man 'filling' a cassette. And that's how I started to experience the materialisation of time, memory and narrative that Asatchaq and other old people imprinted on my little plastic tablets. Casually, I tended to side step this accumulating pile of recorded orality, but was gratified by moments when I could snap a tape out of my SONY and drop it, having scribbled information on the label, into the bag that lay on the floor.

Visits to this village inevitably made white people greedy. And I was no different. Awareness of past realities was overwhelming, rather as when Driggs's temporary replacement, E.J. Knapp, recorded what he called an atmospheric 'weirdness':

> 'a short distance to the southward [of the village] is the weird Eskimo graveyard two miles and more in length by about a third of a mile in width... Exposed to the weather the jawbones have bleached so that they resemble trunks of blasted trees, and the bodies have dissolved. Many of these ancient so-called graves have fallen into utter ruin and the bones and clothes that shrouded the dead lie scattered on the ground.' [Knapp, Letter, July 29 1904]

Like Bishop Rowe, Knapp sketches a picture of strange colouration: the grey/white bones of the Tikiġaq dead with flowers and driftwood crosses rising among them:

> 'It is a curious sight... There are human crania and other bones lying above the surface of the soil, but it is pleasant and hopeful to see growing up among them delicate wild flowers of the most beautiful forms and colors – the daisy, the yellow poppy, the forget-me-not, both blue emblems of the resurrection...when these dry bones shall live. And more hopeful still it is to see the rude wooden cross that marks the more recent graves where rest the bodies of the Christian dead, sometimes buried under the ground, but as often placed above it...' [Knapp op.cit]

And sometimes I felt that while Tikiġaq's interior and anterior history no longer existed, that past exerted so strong a presence that it pulled one down and backward as though exerting a gravitational drag that inevitably would take one with it. We tend to imagine the past as a fantastic and partially comprehensible dream. What happened long ago exists in narratives and memories and even when materialised into contemporary media, it remains dimly out of reach, a film-like, one-dimensional backdrop to the concrete nowness in which we experience tangible and ongoing present movement.

The opposite in Tikiġaq seemed sometimes closer to the truth. While the past – whether it lay in dark, cold tundra or in enigmatic narratives, even when these must be excavated by intrusive ethnographic pestering – was present reality. Some of this, in the shape of burial relics and animal bones, lay visibly on the surface revealed by snow melt and in summer grasses.

But the weight of the past, its vast, dignified and largely unknowable accumulation, lay mostly hidden, albeit magnetically drawing the mind to dwell in its presence, a presence that even given the prior, biological fact of death, refused to die and was still here animated in its own afterlife while the present flitted above it: and that it was the present that constituted the unreality: our shared, changeful and indeterminate now-ness with its transient, mobile, superficial procession of calculable minutes which were haunted by our sense – in comparison with the semi- or imaginatively perceived wholeness of what lay behind – of incompleteness.

*

While in the mid 1970s I still longed to engage young people in my research and create a communal initiative, I soon began to realize that I was really more of their party than that of the elders, and this generated in me a kind of inertia that suggested that I should simply live in a present as experienced by teenagers.

But with this difference. I had the enthusiasm of a quasi-evangelical newcomer. For the kids, any serious curiosity about the ancestors was a fact of life that would outlive elders. And I too was a modern person, hovering between varieties of western cultures. Thirty years later, the North Slope Borough commissioned me to write a social history of the village for high school students. But this would not be published for yet another thirty years. Here was another demonstration of change and the ambiguous impact of a white man's enterprise, though it had been commissioned by Inupiaq people.

*

The history of social change is too complicated to be summarized and the process of change also changes. Here I can only identify two aspects of the transformations that moved through Tikiġaq when commercial hunters arrived in the 1880s. These two mutually connected changes lay in the phenomena of both language loss and secularisation. True, Christianity had partially replaced animism by the early twentieth century. But in so doing, the church had swept aside the mass of spirit lore that had infused existence and whose metaphysical theories connected all departments of life, from whale hunting to the rituals surrounding eating and child birth.

April 1976 Tulugaq Walks out on the Sea Ice

One afternoon at the outset of the whale hunt in early spring, I watched Tulugaq leave the village and launch himself onto the sea ice till he disappeared behind a pressure ridge. Straight backed and alone, he walked fast and purposefully and unlike a seal hunter who would have carried rifle and backpack, Tulugaq strode along empty handed.

What was he up to, travelling that afternoon into the immensity? Tulugaq was a thin young man and, more to the point, he was doing something weird with his arms as if priming his body for take off. He held his arms bent at the elbows and he was pumping them forwards and backwards, as though ploughing the air with wing stubs. Perhaps with his namesake in mind – the Raven Man who had created Tikiġaq – Tulugaq accompanied his progress with a raucous, throaty howling as though hatching himself into a complication of the traditional and the secularly liberated.

Yes, Tulugaq ('raven') was croaking convincingly like the ravens he'd watched circling over carrion on the cliff tops. Maybe he was stoned. He certainly seemed happy and happy to be alone – though he was moving in the direction of the family skinboat where his father and uncles were watching for bowhead, talking Inupiaq.

Whether or not he had tuned in to the Raven myth that he'd read in my notebook, Tulugaq communicated a solitary, euphoric freedom. Liberated from taboo, free like a detached observer, to visit his father's whaling camp, munch doughnuts his mother had fried in seal oil, free to sit and, like his father's anthropologist, observe Tikiġaq's hunting practices as they had evolved, free to come and go, stage fights on dry land, sleep with girl friends and insist on his own kind of food. Free, not least, to squawk and bellow, whether or not he was associating with the mythic namesake he had encountered in my folder of translated stories.

The Coexistence of Tradition and the Modern

It was hard to believe that my ramshackle cabin in modernizing Tikiġaq and the world of Asatchaq's imagination inhabited the same sixty-sixth parallel north. It was as though, once the engine of America had driven into the village, it infused everything it touched. The past had been quiet, tightly interwoven and conducted at low volume in a language impenetrable to outsiders. Tikiġaq's was a culture of gestures and accomplishment which had been pursued for its own sake: difficult things achieved for the reward of continuation and the satisfaction of rightness. It had never been a culture like that of early Buddhists preoccupied with spiritual purity or detachment. There had been vanity, competitiveness and cruelty. But these are global behaviours and Tikiġaq was a place like many others, except in that periodically it had exchanged ideas with other Native societies and patterned them to existing custom.

And just as the language operated its own extravagant and severe coherence, and things in the pre-contact period, in ways locally understood, fitted together, on the arrival of America with its homologising ambition, the culture became asymmetrical and experimental. Some aspects of this lopsided synthesis had been materially beneficial. And most people breathed easily in their freedom from shamanistically supervised taboo limitation which had operated more 'thou shalt nots' than Christianity.

*

I wasn't on the sea ice the day when Tulugaq arrived at his father's whaling camp so I can only imagine his experience.

Tulugaq's father, Kayuktuq, had assembled three men like him in their fifties; the six others were younger hunters. Kayuktuq's was one of the fiercest and most competent of the thirteen whaling crews and expressed an energy that counterpointed the immensity of the whales they anticipated.

I'd visited them once during an idle afternoon when I was on leave from Umik's more modest hunting outfit. And on another occasion watched them paddling between ice floes. The image, during the moments they came into sight, of eight men bent forward and concentrated on their agonizing labour against wind and current was both intimidating and impressive. It was as though they didn't have to succeed. They were already where they belonged and represented, each figure ghostlike but compact in the white snow shirt that covered his parka, an opaque knot of power that was sufficient in itself, an insignia of rightness, performing, in their inherited environment, what Inupiat must do and which defined them.

Projecting from the bow to the right of Kayuktuq's brother, lay the wooden harpoon shaft. Kayuktuq sat high in the stern, while all eight men, with harpoon ropes and buoy, rifles, knives and grapples on the *umiaq* floor, paddled in rhythm. The *umiaq* was a thick-packed artefact, every part of which was lashed, sewn, stretched and minutely adjusted: a composite of sealskins and driftwood, its ribs and framework tense and flexible. A part of the marine environment, like those animals who spent their lives feeding on environmental plenty, its own endeavour was to prey on fellow creatures.

Traditionally there had been year-round rituals that regulated the hunt, though between June and October people could partially forget about them while they were away from the village in the semi-secularizing daylight. The ritual cycle was in the autumn and included singing, masked dances, puppet plays, shamanistic gestes, narrative sessions, competitive games, gift exchange and feasting. This was the period when skinboat owners began to assemble their crews against the spring hunt and also put together the equipment and food that would support the enterprise.

All the *umialiks* who weren't themselves shamans had their personal shamans who communicated with helping spirits such as the moon spirit, the *itivyaaq* spirit family and the spirits of *nuvuk* (the peninsula point) which must be propitiated as the crew moved across the land and sea ice boundary.

Skinboat owners observed dietary and sexual taboos and female *umialiks* both enacted whale behaviour on the sea ice just before the hunt and then retreated to their *iglus* where they sat passively in enactment of submissive whales. The sea ice vigil was, for the male hunter, further ritualised through dietary abstention. Men on the watch ate nothing but raw, often frozen, caribou meat. Each crew member had his own magical songs. And new songs were contributed by shamans in addition to charms sung to the whales, to the wind and to sea ice as well as to the harpoon and the harpoon float with its humanoid face mask and, not least, to the *umiaq* itself. Each part of the subsistence assemblage was thus dignified with otherwordly import.

Kayuktuq and his Crew

In spring 1976, Kayuktuq's crew spoke a mixture of Inupiaq and English. But even their Inupiaq was varied. One man had spent half his life in Barrow and so moved between related, though sometimes identical, dialects. Another had been raised by his monolingual grandmother and expressed himself in a slightly archaic idiom. The dialect spoken by the fifty-year-old Kayuktuq and his brother represented robust twentieth century Tikiġaq. And while the younger men spoke well, their vocabulary was limited. The teenaged Tulugaq and a couple of his near contemporaries knew only a scattering of words.

To a very partial speaker like myself, the sound of an Inupiaq utterance was mysterious and musical: each sentence-length a polysynthetic aria of noun and verb stems linked together with transformative intermediate connectives whose internal structure communicated in an arabesque of mutually coordinated inflexions and whose combined interaction gave rise to the projection of linear, straight ahead sense, albeit with digressive side observations.

For Tulugaq, also, this display of the expressive, represented a mystery that he accepted as the way things had been and part of which remained current for a limited period as partially performed by his father's generation. He understood the issue of language moribundity and regretted it.

When the generation of our fathers is still active, we tend to project longevity, even immortality, onto its existence. We imagine it to be an omniscient regime that intensifies the childish sense we have of our own low status. But that is illusory. Tulugaq knew, that Kayuktuq's represented the last cohort to speak Inupiaq with competence and thereby knew things that only the old language could grasp. The language was what enabled the eye and the mind both to see and comprehend existential complexity. With the death of the language, the realities within that complexity, would become inaccessible.

*

To an outsider, the spectacle of eight men sitting next to their canoe might represent a simple picture. And to a straightforward question, they'd most likely respond that they were just on the look out for whales. Indeed, that's what one might derive from a surface view. Heine, with deceptive simplicity, summarized such an impression in one his North Sea lyrics:

Wir sassen am Fischerhause
Und schauten nach der See [8]

Heine goes on to describe some of the phenomena that crop up in conversation with fisher people as they contemplate the sea: things both observed and imagined: a lighthouse, a ship, distant coasts, unknowable strangers. The poem is filled with the melancholy of inertia, an ambience of enclosure limited by the ordinariness of European weather and intimations of imagined experience.

Tulugaq's experience might likewise have been exotic. For it would have been difficult and perhaps impossible for him to imagine what his elders were seeing and talking about as he absorbed similar views to theirs but without the comprehension that, to them, rendered it recognizable. The ordinary, for Tulugaq, was rendered exotic because he knew, indeed blindly trusted, that there were things invisible to his view that were perceptible to his elders.

I can only imagine what Kayuktuq and his contemporaries observed as they sat and 'did nothing' (*suŋitchut*). The Inupiaq verb form in the negative quoted crops up both in modern conversation and in older narrative. When it occurs, the listener knows that 'doing nothing' describes either a time of peace following work or a hiatus to be followed either by more labour or by an unexpected event. A couple are sitting doing nothing when they are visited by a spirit, or a woman sits on the *iglu* floor during the whale hunt and the spectre of a whale emerges through Tikiġaq earth.

Inupiat are skilled in the art of relaxation and a hiatus between episodes of activity is part of a pattern in the continuum devoted to subsistence, survival and the conduct of a sane life. Indeed, to do nothing signifies knowledge and a control sufficient to letting go.

So far as Kayuktuq himself was concerned, the interval of inactivity had to do both with high status and shared responsibility. To do nothing was to suggest that he and his contemporaries were important enough to abstain from action which would take them down to the level of younger people and that these latter could be expected to look after the details of action.

---

[8] 'We were sitting in a fisherman's cabin and looking at the sea.' The penultimate stanza betrays a Eurocentric attitude to the ethnic other which is of its time:'In Lappland there are dirty people. Flat headed, broad of mouth and small. They huddle round the fire, cook fish for themselves and screech and yell.' Written ca.1825

*

Warum
Soll es eine Vergangenheit geben wenn es einer
Zukunft gibt? [9]

'It's another world. And another view,' said Tukummiq about the sea ice vigil. She was speaking about how the village emptied during the whale hunt, observing in particular the sudden uprush of commitment among younger people some of whom were underemployed. It had been a long winter and sometimes there wasn't much to do. Individuals were now swept into a communal project in which their participation was needed, an enterprise to which they could belong and which offered collective meaning. The whale hunt transcended everything. As a member of a whaling crew, an adolescent could transform into an adult and identify with tradition. 'This is our life. We are whale hunters. That's tradition,' a couple of sixteen-year-olds put it to me.

*

I'll revert later to specifics as observed, as I imagined, by Tulugaq at ice camp. Here, I'll briefly trace two instances of change in ritual practice, the abandonment of, or uncertainty about, taboo regulation in the late nineteenth century. First, as demonstrated by the shaman 'chief' Ataŋauraq. Second, as preached by the anti-shamanistic prophet Maniilaq in the Kobuk region during the same period and whose teachings reached Tikiġaq in the mid-1880s.

Ataŋauraq Violates Taboo

Here, the American trader Charles Brower gives an account of Ataŋauraq's whaling camp when after a two day wait on the sea ice, the crew finally struck a whale:

'We were no time in getting the boat, to chase after our whale, but before we left the ice Ataŋauraq started to sing his whale

---

[9] Why should we be given a past if we're being given a future? From *Warum soll mein Name genannt werden?* Bertolt Brecht

song, as he told me after, it was a very powerful charm and had been handed down to him by his father, and was never known to fail. *Avataqsiun* (a song to make the whale float rise and buoy up a harpooned whale) is the name of these songs. Every man running a whaling (crew) had one and each was different.' [Brower n.d.vol 1 part 1:64]

The next scene contains a sudden innovation:

'After the meat had been disposed of, the [baleen] was divided. Our boat took a fourth and the rest was divided share and share alike among the rest of the *umiat*... While we were working the whale, the old chief thought it would be all right if I sent in to the village and had my oil stove and some tea and hardbread sent out, that we had already killed a whale, and if we lit the stove and made tea back some distance in the rough ice, the whales would not know it. This I also thought would be all right with me, so he sent one of his wives in for what we wanted. They were not gone long and that tea surely tasted fine. The old fraud, however, would let none of the others have any, making them believe that he alone had enough influence with the evil spirit [*tuuŋaq*] to do these things that were forbidden.' [Brower nd. 68]

This was a turning point in whaling practice and it was perhaps inevitable that Ataŋauraq should have been at its centre. To light a fire on the sea ice represented the taboo violation that moved people directly towards pragmatism and convenience. Given the 'chief's' influence, the event led to further breaches which would lead to ritual erosion. Like most of his contemporaries, Ataŋauraq had seen white men catch whales without ceremonial precaution, and Brower's record shows Ataŋauraq acting on this perception. As with Ataŋauraq's cooking innovations, this incident would have its impact on the role of women. Women previously were permitted on the ice only after a whale had been taken. The consequence of Ataŋauraq's decision reached into the modern era. Women subsequently would spend long periods on the ice.

Ataŋauraq soon regretted his taboo-breach, and learning that crews to the north who had remained in taboo had taken three whales, he decided that the spirit which had told him that he would catch three whales may have been displeased:

'At once Ataŋauraq was jealous of their luck, and we had to get everything in the boat quickly, and started up the flaw looking for another place to haul out. He told me he thought that maybe the devil (*tuuŋaq*) was angry with him for letting me have the tea on the ice. At any rate we had not been in our new place more than four hours before we had another whale come right close to the canoe. He finished his spouting and went down just out of our reach.' [Brower n.d.vol 1 part 1:70]

Ataŋauraq now caught a second and bigger whale, and after the crew had towed it in, they returned to the village for fresh clothes:

'…we stayed ashore three days. The first night ashore, a woman died in the village. As soon as she was dead, the body was placed on a sled and taken about two miles up the sandspit. Ataŋauraq was all worked up over the death of this woman, and he told me that it was a bad thing to have her die just at that time, and to make it worse the woman was pregnant.' [Brower n.d.vol 1 part 1:71]

Having vacillated between the pragmatism of the tea episode and a suspicion that he had done wrong, Ataŋauraq now plunged into personal involvement with the latest taboo emergency. Ataŋauraq's relationship with the deceased is unknown. But the death of a pregnant woman during whaling might affect any crew which had a connection with her. As a leading *umialik* and shaman, Ataŋauraq took the woman's death as a matter demanding personal intervention:

'However, as he was a great shaman, [Ataŋauraq] thought he might be able to do something, if he went into a trance and heard what the devil had to say. This he promptly did. As before, he worked himself into a frenzy, and while in this trance said that the woman's body had to be opened and the child taken from her, the body of the child to be wrapped in sealskin and buried separate. If this was not done there would be no more whales taken that year.' [Brower n.d.vol 1 part 1:71]

Ataŋauraq ordered four women to operate on the cadaver. 'Every superstition that these people had', he perceptively remarked, 'seemed to me to have some bearing on their whaling.' It came, therefore, as no surprise that Ataŋauraq now looked forward to the third whale which had been prophesied. Later, Ataŋauraq accomplished this. And while all the other boats remained out on the ice, chief said that 'as he was a big *umialik*, and had enough meat and blubber for the next winter, he did not have to go...' [Brower n.d.vol 1 part 1:76]

Maniilaq – The Kobuk Visionary

Another shift from the forbidden was initiated by Maniilaq in about 1880. Born ca. 1860, the young Maniilaq separated from a childhood shamanistic calling and developed a relationship with a 'source of intelligence' which came to him in birdsong. There were both shamanistic and proto-Christian meaning to Maniilaq's claim that his 'source of intelligence and of thought' lay in *taatagiik,* a father-son spirituality. As recorded in the early 1970s by Christian elders, Maniilaq's mother insisted that her son's experience was shamanistic:

'You must be turning into a shaman or something,' she told him. 'No, mother,' he replied, 'I cannot say I am becoming anything. However I can now understand what the source of intelligence is saying. I listen with pleasure and it tells me that no harm shall come to me. Mother, I am bringing home a ray of light each time I listen to it... Do not worry, it is only the beginning. I want to listen. I want to learn. I know that something is helping us and that the small bird calls from somewhere, the source of which I do not know.'[10]

Following this inspiration, Maniilaq took on southern river shamans in metaphysical combat and at the summer trade fair in Sisualik and Qikiqtagruk (Kotzebue), around 1880,

'he watched [the shamans] with pity, and sat deep in thought. He felt that an evil spirit was among them and controlled them, resulting in an ignorant people who felt no peace, only arrogance.'

---

[10] For this and all following Maniilaq quotations see *Ultimate Americans*: 251ff. and bibliography.

Maniilaq's sayings fall into roughly three categories. There were straight-forward historical prophecies, assaults on the taboo systems which were enforced by shamans, and there were mystical utterances which, as we have seen, proclaimed a new kind of vision.

Like his attacks on shamans, Maniilaq's critique of taboo came from both intellectual and moral positions. First, Maniilaq was able to demonstrate that taboos were illusory and to violate them had no consequence. Secondly, he attacked taboo which he described as inhumane and tyrannical. It was shamans who enforced taboos and often made new ones, so Maniilaq's dissent was an assault both on shamanism and systems they upheld. There are several stories about Maniilaq breaking ancient prohibitions with impunity:

> 'When a poor girl reached puberty, she wore a parka with a deep-faced hood which hid her face so completely that men did not see her for a whole year. She was made to live away from people in a winter home built by her parents... Maniilaq said he felt compassion and pity for the poor girl. He told the people, "The custom of shunning the girl will no longer be practised."'

In a longer story, Maniilaq demonstrates the unreality of taboo regulations by breaking taboo in public:

> '...one time he went across to Sisualik. The people there considered it dangerous to eat fresh beluga skin and blubber mixed with something. To prove that they would not die if they did eat it, Maniilaq mixed the food in front of them. They fearfully moved away from him but...he showed them that there was actually nothing to fear. He did not become ill or die.'

As he said about a previous demonstration: 'There is nothing to fear. I have demonstrated the freedom that is to come...'

Maniilaq's prophecies about the future were relatively straightforward. But his predictions of technological changes seem also to have been sanctified by the divine authority he had reported to his mother:

> 'Everything will change,' Maniilaq said. 'This information I receive from my source of intelligence.'

Looking back, it is as though material progress was being interpreted as an expression of and an accompaniment to, Christianity. But the majority of Maniilaq's prophecies appear to describe air travel, motor transport and the telephone. For example:

> 'He said that people would travel through the air. Hearing this, the people found it hard to believe him. So great was their disbelief that they laughed at him and said that he was speaking nonsense.

> '…he predicted that strange visitors would come from the east and travel down the Kobuk through the sky.

> 'He predicted that people would travel in their boats simply by sitting, without the use of sails.

> '…he predicted that people would speak through the air with ease. If a person spoke from a far off place, people would be able to hear him.'

Other prophecies carried mainly symbolic meaning. The following two pronouncements may suggest climate change and the creation of Kobuk River villages:

> 'The two consecutive seasons, whether they be two summers or two winters, have not yet arrived. It would be a time of great hunger, a time of famine.'

One prediction is in a different idiom: Maniilaq's prophecy that a whale would emerge through the earth near the future village of Ambler on the Kobuk river. A storyteller recalled:

> 'The spot where the whale is to surface is very deep. As children we passed it many times. It is so deep, which makes it all the more probable for a whale to appear there.'

This, unlike Maniilaq's other predictions, has its basis in Inupiaq mythology and relates to stories of hilltop whale bones and to whales that rose from land.[11]

---

[11] Lowenstein 1993: part 1

This land-whale prediction stands apart from Maniilaq's reformist thinking about a taboo-free world. Because the whale prophecy derives from folklore and has its origin in an imaginative medium from which he was separating himself, this like his shamanistic 'swallowing' threat, lies within the magico-religious tradition. There may also be other, unrecorded traditional aspects of Maniilaq's thought.

In a similar vein, Maniilaq predicted ca.1899 that Tikiġaq would be destroyed in a repetition of the 1893 storm. This didn't happen. But Tikiġaq did, as we have seen, move to escape flooding in 1975–76. It appears that Maniilaq did perceive the large-scale, long-term dynamics of change: technological, cultural and even environmental: things that hadn't yet happened, but which would happen.

Maniilaq certainly existed, and there are stories of his later years in semi-exile when he travelled north, perhaps in retreat from home shamanists. But perhaps, after all, initially, he represented people, or a slowly evolving social movement. Whatever the case, Maniilaq was, *par excellence,* a transitional figure. A man who lived in a medium of the non-absolute and perceived present generations as living in a provisional, in-between time.

Maniilaq and uivaqsaat

Maniilaq's references to *uivvaqsaaq* (prophetic cult of ancestral return) come in two parts. On some occasions, Maniilaq identifies *uivaqsaat* as an unknown *people* who will 'come round the bend in the river'. '...You shall receive visitors,' he said 'who travel swiftly along the water in a new way.' These people would 'come from the east...'

These remarks are as arresting as Maniilaq's predictions of technological innovation. Here, in his remarks about new people, Maniilaq appears to express intuition of continental space beyond the home territory.

How might Maniilaq have come to the apprehension that white people would travel down the Kobuk River in high-powered vehicles? The absence of hard dates for Maniilaq's biography renders explanation difficult. But there is a relatively secure chronology for the Euro-Americans. No white men reached the Kobuk valley until summer 1883 when George Stoney explored the Kobuk, returning the next year in a river steamer. Travelling two hundred miles, Stoney further penetrated the upper Kobuk by canoe, returning in 1885 with another steamer. Similarly, J.C. Cantwell of the *Corwin* coast guard team, reached the upper Kobuk on a steam launch in

1884 and 1885. By this point Maniilaq had probably left for the north – both to propagate a modernism which reached Tikiġaq and Barrow in the eighties and also in retreat from persecution. And if the first steam launches were there for everyone to see, there would have been no reason for Maniilaq to prophesy on the basis of what had already happened.

This was one expression of the end of north Alaskan shamanism. In parallel, Maniilaq also preached *uivaqsaaq*. When, in 1890, the missionary Driggs arrived in Tikiġaq, *uivaqsaaq* had spread to most of the northern communities and Driggs assumed it to be the Native religion. Asatchaq grew up in this milieu of change. His Tikiġaq family continued to practise many of the old ways, but they too were swept along by the introduction of Euro-American ideas, foods, artefacts and technologies.

*

Tulugaq at Kayuktuq's Whaling Camp

What were these middle-aged men talking about so vigorously in a moribund language? And who am I to record what I couldn't understand? They talk casually in their ancient tongue. I think of the creature described by Solzhenitsyn, dug up in a Soviet camp, whose extinct meat was consumed by starving scientists. In these Tikiġaq mouths, the language is not a semi-extinct material being. It is the medium with which people express themselves. And would they not be astonished should someone burst into their company to catch, as though in a chalice, precious language remnants? Inupiaq, to them is living currency. Just as they sit on landfast ice in confidence that it's durable, so they inhabit this moment in which history has come from behind and drives unknowably ahead, while they know it will isolate them into the sphere of previous generations.

*

I think of William Blake: 'The fool sees not the same tree that the wise man sees.' But the children are not fools, they are simply different and have been hurried into the future.

The young people of Tulugaq's generation might turn their heads and look behind them in regret. But they are powerless to go back. Nor can they make the effort to refuse what modern America can offer. Like the climate change that's already upon them, the power of transformation is unstoppable. The local language and rituals associated with it lived together, and their dereliction was contained in wider issues. Language loss remains a global phenomenon.

All we know is that aspects of language converged in the most minute descriptive evaluation. How, in what way and when in history, the lexicon and its connecting grammar evolved to provide an interpretation of multiply contingent phenomena, is the mystery. It is, in other words, a component of Inupiaq language and a part of its spontaneous and expressive self-presentation.

But we think about this scarcely at all, no more than we might question a piece of wood that we picked up with the intention of carving it. Reduced and washed smooth by water, was it root, branch or trunk? From which river was this detritus cast ashore? Never mind, it has been transformed from what it had been and we may discard it. No one will notice if it serves no purpose.

*

Imagined: An Umialik's Contemplation

Has the trail been broken? And has the transition from landfast ice to ice pack been examined, negotiated and the information relayed to the women in the village? Which part of the right hand sled runner is off centre? The asymmetry could, if possible, be addressed with a compatible mending material or secured with the addition of ice dressing to secure a peg or two that might transfer from upper holdings. This sugar snow will get quickly wetter whether or not we move further out on this present shelf towards open water. Depending on the height of cloud cover, there will be time-of-year thaw setting in now. Which will make for a slower launch trajectory when we decide to push off. That is, once the ice edge gets unstable and we feel the current under us.

Thinning surfaces condition both direction and velocity. You, Tigluk, put your hand on the third rib from the steersman's starboard. It must be stabilized and mended. The umiaq blanket is nonetheless holding and the women have sewn it properly. It's both flexible and taut. Every one of these stitches is coherent and their relationship conduces to flotation. The women have butchered, flensed, conditioned, dried, stretched, cut, arranged together, oiled, sewn these ugruk skins I took last spring and it's the buoyancy of their carriage that we hunt on.

The umiaq has after all a recognizable anatomy. The ribs, joints, gunwale, the harpooner's and the steersman's seats, keel, bow and deck cohere and overall the impression we carry that it is a species that we animate with our presence, having created a collaboration of driftwood gathered high on the south beach which had its origin on land but which came to land again by sea and which we launch under seal skin. It is integrated and complex and we propel it towards the whale's path as though it, too, in hollowness, like us who fill it, needs feeding. And so our wives performed certain libations and sang over the boat just as the men sanctified the harpoon and the harpoon float, while both these things sang back in their own mystical language that the shamans taught them.

All things come in the particularity of language. When we describe what we see, our mouths express things in concretion as the words materially fulfil themselves. Our words have the lexical weight of articulated pieces: harpoon pole, shaft, point, ropes and toggle. And so we give words to ice conditions as wind and water measure out coincident trajectories and transformations.

Spring follows winter. Hard light hatches. We study the sun's progress from the eastern hills out to the ice horizon. It's light and still cold. Migrating species pass our ice camp. Spotted seal and ugruk, whale, beluga, old squaw duck and guillemot, duck species and several gull types, cranes and jaegers – their names, origins and messages, how to use their wings and feathers, beaks and feet as amulets and insulation. Which migrants fly inland to the cliffs and marshes. We see three kinds of hawk and plovers, turnstones, sandpipers and whimbrels. Puffins, godwits, kittiwakes and phalaropes. Geese, terns, sandpipers and dunlins. So species multiply and come to us.

*

They were transitional hunters – recalling as they did their grandparents' administration from whose complicated regime even their parents had started to separate. The present pursuit represented, to a surface view, traditional practice. And this was part reality. These were today's subsistence hunters working to feed their families and supply the community with meat for next winter. They operated a skinboat which in many respects was identical to the pre-contact form. Kayuktuq inherited his *umiaq* and it may have retained some or all of its driftwood framework. Boat frames used by other crews were constructed in traditional style using imported timber crafted in the village or by friends to the south into laths, planks and stanchions. The harpoon pole was a length of freshly imported pine. The shaft and point consisted of metal forged in a mid-western foundry. The rope and float were recent imports. And the harpooner also carried a 'shoulder gun', a blunderbuss-like weapon, a horrifying blunt thing which shot an explosive shell to deal a *coup de grace* into a wounded animal. The shoulder gun was a hangover from a late nineteenth century commercial hunting weapon. Nor was today's *umiaq* fitted with amulets. No seat on Kayuktuq's benches carried an underside whale carving. A cheerful, sometimes sanguinary subsistence ethic prevailed among the crew members and this replaced ritualized obedience to the skinboat owner, ceremonial house affiliation and custom.

A neighbouring crew managed by one of Kayuktuq's contemporaries sent a representative to Asatchaq who was sitting out the whale hunt in his solitary cabin and requested a charm song from the old man in return for payment. Asatchaq acquiesced but insisted on transmitting his magical contribution with his own saliva through which the song's physical reality could be digested. The runner backed away from the prospect of this ingestion. And while some people, local Christians, atheists and agnostics among them, still wanted to believe in shamanistic magic, the runner's refusal typified community reaction to magico-religious practice that the majority found irrational and anachronistic.

Intermediacy

Two people were openly critical of my work. And later I will allude, in a footnote, to Q's attempt to kill me and thereby put an end to the distraction my work represented. Less drastically, Margaret's attack emerged from an impulsion and she later submerged her regret in a series of friendly gestures.

It took me a long time, however, to understand that there was no way to measure degrees of cultural affiliation. All I could determine was that all of us existed in mildly different spheres of intermediacy that prompts us to look back in nostalgia.

Teenagers at Pool Table

On the first winter evening of my 1975 visit, some teenagers conducted me to one of their games rooms: an ex-Jabbertown storehouse-cum-coffee shop, the centre of which was dominated by a pool table. It was in those first hours that I noticed how kids created polysynthetic sentences out of English words slurred together quickly into self-contained sentences.

These boys were Tulugaq's contemporaries and I noticed later that he operated with the same linguistic facility. Thus as Junior asked his cousin when we headed from the Mission building where I'd left my bags: 'Kaffi-shap-open?' eliding the question into a single word sentence. It was there in the coffee shop that I saw how these kids in blue jeans and piratical head gear had absorbed the rhythms of their elders' speech and the coordinated movements of hunters. Later I evoked what I'd felt of their lives in this fragment:

> I'd watched young men at pool in Rock's Coffee Shop,
> self-confidently rolling with their sea ice cakewalk
> round the table: denims and bandanas,
> outdoor-booted, quietly competitive,
> but less to win than figure a trajectory,
> the likelihood of one uncertainty against another,
> the slice, clack and negotiated tangent
> to the stream of movement,
> a pure line tracked in spontaneity,
> shooting from the mind
> across the intervention, space subverted,
> intersected by a maze of transitory angles.
>
> They were casually so clever.
> As though to comprehend the longitude
> of points at a distance were inherent
> in the eye-hand balance:
> any swivel or contortion regulated
> by a small, quick adjustment,
> so the bones were in alignment,
> ribs and pelvis sprung
> in an elastic parallel,
> bodies drawn like compass needles
> to their polar absolute.
>
> In puffs of chalk dust, the clipped violence
> of breaks, shots, slams and ricochets,
> glances off cue-ball streaking down into the pocket,
> was hunt and dance-play,
> dry, hygienic study,

geometric diagram,
of relations they had known since childhood –
along telescopic sights and rifle barrels –
with animals across snowy mountain-sides,
wild fowl shearing down wind in the twilight,
seals popping up in difficult currents,
all things in the grain of habitat and movement,
and whose sudden appearances, so often awkward,
demanded an instant counter intersection.

Part 8

The House of Time

Asatchaq returns from Hospital

No bells rang, no trumpets blazed for Asatchaq's return. Like many western people, I'd lived by chimes, news time pips and announcements ever since we'd listened to the WW2 news that structured time that otherwise seemed childishly indefinite. Now, as I floated, part in the old man's time, part in indecision, things seemed little different. I was waiting for a climax. What this might be lay far beyond imagination.

Early experience in the middle 1940s was followed in the next decades by school mediated myth that washed through text books, sending the mind round Tritons winding horns and other indistinct reflections. Hence perhaps my sense of Asatchaq emerging like a Triton and his horn intact still, sea ice damaged, but still bravely flourished. His return to the village was normalising, soon got-used-to. Not 'six feet under,' as one man commented.

I'd been walking round in aimless fashion and re-met him by chance. He was crawling towards his cabin and pushing a cooker. Someone had laid the stove atop a piece of cardboard and Asatchaq was shoving this towards his cabin.

He was physically depleted but still had fantasies perhaps, of family life. Mrs Charlotte, though he didn't know this, had died some months back. But Asatchaq still planned a restart. With this in view he'd ordered the cooker from his bed, laying out the money I had paid him and State cheques. A social worker helped him. With help, we shoved the cooker past the cabin's threshold. But the stove stayed unconnected. The generator never could have coped with it.

*

The spectacle of Asatchaq on all fours in the snow was terrible. He'd been grunting with the strain and spent the day exhausted. But glad as he was to retrieve his cabin, he took challenges for granted. Just as once he'd walked out to hunt polar bear, he pursued his business, stoically accepting what experience presented.

I was appalled. The sight of the old man in a baseball cap and muskrat parka pushing that cooker on its cardboard wrapping was horrific. Was this, I wondered, put on for an audience? I didn't think so, but remembered Malvolio rushing out in fury – or at least in the spectacle of one. Silence followed. Or was this Lear, storm-bound outwardly? Inwardly determined. Or Prospero dictating with his staff an end that would conclude politically?

None of this, to Asatchaq, was tragic. It was just what happened. 'Well, th' event...' as someone in *Lear* comments vaguely. As though Asatchaq had torn ahead, pursuing the impossible, more like the tortoise in his race against the hare than Lear, shoving an icon of the super-modern.

I wondered what had changed. The old man's illness, his exit and re-entry were small events in a history of which I had the briefest experience. And in my hunger for an understanding, I must be content with partial comprehension.

This was mortifying subordination. I thought of journalists sent out to trouble spots who found themselves suddenly at the centre of an explosion. Something unaccountable had happened. A space was blown open. Unearthly silence. A child's cry. Dogs. Some passing carrion. The character of one thing changed into another.

I'd been arrogant in my assumptions. Things out of my control were happening. They would happen anyway. Here was Asatchaq. In counter-point, the village. The factor of their separation was the one thing that I understood by simply watching. But while modern people looked ahead, Asatchaq, despite the cooker, gazed backward.

*

Two images continued to preoccupy me. First, was the wound hole that Asatchaq told me lay in grasses we'd identify once the snow had melted. I could feel the wound's presence, as though its putative existence summarised the village history: the wounds Tikiġaq had taken, each preempted by the primal harpooning: that life-promoting promise of stability, identity, discrete society that the myth suggested. The wound was both a curse and blessing. Nor was Tikiġaq alone. Every place on earth was struck thus, somehow. People were likewise. The wound of Amfortas: and Wagner's holy yokel, crying out: *'Die Wunde!'*

*

The second image was more remote. It arrived in my mind like newsreel frames from 1900. Asatchaq aged nine or ten was tonsured, bandy legged, dressed in skins and largely monolingual. Adults still pursued the autumn rituals in the two surviving *qalgis*. Children were excluded, and Asatchaq with all the others climbed their families' *qalgi* roofs and lay on their bellies watching the rituals through the skylight.

What Asatchaq saw in 1900:

Below were the *umialiks* and the shamans, whom Asatchaq knew as ordinary people, transformed to sacred beings. Packed together in the *qalgi* (the largest building in the village, ca. 20/20), naked from the waist up, alternately turbulent and silent. All this was awe-inspiring and enchanting.

Watched by children through the skylight there were gift exchanges – meat, equipment, ivory and baleen – shaman séances, acrobatics, hallucinating transformations, human to animal, animal to human, men whose mouths grew tusks and flippers. The children watched the younger *qalgi* men competing: games of strength, skill and endurance. The kids eavesdropped storytellings: words and silence. Watched masked dancers who depicted whales and spirits.

There were drummings and dancing, sea mammal bladders, effigies and puppets hung from the ceiling. Umiaq and kayak models mobilised on sinew. They saw the effigies, the *quluguġuqs,* while men they knew transformed to figments that their ancestors had carved for them, learned *qalgi* songs and memorized the dances. All this seen through membrane. Packed in the *qalgi* was a concentration of the culture's skills and energies. Everything that mattered. This square of window, an intestine's membrane. All this I saw as though in newsreel, reflected from the old man's childhood vision.

Then each took a feather and dipped it in lamp soot and drew a scene from whaling on the *qalgi* rafters. Then they assembled sacred objects and hung them from the ceiling. There were images of polar bears and whales and caribou that the young men carved and hung up for the sitting. There were also the *qalgi's* collective effigies. Some were mobiles worked with thongs. One showed hunting scenes with whales and ravens. Another showed daylight, night, the stars. At the end of four days, the carvings were burned and bigger effigies were stored.

Every October when the sea ice formed this happened. Once the *qalgis* had been cleaned and dried, the men went in and took their places. We children, said Asatchaq, weren't invited. But watching was allowed. So we rushed to the roof and lay down in the snow with our faces on the skylight.

There were benches round three sides of the house and the older *umialiks* sat in the middle with their shamans. All the *umialiks* who'd caught whales hung bladders from the ceiling. All this for the whale hunt.

The children looked through the skylight and watched 'the sitting'. The men sat for several days and did nothing. The young men hung up images of whales, seals, caribou and walrus. These were the *puguqs*; then they burned them. There were also dead bodies, people killed by sickness, scattered round the village.

*

But Asatchaq was here and I could touch him. It was March '76. The blizzards arrived later – when Daisy's disappearance happened. I sensed, however, Asatchaq was living elsewhere. Perhaps I was projecting what the jammed projector jammed in my construction of him showed me. It seemed, however, he was back there, aged nine, gazing through the skylight. Everything in concentration. There, down below, alive, the rightness, nothing improvised, done correctly.

The Origin Myths and their Derivatives

Following the introductory origin myths, Asatchaq launched more recent history. The myths provided structure, from 'back then'; they enclosed existence. But after his return from hospital, Asatchaq introduced new characters who mimed the archetypes, derivatives of myth: the tricksters, strong men, mystics, conjurers, heroes, fakes and isolates, shamans of last century, their hair raising gestes, their quarrels, athletic power, prowess, chutzpah.

It was as if the orderly turbulence he'd watched through the skylight was a version of more recent histories that filled the old man's earlier recitations. The great *All* he had absorbed in childhood, defying the constraints of order.

And woven in among these chronicles was a preoccupation with authenticity: stories of young adepts, who knew one thing only, real experience, unmasked pretenders whose dependence was on precedent. There were three of these stories of youths who proved that there was indeed truth in the tradition.

There were men who had abused this. Such stories of authentification were perhaps an expression of a sceptical tradition that ran parallel to the sacred. But shamanism could be refined, it could made to succeed both for the sake of a specific purpose and also for its own sake. The value of shamanism itself could be valued as could the possibility of authentic self-advancement.

The shamanistic system might be exploited by magicians who discredited the system's authenticity. Shamanism was after all a social institution that society had developed and on whose truths it depended. But the practice must be conducted with sincerity and without subterfuge. The clarity of childhood vision is a familiar theme to Europeans. It existed in Tikiġaq as when the child Tigguasina unmasks an opportunist. Another shaman child had visited the Itiviyaaq, a spirit family, when older shamans only claimed to do so. Such was the authentication, the renewal process.

Great shamans, as these boys became, could nonetheless be difficult individualists who manipulated both other people and their own ambition in order to make their lives work within the existence of a society that needed them. Personal ambition mattered. Strife was necessary to social self-confidence. Stories of renewal did reveal the existence of institutional weaknesses. But the child stories and the events that they described enacted a process of renewal which was achieved through opposition. Perhaps for authentic shamanism to be established there had also to be corruption. This paradox provided a narrative *raison d'être*.

Asatchaq's zeal in narrating these renewal stories perhaps reflected both the enthusiasm of earlier society for straightforward truth. And also Asatchaq's repudiation of the inauthentic as transmitted by his uncle Samaruna.

Christmas 1975

I was with him during two of the Christmas celebration evenings. Part Christian, part pre-Christian, there were gift exchanges and competitive games. Leaning on his Zimmer frame, Asatchaq sat in a rage. I described these events in a letter to my linguist guru:

'Dear Larry, Here is a brief account of one evening of the Christmas week events. There was dancing and singing, accompanied by games modified from the old ceremonial house. The *uuma*[1] dances were the best thing in that there was a sense of ceremony and spontaneous participation because both clan houses were exchanging gifts with namesakes. The presence of adults dancing together, the men's muscular verticality and the gracefulness of female movement generating order. People exchanged goods ranging from household artefacts and children's toys to whole sides of caribou and promises of whale meat.

'Some of the evening events have been compromised by children running and shouting. A trio of boys once got close to Asatchaq who sat fixated both on past images and in denial of the show around him. Suddenly the old man shouted:

"Get out! ... Children!"

'This was the first time I'd seen Asatchaq with children and it was easy to see why he was angry. Two hundred people wandering round for three or four hours, smoke, pop cans, candy wrappers, kids, little central activity or separation of the *qalgi* groups. In a far corner a group of young men had organized a jumping game. This was *paŋaligaa*, a long jump, feet pressed together like a snowshoe hare. I watched this for a while through moving screens of rush and thought both of the animal fables I'd heard eighteen months ago, and in my ethnocentric way, of these lines from Donne

'Tis all in pieces, all coherence gone.
All just supply, and all relation...[2]

The next night, I was squatting on the floor next to Asatchaq watching another game of *paŋaligaa* when he turned to me and said, "These children. No good. Game no good. Not doing it right. Not like old day. It's no good."

---

[1] *Uuma* means 'spouse of namesake'. *Uuma* relationships are close, affectionate and perpetuated through gift giving and dance.
[2] *An Anatomy of the World*

Continuation of Letter: The Chivalric Episode

'Hello again, Larry, I should be telling you about the *qalgi* games. But I'm upset by disorder. Instead allow me a moment of satire.

'It's a chivalric episode. Yes, Sir P, school Principal, has introduced the forms, idioms and figures of duelling and honour to the knights and their squires of the junior High School population. To be brief, he introduces, with full panoply of rule book, terms, equipment and accoutrement, the art of fencing. Ultimate, new *qalgi* stuff.

'Into the disorder of Xmas evening, thus abruptly steps this nouveau Douglas Fairbanks, reborn, and in ringing tenor requests silence.

'Both *qalgis* are represented. All sit to attention on the floor, as the director of combat, voiced in drawled, self-confident authority, announces another 'Tikiġaq First', and pacing the floor, which has been cleared of babies, outlines the technicalities of combat, scoring, varieties of weapon: the foil and sabre and the epee are enumerated and displayed, a month-old fencing squad history, the promise of a girls' brigade in the New Year, and then with a flourish of his great grey leather gauntlet, ushers forth the fencers, who had been huddled in the storm shed. Out they roll, as though negotiating rotten ice, costumed in chivalric tabards, each with headband with symbolic combat colour tying back their tresses.

'Meanwhile, Sir P is jawing to his audience, which astonished, anent settling of scores, fields of honour, windmill tilting and I don't-know-what-not. He may have quoted Horace even.

'Fencing is then demonstrated, with much judicious head wagging from Sieur P. Crisp 'On Guards!', 'Prêt!' 'Advances!', feints, lunges and raddoppios from the settlers of scores, foil correction by the fencing guru's maklaks, and lastly a redouble-ment. The spectacle is greeted in dazed silence, with an *arraa* ('too much') frozen to each lip pair, followed by a hesitant applause, at which the squires exited, returning to the *qalgi*, shyly.

The Old Qalgi Rites. Dereliction and Destruction

It is hard to assess what Asatchaq remembered. I imagined what he had observed in childhood through that square of membrane. As an adult, Asatchaq continued, albeit no longer in the *qalgi* environment, to perform many of the ceremonials he learned. Nor is it easy not to idealise lost forms. I wasn't there in 1900. My prejudice lies in the notion that the autumn ceremonials represented a great seasonally reenacted art form.

Tradition depends on memory. And as the twentieth century installed its own set of prejudices, the self-disbelief that arrived with Christian humility obliterated what had been of value. The *qalgi* ceremonials concentrated the essence of Tikiġaq's thought and skills. These, to the modernizing observer, were barbaric. But nothing in Christianity corresponded to the logic and the fervour of the old ceremonials. And disbelief in ritual efficacy, scepticism as to its coherence, even the beauty of its accomplishment, was lost on the non participant. No one after all had the language to proclaim *qalgi* validity. An art requires no validation from inside. The language barrier added further distance.

That which is useful will anyway fall to the impact of the more powerful. And just as English, the language of power, would sweep away minority languages, so the powers of state and religion, could never tolerate the impenetrable, internally generated and inexplicable language of the *qalgi,* its dances, singing, stories, games, silences, meat exchanges and manipulation of effigies. One against another, the ceremonial houses competed until they fell both to environmental damage and to modernity. Each house generated its own unity, and in turn this gave birth to the solidarity that would at once bond with the world of the non human and at the same time empower the construction of next spring's whale hunting crews.

Humans and animals thus became separated, categorically in opposition. Both, nonetheless, needed to survive. The rituals otherwise were doomed. To survive they must be repeated. The question of depletion applied largely to the human. Long before contact, many lost their lives to subsistence exigencies. Life was brief. The environment hazardous. But so long as they kept singing, the animals would hear, and there were, so long as society could sustain itself, plenty of them.

This was an art which had both its internal rationale and was utilitarian. Communal and with purpose. And it could do nothing to oppose the pragmatism of the American ethic, which proved after all that hunting was determined by strategy and logistics, not magic. The missionary Driggs did squeeze his enormous bulk through the entrance hole of a *qalgi,* probably around October 1900, but Driggs was more interested in hygiene than in the capability of society to sustain its art. *Qalgi* life therefore suffered a quiet demise. What Asatchaq had seen in 1900 would develop into what he watched at the 1975 Christmas celebration. The children he scolded were not the initiates of 1900. Both groups lived at a remove from what Asatchaq experienced as truth. But the earlier separation led eventually to a comprehensive alienation. This would be the old man's source of pain. But he would nurture this privately and it could not be understood.

The Chivalric Episode

Perhaps unfairly I have satirized the intervention of fencing. This, after all, was an attempt to do something, to offer the new, to fill a void, to motivate and engage the teenage community. In this sense it was worthy. It was also insulting, borrowed from Sir P's taste of hobby. It was an arbitrary stopgap. But the insult derived from the same replacement initiative adopted in the late nineteenth century by the missionary Jackson from the theory practised first in Bengal by Rev. Alexander Duff. This was the idea, scarcely exercised by the not very religious Driggs, that focused on 'pulling down' non European cultures before building up a new Christian, English-language-based culture.

Qalgi values were waning. And perhaps there wasn't much difference between the imposition of the American school curriculum and the arcane specialities of honour fencing. If replacement had partially been achieved already, perhaps it was only a bit madder to introduce the settling of scores and fields of honour to impressionable fourteen year olds and to monolingual elders at school expense during the Christmas celebrations. Further, replacement also implied that an American 'Can Do' expressed superiority. 'Look,' it suggested, 'we're in possession of something that works. We'll offer you a demo.' The audience response was collective bewilderment: 'This may work, but it's irrelevant and we've already been converted to Christianity and this is just one more thing we don't understand.'

Some weeks after Christmas, the same teenage foilsmen attended a weekly Native dance class, paid for by the new Inupiaq University in

Barrow. The students dropped their epees and were initiated into dance moves that were in their joints already. This, perhaps, was another kind of replacement. But it made better sense. Dancing was a cultural and historical fit. It represented both continuity and a future.

*

I mentioned tricksters, strong men, mystics, conjurers, heroes, fakes and isolates. And it's shocking not to have not been more shocked. Perhaps in the most outrageous of Asatchaq's narrative company was Qaunnailaq. And here we enter another major theme. I have mentioned Asatchaq's insistence on authenticity and the old man's recitation of child shaman stories. In this he followed a tradition that explored renewal. The phenomenon of Qaunnailaq's story is different.

I never understood this narrative. But on one level, it exemplifies the spirit of the indomitable. Qaunnailaq's history is of a man who fights, murders, steals a woman. Qaunnailaq also indulges in joking relationships that go too far. A man who travels away, to Utqiaġvik, 350 miles north, to brazen out the consequences of his over reaching. Here in the further north, he escapes revenge through a series of athletic gestures, and returns to Tikiġaq having survived virtually every threat to existence.

There is nothing in the story to make the audience admire Qaunnailaq. At least nothing but what is stubborn and resolute. The determination to fight an opposition that may have existed largely as a result of the hero's infractions. And surely this in itself was a sign of the memorable. Asatchaq doesn't invite our approval. The storyteller demands only that the rascal be remembered. He was larger than life. And like the man who became the Moon Spirit, he crashed against taboo in a gesture of individuality.

What was the meaning of these months of recitation? I hope I'm not wrong that the stories gave the old man pleasure. Pleasure is complex, involving a feeling of rightness, the happiness of identifying with the appropriate, even an illusory sense of permanence, though the actual sensation of pleasure is usually fleeting. Yes: Asatchaq was putting something in place and I offered him the confidence that his effort was worthwhile and would last. His pleasure was, moreover, allied to mine. He was filling a need: a demand from the past to bring the ancestral world back and substantiate a reality that otherwise would be lost and that he would lose touch with.

I too was devoted to the past. I believed its validity, perhaps even its superiority, in that past time had been immobilized into something that could be viewed, analysed at leisure. With a little effort it might be evoked and put on display. This contributed to the investigator's satisfaction and it lent distinction. The past represented a badge of authority based on knowledge. Knowledge that had been acquired with difficulty. And for Asatchaq it was a question of alternatives. There was the alienating experience of the Christmas party. And there was traditional rightness. The stories explained that. They were part of the wholeness I imagined him to have viewed through the *qalgi* skylight. The character of, say, Qaunnailaq, was secondary. It didn't matter whether he was a great athlete, a rascal, a shaman, one of the survivors, a fortunate man in possession of the pretty widow of a man he had murdered. Time justified his resurrection. Asatchaq's satisfaction lay in having disinterred that character. He might have done this without me. But I took credit in having made his happiness possible. Therein lay my own pleasure.

In just such a place we met. It was not unlike the experience of reading. I mean that identification with what remains ultimately a symbolic approximate. Even the act of writing predicated an assumption of the imaginative. Reality, in the imagination, could never be set down in characters, the typed pages of a wished isness. The latter would always be separate from the touch of now. It would be absurd to blurt out its existence without hesitancy and consideration. That latter word, I learned, has its etymology in the influence of stars (*sidera*). Hold, in contemplation, what you see at stellar distance and you may inscribe a starlit pattern. But it will remain a reflection. This was not Trudi smacking a home run. What mattered was what she'd achieved in that moment. Such was the enchanted auditorium. And I was happy to be a spectator. Perhaps there existed another reality within that experience? One of the imagination.

Stamm – The Haphazard

Almost nothing can be comprehensibly explained. Perhaps that's why we settle so easily, so lazily, for the absurd. It is a poverty stricken façade, phenomena crumbling with speed, one thing into another. Little hangs together and less even than that makes sense.

I remembered the Hebrew word *stamm* with which Leah had responded to the miscellaneous, haphazard confusion in Fairbanks life. The self perpetuating and adventitious hedonism of mid-1970 urban

America. All phenomena being random, *stamm*. They happen, just like that, *stamm*, rising and falling in an arbitrary sequence, without an antecedent, sequential basis.

'It is the cause...' Othello suggested. There must be a pattern. This was the hero's agony. A generative motive to the inevitable consequence. Isn't this perhaps at the root of some need for religion? Why else should that love-stoned hippie *lerve* me as he'd claimed to? I was just the nearest object.

Events occur. They're endlessly replaced. Seek for some pattern and you're left with the pattern, not the phenomenon you'd measure. Still, this must be a vision the mind turns away from. Mind refuses the absurd, the arbitrary, the *stamm*. There has to be life. And perhaps it's art that conceals the abyss. A screen round terror.

*

But who could subscribe to that reductive negativity? If it's there, its presence must be acknowledged. Still, one may also refuse to hang over that particular skylight in order to look down on nothing.

Inupiaq people understood these issues but they didn't think they were important. Laughter was one medicine. Another was the power-focused logic of animal fable. Asatchaq knew this and it represented a prop against Leah's vision of the arbitrary.

The animal fable is in fact a response to such a vision of the absurd. The fable is simple. Animals confront each other and come into conflict. Smallness has its value and deceit is permitted. But incorporating the arbitrary, the fable affirms the continuity of life energies.

Most of the fables are ridiculous in their exposition. What remains to be said? Perhaps merely that such fables represent a version of truth: the necessity of survival. And indeed, all Asatchaq's stories represented this determination to transcend difficulty or opposition. That which is not good enough will be taken over and perhaps killed. For one party to survive, the marginal must be submerged.

The Idiot Stories

Least pitying of such indecencies are Inupiaq idiot tales. These derisive satires focus on the incompetent and dismiss the life prospects of a purblind and self-gratifying egotism. Idiot stories are in the same genre as animal fables. And they also have a relationship with other Native American tales. The Trickster of the Winnebago, for example, is after all a figure who both deceives other people and who invites equivalent punishment. This latter is the reward both of folly and the presumption by the non-competent of competence.

Trickster thinks mainly of food and sex. He (usually male) lives in want. But his deprivation is of his own doing. Two old women whom Kinnaq, the idiot, has rejected, curse his *usuk* when he's dangled it into their *iglu*. Kinnaq pushes off in his kayak and tries stuffing his *usuk* into his boot, then dragging it in the water behind his kayak. Children run to meet him when he comes to a camp, and when they imagine that he's caught something, they start chopping it up and eating it. All this flows naturally from Kinnaq's character and it represents a contrary to the hunter/husband ideal. The ideal man generates children of his own and comes home with proper food.

In another story, Kinnaq thinks he sees a girl dancing and singing. He rushes after her and she turns out to have been a Short Eared Owl. The owl flies off and Kinnaq is left with nothing. A further experience of incompetence. Solitude and misprision are both punished. People are expected to live within society and not to mistake one thing for another, hoping to gratify themselves. People are also expected to understand the nature of reality. Kinnaq is a victim of his own egotistical projection, and he is punished for misunderstanding the difference between people and animals. Nor does he comprehend the social nature of sexuality.

*

But as in many expressions of truth, there is ambiguity in this exposition. Poor Kinnaq is not so different from everybody else. Kinnaq is ridiculous, but then life remains difficult and everybody makes mistakes. Kinnaq's blunders, for which he will be punished, leave him empty-handed but what happens also looks perilously like a shamanistic experience of a complex oneness, which is perhaps unified only once paradoxes have been brought together. Earlier I described the experience of the boy Ukuŋniq who wandered off and found himself mistaking a ptarmigan for a young woman. This was part of the boy's progressive accumulation of the power that enabled him eventually to live with the 'woman who won't marry.'

The fact remains that Ukuŋniq was deceived by a ptarmigan and her disappearance left him alone. Reality is deceptive and the world of pragmatism is interpenetrated by imagination. This twoness of life's possibilities was one theme of the *qalgi* rituals that Asatchaq witnessed. People could turn into animals and then revert. This happened because the boundaries between one sphere and another were indefinite. Anything could happen. Kinnaq lived at the extreme end of these possibilities. But he was not alone in the experience. And he couldn't be a shaman because he was unable to combine his susceptibility with the pragmatic knowledge of *qalgi* people and the determination of the proto-shamanic Ukuŋniq.

*

But then many of Asatchaq's story heroes were ambiguous. Reverting to the narrative of Qaunnailaq, I have omitted one feature. This brawling individualist, few of whose actions could be applauded by taboo-observant people, was only semi human. For Qaunnailaq's human body enclosed an animal spirit. The story opens: 'Before he was human he went round looking for a mother… who could give birth to him.' There were known to be two such Tikiġaq marmot children and other marmot siblings were born elsewhere. Qaunnailaq's supernatural origin having been established, the hero progresses first to the status of shaman and then to secular humanity. As mentioned, he travels, fights, breaks partner rules, indulges in athletic feats and exposes himself to revenge. Perhaps because he is actually a marmot (not a major power source) the story does two things. First it represents Qaunnailaq as a figure of the indomitable. Second, it lends the story a tinge of the supernatural which an audience would accept as an aspect of reality. These two characteristics, which to westerners might represent a contradiction, existed in parallel. Just as Tikiġaq religion and Christianity lived side by side, so Qaunnailaq's humanity represented one absolute while coexisting with a non rational counter absolute: that is, Qaunnailaq's supernatural origin and the survival of his non humanity. Thus the man's character was presented. And perhaps this was something that could be experienced rather than explained.

Sallaġin: The Physical and Metaphysical

The story of Sallaġin, another story figure, operates on a similar level. But this late 19th century chronicle is interesting because it expresses so much about old Tikiġaq that is at once materially physical and almost physically, supernaturally concrete.

Surface reality and the supernatural depth implied by the physical presence of that reality coexist. In that it contains both elements, the physical and metaphysical, the story is representative of the simultaneous pragmatic and imaginative that marked much ancient thought. This, today has become remote, threatening, wonderful and perhaps it explains the divided nature of traditional people's response to a past world of magic. A minority, on the one hand, regret that absent region of the irrational. But people who are more securely identified with the modern or with what appears to be Christian pragmatism, are happy to let it go. 'What could you possibly want with those old stories?' asked one sixty-five-year-old. She was outraged that I should depart from a modern world that had swept away the archaic. 'None of that stuff makes sense,' she continued. 'And you can't put it in English.'

Perhaps one thing she suggested was that only the old language could cope with it. Would it, however, make better sense in Inupiaq than in translation?

'We've grown up a lot,' she continued, 'since we buried our grand-parents. We understand that those things can't happen. And I don't know if they happened then. They don't happen now.' This was akin to Umigluk's comment about Asatchaq's great uncle, when Umigluk told me that the old shaman only *thought* he'd gone to the moon: that both Asatchaq the older and younger believed in the truth of old stories, but today it was impossible to collude with a harder American reality.

This was not an argument I could take part in. Imagination, is, however, at the centre of Tikiġaq's narrative tradition. And whether or not one believes in their coexistence, the two cohere. To present these worlds, to acknowledge their existence, must suffice. But a metaphorical dimension has, nonetheless, been lost. This is a poetry of a manifold coexistence: things, specifics, spirits, good and evil forces, a sense of multiple belonging, the attribution of meaning to phenomena which subsequently became dead – like the seal that Margaret butchered – limited things with a subsistence utility. Things that existed only within the edges of their seen concretion. That loss of the unseen and of its complexity continues as an impoverishment. A world that had been alive with both meaning and potentiality became stripped down and, from a condition of sometimes uncertain movement, semi-immobilised: 'reified', in 1960s parlance. People, their environment of things, causality, indeed the whole universe, could now, in the post-contact era, be explained in the language of reason. Animism and shamanistic illusion operated in a continually regenerated world of possible meaning. Whether or not there existed a truth in all that complexity, the attribution of truth was sufficient. If uncertainty, or potentiality was an ingredient, there was room for imaginative improvisation. The shape of that world was therefore largely provisional and its asymmetry quintessential.

Sallaġin's story communicates to a modern audience the representation of a world that is unreal: *weird* in both the older meaning of being spiritually pregnant and in the later sense: eccentric and impossible to fit into the conventions of order. At its basis nonetheless existed a life of continuing subsistence. The two worlds lived together.

These are the contents of this strangely representative story:

There is rivalry at the whale hunt. Sallaġin has the upper hand because he is shaman. But Sallaġin's rival constructs a small *umiaq* with humanoid images that come alive. These images take Sallaġin's son, tie him to a whale float and let a whale sound with him. The boy is cast onto ice and is identified by a semi-shamanistic old woman.

The story contains a multitude of images. There is a cast of anonymous people. But the place names are recognizable. And while subsistence, on the one hand, continues with people needing to hunt and eat, the pursuit of game animals involves both pragmatic knowhow and mystical absorption. The traditional milieu is filled with recognisable artefacts: kayaks, bows and arrows, iglus, harpoons. There are allusions to trading partnerships and trade goods such as tobacco. This world of the limited and ordinary is nonetheless infused with magical potentiality and the uncertainties that reside within that sphere. Amuletic animals such as the loon accompany moments of life and death: conditions that are in themselves interchangeable and subject to magical intervention. We recognise Tikiġaq beaches. But events occur there which might go into reverse, while leaving the beach itself, in the ordinary sense, much travelled. It was difficult to experience one without the other.

In Asatchaq's Cabin

Every sound in the cabin is magnified during Asatchaq's recitations into significance. And because they are being produced here and in the presence of a story, I lend them meaning. It's like being enclosed within the outlines of a sonnet. Just as the sonnet offers a space within which subjectivity and arguments are enclosed within formalities the author has chosen, so the cabin provides symmetrical walls within which security may both accumulate and crumble. There is safety in that space, albeit there's a tension within the structure. The mind fills with meaning. To read fourteen lines is an excursion into knowledge. I am left with the impression of having been elsewhere. A brief, passive excursion.

Just as I enjoy such episodes of removal, so I feel reassuringly enclosed within the space of this cabin, and my nescience is a refuge. This, after all, is a place where nothing much happens. All the anxieties of an outside life, whether or not they have led to this point, drop away. The fetching and carrying of oil and water, the experience of hunger, choosing and wearing clothes – none of these matter. Listening is just a moment. But it's one that transcends, albeit without much comprehension. It obliterates obstacles. A calm has descended. This may not always be pleasant. But there is, for a moment, a partial cessation – what Goethe jokingly (?!) called *Lebensfratzen,* translated for me into 'Goblin-like creatures that attach themselves to your trousers when you come downstairs for a dignified entrance; and you can't easily brush them off.'

Yes. I want the story to continue at least until I'm restless. I get bored quickly. Perhaps this is a fault that marks my generation. Impatience for a conclusion, like the rhyming couplet with which Shakespeare releases you from obedience to a difficult thought. The constraints, nonetheless, had been healing. I return to those limits. It is, after all, the writer or the storyteller who does the work. Nothing else matters during his period of domination.

For with Asatchaq, the process is one of subordination. He is approaching the end of life, the quality of which matters. The experience continues to resemble the consolation of the sonnet. It is simply itself, reassuringly limited.

The cabin is ramshackle but is still a weather-tight assemblage. It's like Sieur P's Americanally imported competence. The cabin does its work. The pine and plywood provide working insulation. The walls lean in the north wind while forcing the wind to stream round its contour.

The wind never ceases. It moves in a long stream, battering on occasion, insistent, as though hurled across sea ice from Cape Lisburne. These sudden blows are extra, as though what's long, and even endless, weren't sufficient. Were the wind not there, this wouldn't be the place it is. Like the sea ice which moves, the air is a part of this environment.

I used the word endless. I would prefer to say eternal. Big things are made of small components. To our limited view, the endless is so old that eternity is easily invoked. The north wind seems ageless. Likewise Asatchaq's speech. His voice enacts archaic patterns. With the wind as its environment, the past comes into being. How did this ancient grammar consolidate? What are these old words, now redundant, unrelated to the present?

The bilingual Tukummiq asks the meaning of old words. Nor does Asatchaq resent her post-shamanic comprehension. He understands well that there remain things out of reach. Such matter recedes further. Why, then, say them? They are frozen. Mean nothing to people with no use for them now. Nor would it make sense for me to learn them. No more sense than holding an old artefact. I think of skulls the missionary forgot to move in 1909. He left them lying on the village surface. Their toothless silence. They have survived reburial. Those jaws once spoke a terminology that's out of date now.

The darkness seems solid. Beyond the window there is nothing. Impenetrable weather. For the time being I'm protected. It's warm in the cabin. Time doesn't matter. Someone who's migrated to the new town site has left a dog team in the old village. You can hear the dogs bark in desperate hunger. Someone is visiting his meat cache. He keeps meat in a dilapidated *iglu*. It's dark down there and cold enough. A snow machine approaches. There goes its vibration. Dogs and machinery. The wind forces them together.

There are also internal, domestic noises. The chimney ventilator and the carburettor. The oil burns efficiently. The old man shifts on his commode seat. I take off a sweater. The fibres creak. Tukummiq breathes out. The old man talks to her. She responds with long '*Ii*'-s. All the little sounds converge. But they don't interrupt the storyteller. The three of us form an artificial *qalgi*. Three separate kinds of solitude. Asatchaq is at the centre. A man reenacting old belief forms. It makes us happy for our different reasons. I write him a cheque. He glances at the digits. I tramp out in the snow and darkness. Asatchaq turns into his alcove where he sleeps on a mattress.

Bird Song and Village Noises

It would be easy to look back and construct an historical melodrama. There would be truth in such a scenario though I'd be embarrassed to render its dramatic significance. The elements are simple. Old Tikiġaq, before contact, operated in an environment of silence. This is not hard to imagine. But complete silence would always be compromised by natural noises, and these, in the great spaces, must have been relatively few.

This isolation of noise made people sensitive to sound. Earlier, I quoted Asatchaq's imitation of the Lapland longspur. Perhaps Asatchaq was reviving a childhood of mimicry. Tulugaq, aged eighteen in 1976, reproduced the croaking of a raven as he walked out to the sea ice in a different key.

Given that the raven was his namesake (*tulugaq*), perhaps closeness to that bird represented a rite. Something he'd grown up with. Still, all the animals were companion species in ways in which today's people remain sporadically familiar. To know an animal's voice was to identify its species. There were scores of species and people sometimes developed their own quiet, complicated language for private contemplation or in synchrony with the non-human.

Silence was therefore punctuated by sounds that were as much a part of the environment as any other phenomenon. Some shamans spoke and understood the songs of marine mammals, caribou and birds. There was a terminology for non human speech. Just as the Inupiaq language was *Inupiaq+tun,* so the suffix +*tun* was affixed to polar bear speech (*nanutun*) or gull and guillemot cries. To approach the cliffs in breeding season was to be smothered both in bird excrement and a vast caul of sound vibration. Within that immersion, which was mostly guillemot language, there were the plaintive calls of the kittiwake, and, paradoxically, the silence of the puffin. Asymmetrically penetrating this variety were eagle, peregrine and raven calls.

For children to move from such experiences to the combative conversations in animal fables involved no great distance. We tend, in the West, to sentimentalise or render animal conversations comic. To Inupiat, the instinct of survival was as strong among the non human as it was among people. To speak was to assert oneself. To be human was to be multilingual.

Music was also important. Asatchaq, like many of his forebears, was a composer and it was as natural for him to sing. Asatchaq composed his first song when he was a child – in his case, falling into summer mud. He took his impromptu song home to domestic applause. Old men constructed drums by stretching semi dried whale's liver membrane over driftwood loops. This was another way of celebrating a capture. The drum spoke from the internal depths, otherwise inaccessible, of the greatest species. Everything could speak. In a story told by Bob Tuckfield, human excrement was overheard singing. If pre-contact Tikiġaq was in one sense silent, it was also a place of voices and music.

The story of the boy shaman Aningatchaq conveys the ambiguous nature of that condition – partly, it has to do with attentive listening. As Asatchaq remarked during the course of his telling: 'I too used to listen to them when I was a boy. I listened to the shamans who came back from the Itivyaaq (spirit) iglu.' One aspect of the boy shaman's story has to do with listening. The story is about awareness of place and time, about appropriate behaviour and carefully judging what both the shamans and the spirits tell out loud.

'*Qamma pigatiin!*: *You are wanted*', one of the spirits called to the boy shaman. 'People gathered at the *iglu* to hear what they'd say'. There is drumming followed by disappearance into the spirit iglu. Before this, the boy Aningatchaq listens. One of the spirits has long ears in order to overhear taboo infraction. Following this, the whole community observed silence during the whale hunt. The use of blunt instruments was forbidden. Apart from drumming, singing and the smaller sounds of activity, the encounter of people with whales was conducted in silence. Tying things together and scraping were permitted. But percussion was for the aftermath of a harpooning. Then it could break out on the great beast's otherwise inaccessible liver membrane.

Nathaniel Hawthorne and the Phenomenon of Noise

I had also been preoccupied with Hawthorne's experience. In July 1844, he sat in Sleepy Hollow, which was a peaceful retreat from the complications of encroaching industrialization. Hawthorne, in the conduct of his rest, was attentively listening to natural sounds when his peace was interrupted:

'But, hark!' he wrote, 'There is the whistle of the locomotive – the long shriek, harsh, above all other harshness, for the space of a mile can not mollify it into harmony. It tells the story of busy men, citizens from the hot street who have come to spend a day in a country village, men of business, in short of all unquietness; and no wonder that it gives such a startling shriek, since it brings the noisy world into the midst of our slumbrous peace.'[3] This moment became famous. And in it, Hawthorne summarized the tensions that Thoreau also identified. Mechanization, as Thoreau wrote in *Walden*, was oppressive: 'We do not ride on the railroad; it rides upon us.'

---

[3] Hawthorne, July 1844, writing of a pastoral moment in Sleepy Hollow, near Concord, Mass. *The American Notebooks*.

There are implications here for most Native societies. Since the arrival of Euro-Americans, incomers had been torn between regarding the virgin continent on the one hand as an uncultivated wilderness and on the other as a bountiful garden. It was relatively simple for eighteenth century pastoralists to gaze marvelling at beautiful East Coast landscape. They also followed Montaigne and Rousseau in hallowing the life-ways of Indian people. As Robert Beverley wrote in 1705, Indians had not been

'debauch'd nor corrupted with those Pomps and Vanities, which had depraved and inslaved the Rest of Mankind… For, by their Pleasure alone, they supplied all their Necessities; namely, by Fishing, Fowling and Hunting…[4]

This vision echoes Gonzalo in *The Tempest*, who himself follows Montaigne:

Riches, poverty,
And use of service, none; contract, succession,
Bourn, bound of land, tilth, vineyard, none…

Apart from James Cook, who made a dash up the Alaskan coast in 1778, no Europeans or Americans penetrated the western Arctic until the nineteenth century. And it would have been difficult even for most devoted primitivist to have written lyrically about either the people here or their environment. The Arctic coast was difficult and bleak. White men were reticent, though John Muir wrote movingly about flora atop Cape Thompson. The awestruck Edward Knapp in 1904, wrote:

'a short distance to the southward… is the weird Eskimo grave-yard …Exposed to the weather the jawbones have bleached so that they resemble trunks of blasted trees, and the bodies have dissolved. Many of these ancient so-called graves have fallen into utter ruin and the bones and clothes that shrouded the dead lie scattered on the ground.'

Knapp also sketches a picture of strange colouration: one of the old, metaphysically ambiguous bones of the Tikiġaq dead with flowers and driftwood crosses rising among them…'

---

[4] Quoted by Leo Marx, *The Machine in the Garden*, 1964:77

Knapp's sensitivity to ambience being dominated by Christianised optimism – which may have been spiritual but also noisy.

Asatchaq and Memory

Asatchaq's voice was grainy, quiet, grave, undemonstrative. The stories were, by contrast, often theatrical. Many of his stories contained unlikely details. Asatchaq emphasized little, though he did laugh occasionally. Generally, however, his recitations were in the manner of how things were. What he said represented an uncritical and fluent version of truth as he saw it: the foundations of a societal reality. This non dramatising of the idiom was perhaps idiosyncratic. I met other storytellers whose performances were more excited and demonstrative. Not Asatchaq. It was as though he was simply letting a tribal history through.

Asatchaq was, in this respect, a conduit. The stories didn't belong to him. They expressed an impersonality not in his ownership. What happened in the past and what was repeated about myth time represented realities he had almost nothing to do with. These things were simply there and he responded to them as he did to the climate.

He once drew me a cartoon of himself with the caption, 'Jim tell true stories.' 'Don't get tangled up,' he warned me, 'and then take them to the Governor.' It was the narratives' authority he respected. Just as he hated the Xmas party with children breaking taboo by crossing the path of an elder, so he had no time for frivolities that were not sanctioned by tradition.

'How did you learn these stories?' I asked him.

'Every night I went to Samaruna's *iglu*. There he told me stories and I listened till I knew them. The words are Samaruna's. I repeated them.' The story took place in an environment of silence.

'We didn't have books and tapes,' he might also have said. He respected those props, realizing that they were for younger people. I didn't respond by confessing the limits of my memory. Nor did I confess that I could never commit such an enormous burden to my own brain. Not only did I come from a generation incapacitated by the absence of memory, but the circumstances were different. Asatchaq had inherited a memory skill that modern people had lost touch with. Even his slightly younger contemporaries were in awe of his capacity. I nonetheless took it for granted that he could reproduce so much with so little hesitation.

Still, I expected this of him. It was almost as though, like a solo violinist, he was of a different species. We were empty vessels that rang and echoed in response to a circumambient series of interruptions while he allowed what was in his memory to issue quietly.

Just as the two origin myths lay at the centre of other Tikiġaq stories, so Asatchaq's voice, its unhesitating progression from one thing to another, held me in suspense. I never suspected that he would hesitate or could make a mistake. The story, after all, represented a particular architecture and he would follow those contours. Thus I sat through the old man's recitations, comprehending little, but aware that something was being built. Asatchaq identified with the issue of authenticity and I colluded with this.

There existed, therefore, these components: the old man with his insistence on authority, the monumentality of an ancient language that, for all its crags, flowed easily from him and third, the intensity, at least between December and April, of the outside darkness. This last was isolating in that it stopped the eye in a depth which forbade seeing beyond it, and became a part of the recitation. The darkness was, for me, a story component, an aspect of the environment, connected to the unknowable past from which it emerged.

Just as performance arose in an unhesitating flow, so darkness remained its context. I sat at the foot of this construction. These things belonged together: a language of the archaic, the old man's insistence on it and a darkness, which was past and present, because Asatchaq brought them together.

It was during these recitations that I became aware of the occasional interruption. There were indoor sounds. The stove, the ventilator, a modern audience. But there was a sound beyond, of a snow machine, a mechanical interpolation, post-industrial, of the present. Someone from the New Town Site had travelled down to his storage cellar. It was a Hawthorne moment. The coexistence of the ancestral and the mechanical.

Here, in that distant machine sound, like a prick of light penetrating opaque darkness, was mechanized America. Sleepy Hollow's invasion. This interruption had started in the nineteenth century. America had driven to the wilderness. Asatchaq was, like the rest of us, a transitional person. Here it was though, diagrammed distinctly. The old world conjured in the architecture of a story, and today's world, coexistent with it.

Asatchaq and Past Time

It seemed right that Asatchaq should thus bring the past back and place it in the present. The process felt no stranger than reading an old book. There was life in those stories, just as life jumps into our faces when we read old novels.

I was also preoccupied with Asatchaq's own age. I respected the nineteenth century factor. Anyone, to us moderns, born then, automatically qualified for the status of venerable. To have known the nineteenth century made you an historical figure who emerged from the darkness of past time. That time was in itself dark. It was a tangible medium with its own colouration.

And perhaps time itself, back then, was, in itself, older. Even better. Time in the twentieth century had speeded up and had become disposable. The days passed. But they didn't matter. They would be replaced with more of the same thing, and these newer, devalued days had little consequence, with none of the import of real time with its slow accumulations.

To have lived even for a short time in and before the nineteenth century bestowed honorific status. We call these people 'old timers' and no doubt the phrase communicates meaning both about people themselves and the times in which they lived.

Asatchaq's age was not, however, an isolated phenomenon. It belonged, to the *now,* and it also had its place on the peninsula. Age had its context here. The entire place suggested age, an illimitable history. Perhaps this is part of what the missionary Knapp identified as 'weird'. What follows is a contemplation of age, both in relation to Asatchaq himself and his place in that old place.

Beringia: Contemplation of Age

Gazing west towards Siberia is to experience a dizzying uncertainty about the extent of space, which, while large, is geographically finite.

But time, particularly in its prehistoric dimension, is more difficult to grasp. And to stand exposing one's face to wind that blows from one continent to another is to feel not just present impact but also to experience the flavour of time itself, the taste of something almost too old to put a name to – as though the wind of this moment arrived from ancient Beringia.

As the wind hits the face, one apprehends cautiously the feeling of a double temporality, as though we, too, had laboured across the ice: and at the same time as arriving, one were also waiting for the present: the now and the archaic collapsed into a conundrum in which Pleistocene and even more ancient and modern periods were mutually identified: today's time encapsulated within the archaic and the archaic, like an icy calyx, carrying seeds of the present.

I have mentioned the Pleistocene as though the Ice Age were our neighbour. And it is helpful to keep one foot rooted in an era that remains close enough to stop us from toppling into what is unknowable, though the latter has been studied by scientists who have analysed fossil pollen, ice cores and mastodon intestines. And their scientific 'Before the Present' dates are inscribed in numbers impossible to grasp except in the unintimidated language of earth scientists and archaeologists such as Frederick Hadleigh West, who wrote:

> The time period of concern is the latter portion of the last glacial episode. The fourth glacial was broadly marked by two major cold oscillations with glacial advances, separated by a rather deep interstadial. This interstadial, the "Eemian", had its onset about 70,000 years ago and gave way to the final glaciation perhaps 30,000 years ago. That final episode is estimated to have begun its climax about 11,500 years ago. The end of the Pleistocene is by common consent set about 10,000 years ago – somewhat arbitrary, but a time around which a number of important Pleistocene-Holocene transition phenomena tend to cluster. (West, *American Beginnings*, 1996)

Scientists have called the 'Bering Land Bridge' Beringia, whose 'most striking feature [in the late Pleistocene] is the contrast between the very restricted, localized glaciation and the vast, uninterrupted expanse of unglaciated country extending across the entire east-west dimension of Beringia. The question that then arises is, what was the nature of this unglaciated environment?' West continues:

> 'At this point there is some controversy. There are conflicting interpretations of the Beringian environment. The argument turns primarily on the interpretation of two ubiquitous observations in the biotic record: the presence of high proportions of *Artemisia*

(Arctic sage) in the pollen profiles and high numbers of ungulate fauna…

'Armed with new data on Alaskan fossil identifications and the ruminations of other scholars, R.D. Guthrie became the most vigorous supporter of the *Artemsia* steppe-tundra position, based upon his interpretation of an abundant, varied fossil fauna that demanded grasses to account for their presence. This interpretation culminating with a full exposition of what he came to call the mammoth steppe'. (West 1996:3)

While only six varieties of mammal migrated from America to Eurasia, twenty-two species came to the American side, nine of these during the late Pleistocene: mammoth, musk-ox, caribou, moose, grizzly bear, polar bear and saiga antelope. West writes further:

'The question of fauna is, indeed, of fundamental importance. The ultimate concern here is human prehistory. It is a safe assumption that it was not the character of the vegetation that brought people into the most difficult environment the genus *Homo* ever came to colonise. But it needs to be emphasized that this is, after all, the period of the Upper Palaeolithic, one characterized across Eurasia by the application of highly evolved, highly efficient techniques for the hunting of this very fauna.' (West 1996:5)

Scientists have agreed that the 'earliest Americans must have entered the continent by way of Bering Strait', and that following the rise of sea levels in the late Pleistocene, human arrival was simultaneous to migrations of mega-fauna such as the mastodon and mammoth: today's maritime people having earlier been plains hunters of the bitterly cold Beringian landscape, enclosed as this was by slowly retreating glaciers.

Ancient Tikiġaq and the Presence of Beringia

Tikiġaq, which lay within Beringia, is saturated by signs of the archaic. Layered with archaeological strata and with human and animal relics, the peninsula is a materialization of time: its stratigraphy, which is formed of beach ridges each completed every eighty or a hundred years by means of the build up of gravel swept west from the cliffs, likewise bears witness to the passage of time, as does seasonal erosion of the north shore and the *iglus* previously excavated there and abandoned – often abandoned by families remembered in stories and whose relics may already have been scavenged.

With the Pleistocene still a palpable backdrop, later, but still old, Tikiġaq narratives were records of both change and memory. And people lived within the complex medium of what could be classified either as myth and local history: this was in addition to what they observed in local geography. One old man remarked that you could see matching land forms opposite each other on the Alaskan and Siberian sides, suggesting that folk memory matches twentieth century science in the comprehension that the two continents had originally been joined. This may not have been everybody's observation. Nor did people know about the submarine and subterranean lakes of oil identified in the late twentieth century. Knowledge that Ipiutak had lain beneath the Tikiġaq surface since ca. 900 CE was also a mid-twentieth century revelation. These discoveries, one commercial, the second historical, added superstructure to a modern people's knowledge of the peninsula's infrastructure.

In a sense, the Ipiutak excavation and the discovery of oil were both materialisations that harmonized with Tikiġaq people's grasp of history as experienced by Asatchaq. People already lived in a present that was interfused with a myth world that was too vague to be dated. Indeed, the continuing present 'reality' of myth existed beyond horizons of imagination and these were as intangible as the speculations of earth scientists and archaeologists.

All humans live in geological and astronomical time, both of which render what we generally understand as history to be comparatively recent. But not all societies have lived with such an intense preoccupation with the past as did pre-contact Tikiġaq. Here the omnipresence of what is historically undatable exists in harmony both with the present and with ancient stories. The stories and a sense of 'that time' are one and the same. The wind blowing from Cape Lisburne is the same wind that swept the Pleistocene. This is what one tastes in local stories.

The Woolly Mammoth (*kiligvak*)

In 1801, Charles Willson Peale excavated a mastodon from a bog in Newburgh, New York State. He painted a picture of this: a multitude of people operating a vast apparatus. He stands at the edge of the crater holding a banner-like drawing of the jointed leg bones. He put the monster on show at his museum in Philosophical Hall, Philadelphia. Labelled 'The Great Incognitum...' 'The ninth wonder of the world!!! Buried since Noah's flood.'[5]

There are submerged mastodon relics all over Alaska and those round Tikiġaq also had a presence. There was however no mastodon *inua* (resident spirit*)* perhaps because people thought this shy and extinct beast had been a rodent that ran underground when it was disturbed.

In 1940, Aġviqsiina told Rainey the following about the *kiligvak*:

> 'There was a man hunting at Aqalulik [ten miles north of Tikiġaq] who saw a *kiligvak* running under the bank with another animal, one of the 'wolves of the *kiligvak*', after it. The *kiligvak* lives underground and the tusks are horns.
>
> 'They are "backwards animals". When you see a tusk sticking out and you say 'go down' it comes up. When you say 'come up' it goes down. When people are boiling meat and it cooks very slowly, they say "it is *kiligvak* meat." Because in the old days people ate this meat and it cooked faster on a wet wood fire.'

Little more has been recorded. Inupiat assumed, as suggested by Aġviqsiina, that this ancestral elephant which migrated through the corridor of unglaciated Pleistocene steppeland in pursuit of Artemisia, had been an inoffensive creature.

The upside-downness associated with the *kiligvak* nonetheless places it in mythological time, the environment of Tikiġaq's Raven Creator when 'people walked on their hands' because they didn't know how to do things properly. What survived into the historical period were ivory and bone relics: molars, tusks and bits of skeleton. Real people walked upright.

The underground presence of mammoth relics points in two directions. On the one hand it belongs to Tikiġaq's subsurface. On the other, it offers an image of the archaic and stands monumentally within the discussion of age.

---

[5] Thomas Jefferson referenced the existence of 'mammoths', which he believed still roamed northern regions of the continent, as evidence for a greater biodiversity in America [than that in Europe]. Peale's display of these bones drew attention from Europe, as did his method of reassembling large skeletal specimens in three dimensions. https://en.wikipedia.org/wiki/Charles_Willson_Peale

And whereas the *mastodon* had migrated much earlier to the American side and had died out for lack of woody forage, early Alaskan grasslands had sustained the hairy mammoth until it too became extinct about ten thousand years ago – long before Tikiġaq established a culture in about 800.[6]

Whereas it was clear that the whale was both a prey animal and centre of a cult, there is no evidence of a prehistoric mastodon or mammoth cult. Perhaps, had the mammoth survived longer, there might have been such a cult.

In an earlier book, I suggested that the Tikiġaq *iglu*, which was partially constructed of whale bones, functioned as a whale symbol during the whale hunt.[7] The brown bear may also have had cultic status as it did in northern Japan.[8] The mammoth, whose extinction predated Tikiġaq, appears not at all in local myth. And perhaps the nearest thing to a mammoth-centred religion was excavated at Berelekh, Yakutia, where mammoth relics, among those of other Pleistocene fauna, were discovered in what may have been a mammoth bone house. Here is a partial inventory of the Berelekh excavation:

'Bone and ivory artefacts include mammoth tusk and bone tools… Among these are 4 mammoth tusk knives, one spearpoint of mammoth tusk, and two scrapers… Certain mammoth rib fragments have been smoothed… N.K. Vereshchagin identified mammoth, woolly rhinoceros, bison, horse, reindeer, cave lion, wolf, glutton, and hare. The recovery of an entire hind leg of a mammoth, with flesh and wool [was possibly] separated from the carcass in ancient times. It is possible that the numerous mammoth bones at the Berelekh site are the remains of prehistoric dwellings, rather than an accidental accumulation.[9]

---

[6] I have switched from 'mastodon' to 'mammoth' at this point. The mastodon was the earlier species and may not have reached north Alaska. The relics in Tikiġaq's subsurface were probably mammoth.

[7] Lowenstein 1993

[8] There is a mysterious locution that suggests that the brown bear (*aglaq*) had cultic value. In Tikiġaq dialect, people were either *aglagiituq* ('good brown bear' or 'not in taboo') or *aglagiitchuq* ('bad brown bear' or 'in a dangerous condition of taboo').

[9] *Berelekh, Allakhovsk Region,* Yuri A. Mochanov and Svetlana A. Fedoseeva, in West, 1996:218–21

Disregarding self-promotion – he was a serious portraitist and museum creator – Charles Willson Peale and also Thomas Jefferson were responding to American discoveries that lent dignifying status to the continent. America was old and this fact rendered it important. In the western regions, mammoth relics were also more recently excavated all over Alaska, notably at Big Delta and Cape Espenberg, while small mammoth populations survived into the years ca. 5,600 years ago on the St Paul and Wrangell Islands.

Siberian and Alaskan Natives have used and traded mammoth ivory since the seventeenth century and the Siberians had a mammoth mythology parallel to the Alaskan. Relevant here is that in Tikiġaq, *kiligvak* relics were evidence of life in deep time. The *kiligvak's* material scale mattered little. But whether the mammoth had once held sacred value, was a contemporary of Beringian migrants or was hunted for its meat and skin, remains unknown. So far as later people understood, the mammoth had lived in the remote past and its remains surfaced occasionally to confirm an archaic stratum of existence.

Asatchaq as *monstre sacre*

Just as the young American Herbert Aldrich in his 1889 narrative of Arctic America and Siberia learned, maybe wrongly, that the *kiligvak* may have been a sacred animal in maritime Siberia, so Tikiġaq people regarded Asatchaq as a *monstre sacre*, psychologically dangerous but also, partly because he was quasi-sacred, someone to be avoided with honour. This latter, perhaps because he was a relic of a period from which twentieth century people wanted freedom. The past is wonderful, but potentially suffocating.

Ownership of Tikiġaq songs and stories was traditionally regarded as a mark of power. Songs and stories had lives of their own, they were charged with *qila,* spirit energy, and the same *qila* was shared by men and women who were stalwart enough to transmit what they had memorized or ingested. The word *ingested* is used non-metaphorically: it denotes physicality, although the physical also suggests the metaphorical transaction. To transmit a song, the singer would donate it with saliva. Singer and song thus mutually identified.

To be a shaman in old Tikiġaq you were either formally initiated or old age bestowed on you quasi-shamanistic authority. An old person was routinely regarded as having shamanistic power and was therefore *irigii* (frightening).

Asatchaq, who had not been formally initiated, was in possession of the latter. He was old and knowledgeable. Many found him *irigii*, and part of the fear he inspired (and which I shared) derived from his association with archaic traditions.

Because I was an outsider, I was immune. But I was drawn to the notion of the old man's sacred character partly on account of his surname, Killigivuk, which the missionary Driggs had created as a means of linking the boy to his father, whose Inupiaq name was *kiligvak* (mammoth).

Mythologising the Past

Whereas the missionary Driggs had been intent on introducing Tikiġaq to aspects of modern America, I tried, without comparing myself to the doctor, to look in the opposite direction. I had no illusions about changing anything. But I was preoccupied with the ancient and wanted to look at everything backwards, as though perhaps to create a patchy, out of focus panorama, a semi-exposed period newsreel in which Asatchaq and his elders expressed a version of time that corresponded to my idea of what had been authentic.

And while I understood that the late 19th century had been a period of deprivation, I colluded with Asatchaq in the view that it had also been a time of optimism when traditional lifeways could still be preserved.

My inclination to mythologise even the living was triggered partly by a tendency that was inherent in Asatchaq's own ancestor veneration. Authority and cultural continuity were part of the same thing, and together they amounted to a good that drew to itself respect both for recent forebears and for past generations.

In 1976, this respect still existed, inherited almost automatically by modern people, because it had been implicit in the old culture and could be adopted without abandoning the present. But loss of culture intensified modern people's tendency towards a sometimes negative self image, rendering respect to a lost ideal thereby firmer but more anxious. That which was lost was obscured by a complex, many-dimensioned darkness of which the light of the present was an unavoidable transmitter.

Firmness and hardness had, in one way, a self-abasing influence. In another sense, it added validity to the present in that the past amounted to value that was ineradicable and contributed a belief in the legitimacy of the now: this was partly because the now had risen from greater origins. Two sources of validity thereby existed: on the one hand, the urgent and real demands of the present, on the other the justification of the present by means of precedent.

It is perhaps from these present time disappointments that the tendency to mythologize arises. To create a myth is to banish the inconclusiveness of open-ended existence. One function of myth being to assuage the anxiety of being provisional, being an inhabitant of now time, far from the sphere of what has, all along, been complete.

Cosmopolitan Whites

Euro-American arrival in the Inupiaq world was to bring a combination of industrializing commerce and Protestant Christianity. One thinks contact between America and its indigenous peoples as the interface between Anglo Saxons and non European Natives. This, in Tikiġaq by the 1920s, became largely the case: the white man was represented by just that demographic constituency because the newer incomers (teachers and government officials) were generally as Wasp as Episcopalian preachers had been.

Before the 1920s, 'whites' had been a cosmopolitan lot, swept north by personal indigence, interest in adventure, American market forces and frontier ideology: but like the immigrant populations of the later nineteenth and early twentieth centuries, mixed. Central European and Scandinavian populations in Nebraska, Ohio and Minnesota formed societies that wanted land in which to develop their economies and had no desire to carry their ambition to the Arctic. The prospectors who crowded into the Dakotas, the Yukon and the beaches of Nome, had been a society recognizable to missionaries because they represented the obverse of elite character.

Most remarkably, however, in the years around the turn of the twentieth century, Tikiġaq people saw Germans, Black men, Scandinavians, Irish, Welsh, Canadians and Hawaians coming and going. Certainly, these represented the new American frontier forces, but they were not homogeneously white. And while these were generally lumped together in Inupiaq eyes as whites, they were a changing crew of many ethnicities. These days, as I'd mentioned to Daisy, everyone is a mixture.

The Death of Daisy – Long *unipkaaq* (myth story)

Asatchaq said nothing about Daisy after her disappearance. Daisy had been a child who called the old man *ataata,* grandfather. The event was too horrible to talk about and I couldn't introduce the subject. I was a bystander. The tragedy of that death affected me, but I didn't feel like intruding.

Asatchaq's silence was impenetrable. And his feelings were no doubt more profound than he wanted to express. I wonder, too, if his response was perhaps complicated by memory. He had lived through the period of the 'Great Sickness' and had witnessed many deaths. While he and his family had survived in good health, Asatchaq had grown up surrounded annually by the deaths of about one sixth of the village. Present instabilities, the uncertainty of life in 1976, perhaps seemed to him a repeat, in a new form, of the years around 1900. 'Confusion now hath made his masterpiece', the line from *Macbeth* occurred to me. And the moral emptiness of material America with its self-justifying prop of Christianity, had materialized in horrifying climax. Dope, alcohol and the dollar economy had arrived even before the pipeline.

The other line that inevitably occurred to me was from Eliot's *Wasteland:* 'These fragments I have shored against my ruins.' The passage preceding this was also one of horror and defeat:

> What are the roots that clutch, what branches grow
> Out of this stony rubbish? Son of man,
> You cannot say, or guess, for you know only
> A heap of broken images.

It is easy to contemplate the meaning of such lines. But to live in their midst: that was no doubt how 'Old Tom' despairingly existed in the limited shelter of a tradition whose forms he'd watched break. And this is how Asatchaq lived in the after shock of Native and American contact. The line from *Macbeth* made more sense than its abstract implication. Against the culture of death, did Christianity, after all, offer the social or psychological succour I imagined? This was a moment when I needed at the very least to hear the voice of Mrs Charlotte. But Mrs C had gone. And we dwelt in the space that she'd understood better than most. This was comfortless and hollow.

If *confusion,* in the sense of *disorder* in *its* wider sense, was what Asatchaq experienced in modern life, then perhaps the narrative tradition represented order. Without hesitation, therefore (so I thought), Asatchaq launched into the longest and most imposing story in his repertoire. He didn't, characteristically, comment on or introduce what we called 'the long *unipkaaq',* beyond prefacing it with the words 'this story is a long one.'

Nor did the old man suggest that the recitation had to do with Daisy's disappearance or the disorder in which this happened.[10]

The long *unipkaaq* is a narrative of travel, transformation, human survival and shamanistic initiation in the form of death and rebirth. Yes, storytelling is about knowledge and it's this knowledge for which Asatchaq was respected.

But the storytelling process also has to do with healing. And I believe that this may have been Asatchaq's motive in launching the long *unipkaaq.* The people whom the storyteller might try to heal may have been out of reach. In the past, perhaps, a community that came together might well have achieved the reassurance that life was worth living, that social existence continued.

The long *unipkaaq* represented a foundation. It was ancient and it continued to abide. The horrors of loss are not possible to comprehend. Wounds can't be salved. There is no consolation, only grief. 'All dark and comfortless', as blinded Gloucester cried out at the hand of cruelty. But still there remains the communal foundation. It persists. It is there. It may be visited.

---

[10] I was threatened, bizarrely, during the same period, and escaped the person I described as 'my murderer' by a fluke. I'd been locked in my unheated cabin during the same period of confusion and emerged in good health to learn that the next translated 'long *unipkaaq'* sentence would be 'he was then shut in his iglu.' And although that event represents another story, the narrative involved me in the turmoil of which I was otherwise a spectator.

Part 9

Atom Bombs at Aggutauraq

I've written a lot about culture contact and the changes Asatchaq had seen. But the word 'contact' doesn't adequately express the process. The word 'change' is also misleading. Even during the traditional period, change had been continual. And local culture had always been a slowly evolving phenomenon. Once the Caucasian presence had been established, these changes in Inupiaq society were bigger and more rapid. In this connection, I have also described aspects of the American presence in the northwest Arctic. Perhaps the word 'impact', in addition to 'contact' might be introduced into the discussion of this complex but accelerated course.

The climax of the contact/impact process came in the late 1950s. This was the phenomenon of Project Plowshare or Chariot: a plan to detonate five nuclear bombs at the southern end of Cape Thompson. I have outlined this project in the text below and have woven it into the narrative. At best unrealistic, the project was a dangerous plan which abandoned every humanitarian concern and whose abandonment, unfortunately, had little impact on the global issue.

*

It's late June, and bank rolled by Mobil Oil to investigate coastal birds, McDuff, an ornithologist, has flown into the village. McDuff's an easy-going Fairbanks giant, with a cabin in the spruce woods, a dog-team, half a PhD, and knowledge of Alaskan birds. Within hours of arrival, and free from qualms about paying locals, McDuff has organised a trip, and suddenly I'm off with him along the south beach on a rented snow-machine.

Two problems arise. First, there's no snow, and so Ambrose, our guide, an Inupiaq visitor, has to drive the machine over rotting ice floes. The other problem is the snowmachine itself. An ancient discard, it's reduced to its innards, skis awry, the rubber track tattered. The sled, on which McDuff and I take turns in choking exhaust fumes, is likewise on its final journey: and since the sled drops under water as we attempt leaping between ice pans, it's easier to run alongside, our backpacks strapped neatly under sea water.

When finally the machine gives out, we drag it to the beach and try, unsuccessfully, bleeding the slush from its gills. Ambrose trudges back to Tikiġaq and a teenager will presumably gun out to scavenge the Snow Go carcass.

We're twenty miles from the cliffs and McDuff's no longer in a rush. We walk. I ask him – as I do of myself – 'What was the hurry?'

'I can't remember,' he says cheerfully. 'Maybe something about money. The oil man: he pays good: but only for a week.'

He gestures to the cliffs. They're still distant: dark blue with ice streaks. 'It's wonderful,' he says, 'to be out in shared territory. Among Eskimos and summer birds.' He raises his glasses and rushes through the fringes of the tundra. 'A knot,' he returns, scrawling in a notebook. 'Alaska's wonderful!'

We walk in silence, broken by McDuff's short, rushing exits. Each time he comes crashing from the tundra with his notebook flapping, it's a whimbrel, phalarope, longspur, old squaw: the list soon extends to forty species.

We have very little food, but McDuff with his shotgun bags a pair of ptarmigan and at midnight we camp, build a driftwood fire and eat, washing down the hot dry meat with brackish water.

When we lie down to rest, we lie on cold stone. I raise my mat on wood and grasses. But it's hard to relax. My sleeping bag is damp and salty. And then it's dream I enter: a half-world of the present, of birds and old stories.

A Short-eared Owl – *nipailuktaq*, 'silent flier' – floats over the lagoon. It chews lemmings in the dreamlight and coughs up hair and vertebrae. I, too, want to hunt. But also to sleep, and urinate the salty water. I'm hungry and exhausted. Behind my ribcage springs the charred dismembered ptarmigan. The owl travels the low sunbeams. The rays lead down to my colon.

'Hungry?' I ask it. The owl says nothing, so I raise my fingers, drawing it to me. When I shake a little, the owl's claws dip, and the pain is exquisite.

'No need to come further,' I decide in the end, 'I'm only a white man.' The small owl in the pale light frowns.

'You know my name's meaning – *nipailuktaq*?'

'Yes: "it flies in silence".'

'Put that, when I leave you, in your story.'

'We're already there. The old stories still happen. Look: here's Ukuŋniq.'

The young shaman lopes towards us in torn boots and dog-skins.

'Not just Ukuŋniq. I'm Raven too, and Moon Boy,' Ukuŋniq mumbles, saturated with his mixed, convergent myth identity.

'How they roll into one!' I want to exclaim. The owl preempts me:

'They're all lonely, those travellers. With no-one to talk to. Their loose bits of soul discharge at random. They drift round starving. Always singing. Then other souls – like here in driftwood – sing back to him. When the boy feels better...'

'Or worse,' says Ukuŋniq. He's become a shaman. Ukuŋniq's parka drops onto the beach stones. Its meaty odours are disgusting. Coughing badly he shuffles to the side. Not wanting his cold, I wrap his skin around my jacket.

'Come on!' McDuff struggles to his feet, 'it's too cold to stay here.'

'I can't,' I explain, 'I'm stuck. Tangled in Ur-time.'

'You're raving,' McDuff barks, laughing away his irritation.

'It's the shaman who's crazy. He ran away without his parka.' We walk on for five miles to the edge of the cliffs. Isuk stream runs over the beach from a patch of willows. Here the low land ends and the cliffs rise abruptly. Camped by the stream, and sitting with their legs towards the sea are Umik and Sarah.

'Hi Tom,' says Umik. 'You brought a white man.'

'Hi.'

Silence.

'Hi.'

Silence.

'Hi.'

Silence.

We settle our packs and sit down with them.

The growl of cliff birds fills the wind. Lines of murres speed out to forage.

'This is McDuff.'

'Howdy, Mister D.'

'Howdy,' says McDuff.

'He's come to count birds,' I introduce him.

'Lots of birds round here. You'll need a lot of paper.'

McDuff explains. 'Not the *number* of birds on the cliffs, but...'

317

'Who pays you to count birds?' asks Sarah.

'A company. Oil men.'

'Ah,' says Umik.

'Will they drill into the sea?' asks Sarah sharply.

'I hope not,' McDuff says.

'I can see it,' Sarah goes on, 'in my head-dream. I see oil. Black. Black oil. Spouting from the sea. I've seen pictures. Out of Texas. First the white man came and killed our whales. Then when the whales have gone, they'll make the sea spout…'

'Make sure whose side you're on,' says Umik. He and McDuff avoid looking at each other.

A silence follows. Then:

'How many birds come to nest on these cliffs, you reckon?'

'About quarter of a million,' says McDuff.

'Used to be more,' says Umik bleakly.

'Yes. Way back, there were twice that many.'

'Why?' asks Umik. He stares at the sea. We follow his gaze to a line of murres disappearing on the south horizon. 'I'll tell you,' says Umik. 'The atom bomb. And atom bomb people.'

'You mean from bomb tests in the 1950s? In Siberia? I guess that's possible.'

'Not that,' says Umik getting warmer. 'I mean Washington. America.' Another silence.

'Have you ever heard,' I ask McDuff, 'of Project Chariot?'

'Can't say I have,' McDuff says quietly.

'It was national news in 1960. But it centred right *here*. The big Alaskan scandal of the century.'

'Tell me,' McDuff says.

'Perhaps you won't believe us. But when you're back to the Fairbanks library, you'll find the archives…' I tell him where to find it.

'I guess he'll believe us,' Sarah says gravely.

'You've heard of the AEC: Atomic Energy Commission,' I start uncertainly. 'But maybe you don't know the name of "Ogotaurak"?'

'Nope. Means nothing.'

'Aggutauraq's the name of a stream. The last valley in these cliffs. Just ten miles south of where we're sitting.'

'You mean,' says McDuff, 'the place with some huts at the end of the cliffs? I saw it from the plane here.'

'That's it,' says Umik.

'Well, back in 1957 a plan was devised for Aggutauraq. The AEC thought they'd build a harbour there.'

'Sounds crazy,' McDuff interrupts. 'Who'd want a harbour when the sea is frozen – all but in summer?'

'It was madder than that. They planned to excavate this harbour with...'

'Atom bomb!' says Sarah bluntly.

'You're kidding,' McDuff whistles.

'Not one bomb. Five. Four in a line. Then a big one at the end. A keyhole shaped harbour, the designers described it.'

'*Jesus Christ*,' McDuff says slowly. 'The bastards.' The first harsh words I've heard him utter. 'I mean...' he stammered, 'How...? what...? why...?'

'Oh they didn't care,' says Umik, 'what got in their way. About Eskimos who lived in villages. They wanted to bomb us. Their very own people. These cliffs, the animals, birds and fishes: atom-bombed by white men, scientists and politicians.

'You asked me why the birds have cut their number. I answer: the birds knew. They heard those men talking. The birds decided: "We'll go and nest in other places. Then if they bomb Imnat (the cliffs), some of us will live. Then in a thousand years we'll come back to Imnat." That's what the birds thought.'

*

I walked home with McDuff and then he left. I wrote to him as follows

Tikiġaq July 2 1976

Dear McDuff:

By now you'll be back in your cabin in the spruce woods with your axe, your microscope and huskies. I hope the Fairbanks spring continues fine. Here we have wonderful sunshine: about 50F with the wind from the south. As for me, I've retreated from our walk and write to you in my cabin's half-light.

I've been thinking about bombs, birds and stories, and the conversation we had with Umik and Sarah. You understood, I think, the source of their suspicion. People here will rightly perhaps always be wary of outsiders. Whatever our intentions, we white men are the heirs to earlier intruders. And whether we're teachers, dentists, bird men or ethnographers, we can't disengage from the historical process which brought the US up here.

I had pious hopes when I first arrived that I was to be some sort of old-ways-rehabilitation-saint, 'working for and with the community' etc. Some locals treated me at first within those terms. But this was temporary and born of a sort of a wish-fulfilment about 'giving culture back' – an issue far too difficult to address here. As for my own role in reclamation, I realise that my work is largely clerical, and that at bottom I'm simply the old man's amanuensis.

But even in this small capacity, I'm part of a continuum. After the traders and missionaries have pacified the country and neutralised its inhabitants, then ethnographers rush in and accumulate the fragments to put in museums. Whether these are masks and pots or stories and kinship charts, the culture 'reclaimed' is thereby spray-varnished and given its place in history. This helps assuage a majority guilt at having ruined what it now seeks to preserve.

Of course, you counting birds for Texaco, are as anxious to protect the eagle and the knot as I am to canonise – or fossilise? – my storyteller in a book. Whereas what you seek to protect is alive, I collect verbal ammonites: organisms which no longer live in community tissue. You are, still, as I remain, part of the imperial sweep. So long as Texaco can provide a convincing statement of likely development impact to reassure the public that industry has taken nature and local culture into consideration, then they will come in – as Sarah visualised – and start drilling to hell through the seabed.

In this connection, I was preoccupied in the spring, following a young woman's death, with some verses from St John: 'Horror! Horror! Horror!' The village was exploding with tension, and people were talking about the end of time. Christ's dawn was here. Angels stood on the schoolhouse roof. The future erupted in a brimstone of horned beasts, war in heaven.

I got caught up on the periphery of these apocalyptic strata. Partly because events in the winter suggested that something was wrong. Partly because the incidents in one of Asatchaq's stories seemed to reflect these events: as though stories represented a subterranean consciousness of was happening on the surface: and that archaic versions of the same energies, stored in ancient, frozen roots, were bursting through the floors of modern houses.

Then just as the past seemed to rear up to address us – maybe even to reassure us that *the disorder had all happened before* – I had my own small visualisation, though this time it was the future and not the past that was revealing itself:

In March, I'd walked out one afternoon onto the sea ice, and looked back at the village. Instead of a geometry of roofs and meat racks cresting pressure ridges, I saw, through an effect of light, the city of the future: Tikiġaq inland, in white/blue ectoplasmic mirage substance: storey upon storey of office and municipal housing (I'll quote, if I may, from a poem I started)

    arrayed in a cross-hatching of
            crane necks and derricks,
the time-vandalised multiple elongation of dwellings
          a vague
run in the air meta-city
            on the latitude of the Standard Oil building
in Chicago:
         unusable high-wind sun-balconies
               cluttered with
transport damaged condominium accessories –
             It leapt, yes,
as does Las Vegas out of a basin
         in the Mohave desert at nightfall,
or Denver glazed suddenly
         against the Rockies from an aircraft cabin,
and like those centres,
        Tikiġaq upstretching
           on exchange of metal.

Not precisely Armageddon. But, taking off from Sarah's vision, an optical impression of what might become of this place in the not distant future.

But now from apocalypse 1976, let me return to 1957. I have quoted *Revelation*. Now turn your mind back to the prophet who cried the following:

> …they shall beat their swords into plowshares, and their spears into pruning hooks; nation shall not lift up sword against nation, neither shall they learn war any more.

It was this celebrated verse from *Isaiah* that Lewis Strauss had in mind in 1957 when the US Atomic Energy Commission, of which he was president, decided to explore 'the peaceful application of nuclear explosives'. In a casual mutation of the Hebrew ideal – the 'sword' of US bombs in continuing manufacture would after all be *accompanied by, not converted into* the 'plow' of atomic excavation – the AEC therefore called their 1957 programme 'Project Plowshare'. And Project Chariot – a reference to Elijah's ascent in a chariot of fire – was to be one of the first experiments in the Plowshare programme.

As you know, the AEC did not detonate atom bombs at Cape Thompson. Such, however, was their original plan, and I've brought with me from Fairbanks a box of photocopies about this and have been re-reading some of them. So here I am floundering in bulletins and news clippings from the early 1960s one sunny midnight, when my teenage friend Sharva bursts in.

'What you doing?' he asks between munches of the sandwich I've constructed. I identify my cache of xeroxes and he says, 'Oh yes: Dad once told me about that deal. When the atom people tried to blow up Aggutauraq.'[1]

Sharva's father had worked at the site. While most of the village stood against the project, a small number worked there as labourers and carpenters.

---

[1] The other major Plowshare project was to detonate some bombs in a salt dome near Carlsbad in New Mexico. They called this Project *Gnome*, perhaps to rhyme with 'dome'. Or maybe as a complement to the plowshare-and-chariot vision of the Jewish apocalypse, there was in the lower depths of the San Francisco AEC office an earth-mysteries specialist or an early devotee of Tolkien. But I think 'gnome' is good in that it represents a semi-domesticated version of the Nibelungen: dwarfs who mined the bowels of Wagner's imagination and led eventually to the death of gods.

'What would you have done?' I ask. Sharva kicks out with a high left boot and a crust of snow flies onto my table. Growling explosively he rakes his arms in a violent half-circle.

'They wouldn't come back with *hydrogen* bombs even!' he laughs joyfully.

Hydrogen bombs. Not 'just' A-bombs. Was that the plan? To clarify my thoughts, McD., let me outline this history for you.

First to names. The documents and map read 'Ogotaurak'. It's easy to be snobbish: but contemporary spelling, Aggutauraq, takes you closer to the place, which means 'little *aggutaq*': a seal stomach bag, a name derived from the name of a hilltop north of Aggutauraq creek shaped like a seal stomach.

And to history. Plowshare came into being in 1957, and the first underground test, 2,000 feet into a mountain, happened that September in Nevada. Since this bomb yielded no atmospheric fallout, the AEC decided to shoot for more. One impetus came from the University of California's Livermore lab's Edward Teller, who talked about what he described as 'nuclear landscaping'.

'We'll make deserts bloom,' he wrote. 'We'll landscape the earth's surface to suit U.S...' The project was launched in cold war time.

On the one hand, there was public support for the development of nuclear weapons. On the other, there was national anxiety about testing. Besides the horror of August 1945 in Japan, there was, for example, the episode of the Lucky Dragon boat. Unbeknown to the American public, there had, since 1944, also been radiation leaks in the USA, some unintentional, other less so.

In an attempt to neutralise revulsion against 'death dust', the AEC said it would: 'highlight the peaceful uses of nuclear explosives and thereby create a climate of world opinion that was more favourable to weapons development and tests.' Teller, who was Plowshare's most vigorous propagandist, met public anxiety with a curious mixture of plain speech and vague promises.

'I believe,' he wrote in *Popular Mechanics*, March 1960, 'that the dangers from fallout in the weapons-testing programme have been greatly exaggerated; nevertheless, this worry exists and so we are trying to develop 'clean' bombs... with no radioactive fallout and no local residual contamination.' And in this respect, the value of the H-bomb (or 'hell bomb' as it was described by some) was that it produces no fallout. Only the A-bomb used to trigger the thermonuclear explosion throws up waste.'

Back in 1958, the AEC contracted with Longyear, a Minneapolis firm of consultants, to study 'mineral potential and proposed harbour locations' in northwest Alaska. After nine weeks of work, but without having visited Alaska, Longyear suggested the cliffs we walked to earlier this month. But at the south end, where Aggutauraq creek runs to the sea. There were shale-oil and coal deposits in the area, and a harbour was judged economically viable.

Longyear's proposal seemed to meet the four AEC criteria 'for the selection of an appropriate site':

1. Location in the United States
2. Location that assures protection of people and wildlife
3. Conditions satisfying geologic and engineering requirements
           for experimental data
4. Possible long-term utilitarian value.

The first criterion was accompanied by Alaska's entry to statehood in 1958. Criterion 2: Tikiġaq, with a population of 320 was 32 miles away, the smaller villages of Noatak and Kivalina were forty and fifty miles from Chariot. Criterion 3 could only be satisfied through research. The fourth criterion was easily fulfilled by the proposal to excavate a harbour. This was would be the 'keyhole shaped crater' I described to you: 300 foot deep, 1,500 feet in diameter, with a 2,000 foot channel leading to the sea. To this end, one 200,000 ton H-bomb and four 20,000 ton bombs would be exploded roughly as shown in a diagram provided by Teller for his article in *Popular Mechanics*.

These explosions would exceed the power of the Hiroshima A-bomb by a factor of fourteen. To reassure the public, there is an artist's impression of the Chariot explosion on the same page as the diagram. It shows two rugged pilots dressed in flying suits and helmets at the controls of an aircraft cabin, gazing – a mere hundred yards from a comic strip wilderness – with benign impassivity at five white plumes of nuclear smoke rising like cotton-wool. Undisturbed, a windless sea laps the moony cliff base. There would be, after all, only thirty million cubic yards of earth being blown sky high.

Chariot's purpose was conceived as both practical and experimental. On the practical side lay the possibility of transporting mineral resources down the west coast, although just a few months later, geologists concluded that the only stuff worth extracting was a low grade coal. It was further demonstrated that a harbour, once explosively dug, would quickly silt up with mud and sand. Lastly, as any Tikiġaq child could have told them, the sea is frozen between October and July, and thus shipping could only reach this area between July and September. These simple facts put the kybosh on the economic pretext, and the AEC laid them aside.

But the experimental rationale lost little of its urgency. The blast would, according an AEC bulletin, constitute a 'harmless experiment in nuclear engineering (NE)'. This would open the way to future uses of NE for the excavation of canals, harbours, building sites and recreation areas in other parts of the country. There was an economic purpose behind this too. Nuclear explosions could *dig* in a fraction of the time and at a third, or even a tenth of the cost of chemical explosives. It was just a question of finding out how to do it in reasonable safety and with minimum fuss – and/or public interference.

None of this business in remote northwest Alaska was taking place in isolation from the international arena. As early as 1958, the AEC presented their Chariot proposal to the Second U.N. International Conference on the Peaceful Uses of Atomic Energy. To accompany their presentation they showed a movie which included a mock detonation placed in a model of Aggutauraq valley. But despite the success of the movie, the plan met with opposition from both eastern and western delegations. While Chariot was on the drawing board, the USA, the Soviets and Britain were negotiating a Nuclear Test Ban Treaty.

The Russians viewed Chariot as an American ploy to sidestep this projected test ban. By 1959, they were accusing the US of planning a 'camouflaged hydrogen bomb test' only 175 miles from the Soviet frontier. 'Whatever the US press says,' claimed *Sovetsky Flot*, 'it is clear to all that a test of death-dealing weapons is to be carried out under the guise of building a seaport.' And only when the US abandoned the Chariot project in 1963, did the test ban treaty go through.

In the meantime, Chariot had to be sold to the Alaskan people. In July 1958, Edward Teller toured Juneau, Anchorage and Fairbanks to elicit support in government, business and academic circles. Alaskan opinion was, as the lawyer Joseph Foote wrote, 'sharply divided.'[2]

---

[2] *Background Materials on Project Chariot*, an unpublished paper by Joseph Foote, 1961. Don Charles Foote Collection, in the Archives of the Elmer E. Rasmusen Library, University of Alaska, Fairbanks. All further Chariot materials, including partial transcript of the meeting in Tikigaq are likewise from the Don Charles Foote archive.

Many of those not in opposition to the blast simply wanted to excavate a dam or a harbour where it would be accessible. 'Government officials,' continued Foote, 'scientists and top level business men thought Teller's scheme was ridiculous. Opening northwest Alaska to economic development was low on the list of things to get done. But Chambers of Commerce in areas sensitive to federal spending were enthusiastic.'

Teller's Alaskan speeches sounded feverish and exaggerated. Alaska, he claimed, had been chosen because it had 'the fewest... and the most reasonable people.' NE, he said, could be controlled so precisely that they could 'dig a harbour in the shape of a polar bear.' Some of what he said was simply misleading. For example, while the idea of Chariot as an economically feasible project had been shelved by January 1959, Teller was assuring Alaskan business that while the project had to 'stand on its own economic feet', two-thirds of the $5 million budget would be spent in Alaska.

The following summer, when Chariot was in danger of being abandoned through lack of support, Teller returned to Alaska, still claiming, despite contrary evidence, that a harbour at Aggutauraq would be usable. Joseph Foote writes: 'Asked if other harbours could be blasted in Alaska, (Teller) says: 'That's like a little girl asking what do I want for Christmas. It's up to you... If your mountain is not in the right place, just drop us a card.' In an address at the University of Alaska that autumn, Teller cried: 'Please God, that by making harbours here... perhaps near coal deposits, by exporting this coal cheaper to Japan, the Japanese might become the first beneficiaries of atomic energy, of atomic explosions, as they have been the first victims.'

In January 1959, Chariot was in fact temporarily shelved. At the Second U.N. International Conference on the Peaceful Uses of Atomic Energy, western scientists 'were sceptical of the US programme.' The main objections were over fallout and over injecting a new controversy into the picture before a test ban had been negotiated. The next six months saw major barnstorming exercises both from Teller's laboratory and those AEC personnel who still supported the blast. By spring 1959, Alaskan opinion, spurred partly by a resolution from the Alaskan House of Representatives, had come down in favour of Chariot. Equally important, by promising large-scale contracts for pre-shot scientific research at Aggutauraq, the AEC persuaded the top brass at the University of Alaska to put its weight behind the project.

June 1959: barge-loads of equipment started to arrive at Aggutauraq for the start of the pre-shot scientific survey. This was to be the first ever

US Environmental Impact study. At this wonderful opportunity for scientists to get into the field and be paid to produce data on one of the least explored areas on the continent, small planes droned down onto the airstrip that had been laid at Aggutauraq. Up went insulated quonset huts and cabins. And – despite reluctance from the AEC, and the fact that bulldozers and weasel tractors had, by the end of July, wrecked extensive areas of tundra cover – archaeological work at Aggutauraq also started.

> Personnel: Senior Scientist, Frederick Hadleigh-West
> Field Assistant Kenneth E. Howell
> Field Assistant, E. I. (Kivalina)
> Labourer, H. N. (Tikiġaq)

It must have been an extraordinary scene. I think of you, McD, alone with your binoculars, sitting with Umik and Sarah at the cliffs last week. But in summer 1959, a scientific kibbutz swarmed here. First was the US Geological Team which returned from its previous summer's work to sink shafts through the tundra to explore the bedrock. Then, besides the teams from the AEC and the US Public Health Service there are groups from the Universities of Washington and Alaska to whom the AEC had granted research contracts. Offshore lay the UW's research ship *Brown Bear* with marine biologists, fishery investigators and invertebrate zoologists. Then in camp, besides thirty-odd construction and maintenance staff, there were ornithologists, botanists, geologists, geophysicists, caribou and small mammal scholars, brown bear students, marine mammal experts. Anyone with anything to do with anything from tundra cotton to peregrine falcon diet was there checking, tracking, trapping, mapping.

To give you a sense of the sheer diversity of life at the cliffs: in forty studies from data collected by a hundred scientists between the summers of 1959 and 1961, half of the sixty known Alaskan mammals were recorded; 120 inland bird species, and 1400 species in other groups, several score of these new to science. As you will agree, this would clearly be an ideally uninhabited environment in which to detonate fourteen Hiroshimas. And if you can do this to non-human species, why not bring it closer to home? Indeed, as President of the University of Alaska, Ernest N. Patty, proclaimed: this dramatic method of excavation could one day be used even near cities. But first it had to be demonstrated 'in the boondocks'.

In January 1960, the AEC's Environmental Studies Committee met and reported that 'the best time for firing is spring.' This, according to the

AEC, via the *New York Times*, was when 'most plants and small animals would be under snow, few birds would remain in the area, hunting activity on the land would be minimum and radioactive debris would be flushed off the frozen landscape by spring run-off. Once this had happened 'much of the debris would decay appreciably before entering biotic cycles through the sea after breakup'. Since no scientific studies in spring had yet been done, this appraisal came as a surprise to Alaska residents. It hardly required a PhD to observe there is virtually no snow cover at Aggutauraq. The frozen tundra with its grass, sedge, lichen, moss and willows is wind-scoured all winter.

Four Alaskan scientists accordingly protested, and two of them resigned from their AEC contracts. They had been asked by an agency consisting of scientists to produce scientific data, and now their contributions had been aborted before they could produce anything. The Alaskan Commissioner of Fish and Game likewise protested that the AEC's decision 'shows signs of predetermination.' He complained further that the environmental programme was slanted towards cataloguing biological life and measuring background radiation levels – which are mostly of interest in making post-shot comparisons. 'The Home Chamber of Commerce might be satisfied,' he concludes, 'but the scientists of this Department are not.'

On 5 March 1960, the *New York Times* reported that 'the AEC's proposed nuclear explosion on Alaska's Arctic coast is at least a year away. The original plan of blasting out a usable harbour near Cape Thompson has also been abandoned as unfeasible… Instead, a mile-long, keyhole shaped excavation in the tundra is contemplated.' Thus in contemplation, a party of three from the AEC arrived in Tikiġaq and other villages to talk to native community councils. It had been reported that they [village people] were 'afraid of what the blast will do.' But this was the first and last time the AEC approached any local people.

Now imagine this scene. It's March 14. A Cessna 180, piloted by the Inupiaq Tommy Richards takes off from Kotzebue and flies east and then north on its hour's trip to Tikiġaq. On board the Cessna are Rod Southwick and two colleagues: Russell Ball, in charge of Chariot's general planning, and a scientist, Bob Rausch of the US Public Health Department.

Inland, then up coast they tack until they almost reach Cape Thompson. 'Aggutauraq coming up to your right, gentlemen,' shouts Richards over his shoulder. The men crick their necks. The Cessna banks, and to starboard they gaze down on the little valley. Ahead stand the cliffs. On each side of the valley are ridges. Otherwise the valley is flat and brown and streaked with snow. The creek is near invisible. What stand out are the air strip and wind sock, and the little colony of huts and shelters (a few ruins remain there).

'That's where my ancestor Samaruuraq caught two whales and two walruses, all in one day,' says Richards, nodding down at Aggutauraq. 'Walked there from Kivalina in the 1893 famine.' But nobody hears him.

'One helluva wasteland!' mutters Ball, still fresh from Frisco.

'Gee willikers!' chimes Southwick. 'But not,' (recalling Introductory Studies 101: *The Sublime*) 'without its elevated grandeur!' Rausch, who knows the Arctic, keeps his council.

On they drone and touch down in Tikiġaq. The men, kitted out in Fairbanks in heavy weather gear, trudge into the village from the air strip. They glance at their watches, anxious to get back to Fairbanks.

The Community Hall of St Thomas's Episcopal Mission is a long low clapboard building. Like the church and the clinic, it's painted dark green. Richards leads his trio through the storm shed. Seated already for over an hour, their boots stretched on the floor in front of them are one hundred middle-aged and elderly Inupiat. Besides the Inupiat are two white village residents: Keith Lawton the Episcopalian priest, and Don Charles Foote (brother of Joseph), a historian working in Tikiġaq for a PhD at McGill. A brilliant scholar, he and Berit, his artist wife, have lived in the village for a year already. The AEC have employed him to compose a human geographical study of the area. This he has done (a distinguished work, available online). He has, at the same time, mobilized opinion in the village to oppose Chariot.

At the end of the hall, three chairs are waiting behind a tressel. Square on the tressel stands a tape recorder. A box of reels and a backup recorder are stacked under the table. Despite intense heat thrown out by a coal-burning stove, most of the Inupiat wear parkas. The air is heavy with cigarette smoke.

The Tikiġaq mayor, Umigluk David Frankson, aged fifty-six, opens the meeting. He speaks in Inupiaq and introduces the visiting party. Rod Southwick then begins his reply. And here, for your interest, McD, are some extracts from an extraordinary transcript which you can read in the Foote Collection in the University Library archives. As you will know, Don Foote was killed in a car accident in 1961. Here is a partial transcript:

Southwick: Thank you… It is our purpose to tell you what the status is of the project at Aggutauraq creek. The AEC early this month authorised the continuation of studies about the land, the sea, the fresh water, animals, fish and mammals. I want to emphasise that the Commission has *not* approved any explosion. The decision will be based solely on these studies that are going to show if such an experiment can be conducted safely. In the (Pacific) Bikini tests that were carried on above ground, the amount of radioactive material was many times greater than will be case here. The immediate area round the excavation will be dangerous for a short period of time after the explosion… if it is done. But the effects of this will not be very far-reaching in many number of miles and within a relatively short time, just a matter of several weeks or a few months at the most.

Ball: We now have available to show you a brief moving picture which describes several of the ways in which we think it will be possible to develop peaceful uses of these nuclear explosives. You will find that the movie talks about the creation of a harbour. This film was made at a time when thought was being given to the creation of a much larger harbour than is now considered. Because of this the explosive devices which the film mentions are much larger than the one we now propose to use.[3]

The film is presented and an explosion is shown in an area modelled to resemble Aggutauraq.
Thehere is silence, though the audience intermittently cries in horror: 'Yeee! Aah!' Southwick now invites questions, and the tough and clever Rev. Lawton quizzes Ball:

What type of rock has been found in core samples? What do the mudstone and shale you've found – as against limestone or granite – tell us as regards safety? What about shock waves? What would be the blast's effect on tides? What percentage of the radiation would be expected to break surface?

Ball: No difference this (speech continued in archive typescript)

---

[3] Don Charles Foote Collection, University of Alaska Archives, Fairbanks, AL.

Lawton: Is there still any thought that this will be a usable harbour?

Ball: As our studies progressed, it became clear that there is not, at the present time, an economic need for such a harbour. It is not exclusively viewed as a very worthwhile experiment to help us learn how to dig craters.

Dan Lisbourne (Tikiġaq man and village council representative): Mr Ball, why was Cape Thompson chosen in the first place?

Ball: It met quite well a number of criteria. One of the types of excavation which is of rather obvious value is in the excavation of harbours. Ah, harbour and channels particularly seem attractive. Hence we wanted a coastal location. Second it was of course obvious that we find one remote from large centres of population for such an initial experiment. Cape Thompson was a location which seemed very well to fit with these criteria.

Lisbourne: The Barrow to Barter Island area [Alaska north coast] is the most remote place I've seen. Couldn't they choose such a place?

Ball: Ah, we didn't want to get into an area where the winter would be too severe. After all, we're a bunch of southerners up here. This climate is kind of hard on us, you know?

Anonymous voice: When this blast was considered was our livelihood and living considered?

Ball: Well, the Commission recognized that detonation of this sort, producing radioactive material as they always do, must always be conducted with the welfare of the citizens in mind. The Commission will proceed only on the basis that the studies conducted prove conclusively to the whole scientific world that it could be done without hazard to the Eskimo people in any way.

White man on visit for guided polar bear hunting: Will radiation be checked during the experiment?

Ball: We will have men and instruments here and in several other villages, to give you information as to whether there is any fallout or none at all. We don't want to leave you in ignorance.

Lawton: What precautions will be taken to prevent trout, which migrate past the keyhole-shaped harbour, from entering and then later being caught in Tikiġaq nets?

Ball: Well, there will not be any need for precautions. We have not planned any.

Lawton: This was my question. Would there be any danger for fish going into that area?

Ball: No.

Rausch: Marine biologists at the Eniwetok test [central Pacific][4] made very careful studies as soon as it was possible to go into the area. And, ah, I believe in one instance they suggested that the people should not eat the fish for two or three days after the test... And that was a shallow lagoon with radioactive material a thousand times greater than that which would be released here.

Lawton: If someone strayed into the area of the test, or some pocket of radioactivity due to a wind-shift, landed on a particular portion of Tikiġaq, what kind of reparation would be possible for any damage that was done?

Ball: At this distance the amount of airborne radioactivity which could reach here could not possibly be enough to cause any injury to the people or the animals. Ah, around the hole there will be an area that will be sufficiently contaminated that it will be necessary for a period of time to restrict access. We will station people there, post signs or fences, whatever appears to be the most convenient way to do it. So that, er, there will not be an

---

[4] Atmospheric tests were conducted on the Eniwetok atoll between 1948 and 1962. The first hydrogen bomb test took place here in 1951. Residents who had been removed by the US military after WW2 began returning only in 1970. For the next decade, the US authorities worked to remove contaminated earth and other materials and declared the atoll safe in 1980.

opportunity for people to wander into an area where it is not safe for them to be. After a period from a few weeks to a few months... it will be possible to remove all restrictions on access.
Lisbourne: In that period of time, even two or three weeks, it'll cripple the hunting at Tikiġaq.

Ball: No, you needn't be restricted. All you need to do is avoid going across the immediate area to get where you want to go hunting. You may have to go around the backside of a hill instead of going along the shore... But your animals will not be... You don't hunt the animals down near the beach. I presume you hunt them back in the hills.

Charlie Tuckfield: How can we avoid going around that area where we hunt all the time, that's Aggutauraq Creek?

Lisbourne: That's where our hunting ground is, Mr Ball.

Ball: Right, er?
Lisbourne: Right close, right around in the Aggutauraq Creek.

Southwick: Right on the shore?

Ball: Close to the shore?

Lisbourne: Yes. Right there.

Ball: How close? You don't go hunting caribou on that location, do you? Do you shoot the animals right there at Aggutauraq Creek? Or do you mean to say you go by there to go to the animals?

Lisbourne: Ya: we shoot them there. There were nineteen dog teams there just this week.

Rausch: How late in the spring do you hunt there for caribou?

Lisbourne: Oh, as long as the trail is available to us, with snow.

Ball: Of course, an important part of our programme will be to learn the location of caribou before we decide to shoot. And so far as possible choose a time for the shot when the caribou are not in that immediate area. So we hope by this means to avoid any inconvenience to you by picking a time for the detonation when that's not a good time to find the caribou.

Southwick: That's one of the reasons Don Foote is here: to find out these things for us.

Lawton: Would there be any precautions taken to keep the caribou out of a contaminated area after the shot? Caribou might wander in and several weeks later be shot while contaminated.

Rausch: With all the activity that will be going on in the camp, in the immediate vicinity of the camp, I think that there won't be any caribou in that vicinity close enough in where they are likely to become contaminated in any way. In other words, if they're going to be back in the hills there, some distance, it's not going to make any difference.

Ball: We might mention our experience with the herd of cattle in Nevada. Some of the cattle near a nuclear explosion had enough fallout on them to get some skin burns from the fallout. The herd there was brought in after the detonations to graze on the contaminated areas to provide evidence to the ranchers that it was safe, that the fallout, such as it was, would not provide any hazard to the animal or effect its safety in consuming the meat.

Tuckfield: Down in Nevada they don't use dogs for hunting, huh?

Ball: No.

Tuckfield: Suppose a guy went out hunting and got all his dogs killed and had to walk home?

Ball: (seriously) It would be a long walk, wouldn't it? Well, ah, we will ensure that no one or his dogs are in the area where they could possibly receive any injury at the time of the shot... You will know long in advance the precise day and time of the shot.

334

We will have airplanes flying, sweeping the area, so we will know, can assure ourselves that all the people are out of the way. So we'll know for sure where all the caribou are at that time. And so on.

Lisbourne: I should think that we'll be kept away from our hunting ground for a few days. I'm sure of that.

Ball: For a few days, this is possible.
Lisbourne: The people, all of us are, well, dependent on the food, the animals.

Ball: How many, how many days during the year, ah, do you hunt?

Laughter from the audience.

Lisbourne: We have to go out hunting all the time. We have no provisions like you have now out there. Just have to go out and get 'em.

The discussion continues into the nature of the biological studies that the AEC plan.

Lisbourne: Wouldn't it be feasible if the biologists were to stay up here whole year long and study what they should study. Like for instance Doc Johnson. He stayed here just four days. I don't think you could learn much in just four days.

Rausch: I certainly agree with you, and the plan is to have full time people in this area during the coming winter. We didn't plan as adequately the first year because we weren't certain how things would go and so everyone concerned should able to use more judgment in the coming time.

Lawton: Who is the radiation biologist with the AEC?

Southwick: Dr Allen Seymour is a member of the Committee.

Lawton: And he wasn't available for tours around the villages at all?

Ball: He was with us at the three-day meeting which the Commission held at Anchorage. But, ah, we didn't at that time consider it important enough to bring him up here.

Southwick: We didn't think it was necessary to pull him off the job he's on right now. Are there any further questions? If not, I would like to, ah, thank you very much, Mr Mayor, the people who have come here, ah...

A woman's voice interrupts in Inupiaq. Then a man's. Then another woman's.

Lisbourne: Ah... the woman here said all these people here, all of these people, most of them are just silent right now and they have great fear in this detonation. And the effects, and how the effects of it will be.

Southwick: Internationally?

Lisbourne: No. *Here*!

Ball: What? I don't, ah, quite under-, get what her question was.

Tommy Richards: The effect of the blast on the people.

Ball: On you, on your own Eskimo people?

Silence

Ball: Oh, well, ah, I believe we've covered that already. (*Turning to pilot Richards about return flight*). Ah, I think we'll have...

Richards: I don't think that's true. You haven't.

The audience begins to talk in Inupiaq. A man's voice. A woman's.

Richards: Are you gonna go through with this thing when you know that people here are afraid of the explosion?

Silence

Ball: Oh! As we have said, eh, the AEC is making very *careful* studies to make absolutely *sure* neither that you nor any of your people will receive any harm from this experiment. If we cannot assure that, we will not do it! *Only* when we can do it safely would we consider going ahead. Does that reassure you?

Voice in Inupiaq. Silence. The voice continues. End of meeting and of transcript.

Well, Mr D, my conversation with Sharva remains in memory. I will repeat it here. Sharva'd riffled through a box of papers that I had on Chariot.

'What would you have done?' I ask him. Sharva kicks out with a high left boot and crusts of snow fly onto my table. Growling explosively he rakes his arms in a violent half-circle.

'They wouldn't come back with *hydrogen* bombs even!' he repeats joyfully.

Beechey, Frederick William. 1831 *Narrative of a Voyage to the Pacific and Beering's Strait*

Bockstoce, John R. 1977 *Eskimos of Northwest Alaska in the Early 19th Century*, Oxford: Pitt Rivers Museum

——, 1986 *Whales, Ice and Men*, Seattle, WA: University of Washington Press

Burch, Ernest S., Jnr. 1981 *The Traditional Eskimo Hunters of Point Hope, Alaska: 1800–1875,* Barrow: North Slope Borough

Dobyns, Henry F. 1992 in *Disease and Demography in the Americas,* Seattle, WA, University of Washington Press

Driggs, John B. 1889–1908 *Letters from Point Hope, Alaska*, Austin, TX: Archives of the Episcopal Church

Fienup-Riordan, Ann, 1991 *The Real People and the People of Thunder,* Norman, OK: University of Oklahoma Press

Foote, Don Charles, 1959–61, *Unpublished Field Notes,* Foote Collection, University of Alaska Archives

——, 1965 *Exploration and Resource Utilization in Northwestern Arctic Alaska,* McGill University, Montreal

Kehoe, Alice, 1989, *The Ghost Dance,* New York, NY: Holt, Rinehart and Winstone

Larsen, Helge and Rainey, 1948 *Ipiutak and the Arctic Whale Hunting Culture,* New York, NY: American Museum of Natural History

McLean, Edna Ahgeak, 1980. *Abridged Inupiaq and English Dictionary,* Alaska Native Language Center, University of Alaska

Maguire, Rochfort. 1988, *Journal 1852–1854,* ed. J.R. Bockstoce, London: Hakluyt Society

Newlin A., Loon H, Ramoth-Sampson R., and. *Maniilaq Stories,* Online, www.alaskool.org

O'Neill, Dan, 1992, *The Firecracker Boys: H Bombs, Inupiaq Eskimos and the Roots of the Environmental Movement,* New York, NY: Basic Books

Rainey, Froelich G. 1940–41 *Unpublished Field Notes*, Archives of Elmer E. Rasmusen Library, University of Alaska, Fairbanks

——. 1947, *The Whale Hunters of Tigara,* New York, NY: American Museum of Natural History,

Ray, Dorothy Jean, 1967, *Eskimo Masks, Art and Ceremony,* Seattle, WA: University of Washington Press

Spencer, Robert F. 1959, *The North Alaskan Eskimo,* Washington, DC: Smithsonian Institution

Stefansson, V. 1912, *My Life with the Eskimo,* New York, NY: Harper and Brothers

Stuck, Hudson, 1920, *A Winter Circuit of Our Arctic Coast,* New York, NY

Trigger, Bruce G. *The Cambridge History of Native Peoples of America, Vol. 1,* Cambridge University Press

Vanstone, James W. 1962 *Point Hope, an Eskimo Village in Transition,* Seattle, WA: University of Washington Press

Wilimovsky Norman J. et al eds. 1966, *Environment of Cape Thompson Region, Alaska,* Germantown, MD: U.S. Atomic Energy Commission,

Wolfe, Robert. 1982, *Alaska's Great Sickness,* Philadelphia, PA: American Philosophical Society

Wyatt, Victoria, 1994, *Alaska and Hawai'i,* in Milner et al. *Oxford History of the American West,* Oxford University Press

Notes and Acknowledgements

The front cover image, in a design by Ewan Smith, uses a photograph courtesy of the Pitt Rivers Museum, Oxford. The photo is of a northwest Alaskan whale hunting mask which was fixed to one of three floats attached to the harpooner's line, which the harpooner and/or a presiding whale boat owner sang to, and which sang back once a whale had been harpooned. In the Inupiaq language, this was an *avataqpak,* a component of hunters' magical relationship to both the whale and to themselves. The mask, in dimension, is about 135 mm long and 115 mm wide. It is made of light brown wood (driftwood probably), with baleen and sinew reinforcement. The eyes are blue glass trade beads, with a piece of intestine hanging from the chin. It was collected by Frederick William Beechey of HMS Blossom, who was probably the first European to set foot in Tikiġaq, summer 1826.

Just as the beads bespeak previous Euro-American contact, so the museum number also suggests ways in which the original culture had, like that of many Native societies, been catalogued and described. This latter element, sometimes unspoken, is one theme of this book. And so many histories coexist within Tikiġaq that the form of the book is governed by that convergence and simultaneity.

Acknowledgements: I would like sincerely to thank everyone who has contributed to this publication: The people of Tikiġaq, and especially to the late Asatchaq Jimmie Killigvuk, and the late Carol Tukummiq Omnik who translated texts so ably. And not least the many who have supported me with comments. These include Ewan Smith, Anna Lowenstein, Elizabeth Lowenstein, Robert Saxton, Richard Bready, Patricia Partnow, Lawrence Kaplan, Jonathan King, John Bockstoce, Art Oomittuk, Ellis Doeven, Kristi Frankson, Brigid MacCarthy, Kate Wheale, Margaret Simonot, Alan Murray, John Wakefield, Denise Riley, John Welch, Tony Frazer, Denis Boyles, Leah Jordan, Greg Jackson.

www.ingramcontent.com/pod-product-compliance
Lightning Source LLC
Chambersburg PA
CBHW020335270326
41926CB00007B/193